Strategies for Improving Economic Mobility of Workers

Strategies for Improving
Economic Mobility of Workers

Bridging Research and Practice

Maude Toussaint-Comeau
Bruce D. Meyer
Editors

2009

W.E. Upjohn Institute for Employment Research
Kalamazoo, Michigan

Library of Congress Cataloging-in-Publication Data

Strategies for improving economic mobility of workers : bridging research and practice / Maude Toussaint-Comeau and Bruce D. Meyer, editors.
  p. cm.
  Includes bibliographical references and index.
  ISBN-13: 978-0-88099-352-4 (pbk : alk. paper)
  ISBN-10: 0-88099-352-9 (pbk : alk. paper)
  ISBN-13: 978-0-88099-353-1 (hardcover : alk. paper)
  ISBN-10: 0-88099-353-7 (hardcover : alk. paper)
  1. Migration, Internal—United States. 2. Occupational retraining—United States. 3. Housing subsidies—United States. I. Toussaint-Comeau, Maude. II. Meyer, Bruce D.

  HB1965.S76 2009
  331.12'70973—dc22

                                2009022482

© 2009
W.E. Upjohn Institute for Employment Research
300 S. Westnedge Avenue
Kalamazoo, Michigan 49007-4686

Cover design by Alcorn Publication Design.
Index prepared by Diane Worden.
Printed in the United States of America.
Printed on recycled paper.

Contents

Acknowledgments   vii

Part 1: A Conference and Research Summary: Lessons from Diverse Perspectives

1 **Introduction and Overview**   3
  Maude Toussaint-Comeau and Bruce D. Meyer

2 **Bringing Together Policymakers, Researchers, and Practitioners**   7
  to Discuss Strategies for Improving Economic Mobility
  Maude Toussaint-Comeau

Part 2: Trends, Policies, and Programs Affecting the Poor

3 **Past Trends and Projections in Wages, Work, and Occupations**   51
  in the United States
  David Autor

4 **The Earned Income Tax Credit, Welfare Reform, and the**   65
  Employment of Low-Skilled Single Mothers
  Hilary Williamson Hoynes

5 **Reflections on Economic Mobility and Policy**   79
  Bruce D. Meyer

6 **Helping Low-Wage Workers Persist in Education Programs:**   89
  Lessons from Research on Welfare Training Programs and
  Two Promising Community College Strategies
  Lashawn Richburg-Hayes

7 **Financial Aid and Older Workers: Supporting the**   109
  Nontraditional Student
  Bridget Terry Long

8 **Can Residential Mobility Programs Improve Human Capital?**   127
  Comparing Social Mechanisms in Two Different Programs
  James E. Rosenbaum

9   What Might Improve the Employment and Advancement   153
    Prospects of the Poor?
    Harry J. Holzer

10 What We Know about the Impacts of Workforce   165
    Investment Programs
    Burt S. Barnow and Jeffrey A. Smith

11 Correctional Programs in the Age of Mass Incarceration: 179
    What Do We Know about "What Works"?
    John H. Tyler and Jillian Berk

12 Comparing Apples to Oranges When Evaluating   199
    Community-Based Programs and Services
    Robert J. LaLonde

The Authors   211

Index   213

About the Institute   227

Acknowledgments

The conference "Strategies for Improving Economic Mobility of Workers," held in Chicago on November 15–16, 2007, and the publication of this conference volume are a joint project of the Federal Reserve Bank of Chicago and the W.E. Upjohn Institute for Employment Research.

Maude Toussaint-Comeau originated the idea of the conference. Her efforts, along with those of Chicago Fed Director of Research Daniel G. Sullivan, Vice President of Consumer and Community Affairs Alicia Williams, and State Community Affairs Program Directors Jeremiah Boyle and Harry Pestine, helped to bring this project to fruition.

A host of individuals at the Federal Reserve Bank of Chicago and the Upjohn Institute provided invaluable help with the conference project. We would like to acknowledge especially our colleagues in Consumer and Community Affairs at the Chicago Fed, headed by Alicia Williams. In addition to the aforementioned Boyle and Pestine, Community Affairs Manager Harry Ford, Community Affairs Program Directors Helen Mirza and Desiree Hatcher, and Consumer Regulations Director Steve Kuehl ensured that on-the-ground experience was reflected in the conference. We are grateful to Chicago Fed economists Anna Paulson, Bhashkar Mazumder, Lisa Barrow, Dan Aaronson, and Gadi Barlevy for lending their advice and expertise to help us identify speakers for specific sessions of the conference.

We express our gratitude to Chicago Fed staff MaryJo Cannistra and Sandy Schnieder for managing the long administrative and planning process for the conference.

We also want to acknowledge other colleagues for their many contributions: from the Chicago Fed, Barbara Shoulders, Katherine Ricca, Edwina Davis, Ella Dukes, Daniel DiFranco, Nathan Marwell, and Nisreen Darwish; from the Upjohn Institute, Robert Straits, Timothy Bartik, and Kevin Hollenbeck; and from DePaul University, Ludovic Comeau Jr.

We thank the distinguished keynote speakers, Alan Blinder, Edward Lazear, and Alex Kotlowitz, for their dynamic and thought-provoking presentations. Last but not least, we thank the participants, panelists, and discussants at the conference for a stimulating and highly informative discussion of the critical issues facing low-income workers and vulnerable populations.

We are grateful to Helen Koshy of the Chicago Fed for providing valuable editing services. Many thanks also to Ben Jones, Erika Jackson, and Allison Hewitt Colosky of the Upjohn Institute for the editing, typesetting, and proofreading of this book. Any remaining errors are those of the individual contributors.

Part 1

A Conference and Research Summary: Lessons from Diverse Perspectives

1
Introduction and Overview

Maude Toussaint-Comeau
Federal Reserve Bank of Chicago

Bruce D. Meyer
University of Chicago and NBER

On November 15–16, 2007, the Federal Reserve Bank of Chicago and the W.E. Upjohn Institute for Employment Research cosponsored a conference at the Chicago Fed, "Strategies for Improving Economic Mobility of Workers." The conference's purpose was threefold: 1) to bring together researchers, practitioners, and policymakers to discuss policies affecting low-wage workers and other vulnerable or disadvantaged populations; 2) to identify best practices in workforce development initiatives; and 3) to extract lessons for devising effective policies. This book is an outgrowth of that conference.

The chapters in this book aim at offering a fresh review of the economic circumstances of disadvantaged segments of our population, as well as providing a provocative but nuanced assessment of the effectiveness of various policies and practices geared to redress a number of issues affecting them. Examples of programs discussed include housing allowances that address the spatial mismatch between poor inner-city neighborhoods and areas with job growth, education retention programs and financial aid for older low-income students, employment and training programs for former welfare recipients, and labor market reentry programs for the hard-to-employ/ex-offenders in distressed communities. This diversity of programs reflects the variety of challenges and varying issues that vulnerable populations and communities confront; it also reflects the many creative ways of approaching these problems.

CHAPTER CONTENT

The book presents a compilation of chapters from leading experts commissioned to present papers at the conference, in which they discuss key ongoing and emerging issues facing policies affecting the poor. The chapters include studies that address the following specific questions:

- What are the trends in wages, work, occupations, and economic resources—the "material circumstances" of low-income workers—and what are their implications for economic mobility?
- How effective are the Earned Income Tax Credit (EITC) and welfare reform in improving the lives of single women with children?
- How well do education retention programs work in meeting the needs of low-income adults?
- What are the shortcomings of financial aid policies in serving nontraditional students, and how can policies be altered to better serve them?
- How effective are residential mobility programs?
- How effective are various workforce investment programs in linking workers to work and to greater economic opportunities?
- How well do correctional programs work in helping ex-offenders reenter the labor market?
- In evaluating community-based programs and services, what should practitioners know about the limits of such evaluation, and what should they do?

The first part of the book comprises this brief introductory chapter and the lengthier chapter that follows, which contains an overview of the research and discussion from the conference. In this introductory chapter we will quickly run through the book's authors and their topics, but in the next chapter Maude Toussaint-Comeau will address in greater detail the specific contributions of the papers that make up this volume, as well as the substance of the remarks by speakers at the conference. Then she will identify key challenges and opportunities for moving forward.

The second part of the volume is formed by the 10 remaining chapters; each tackles specific aspects of the questions outlined above.

The first chapters in Part 2 of the volume provide an overview of the data analyses and research surrounding the trends in the wages, income, employment, and poverty of low-wage workers in the United States. These trends provide the background for policy considerations discussed for the situation of workers today.

David Autor sets out the main facts about the trends in wages and occupations for low-income workers in his chapter, "Past Trends and Projections in Wages, Work, and Occupations in the United States."

Hilary Williamson Hoynes, in her chapter, "The Earned Income Tax Credit, Welfare Reform, and the Employment of Low-Skilled Single Mothers," analyzes the trends in employment for less-educated single women with children in comparison with other groups and discusses the role of the EITC and welfare reform in shaping these trends.

Bruce D. Meyer, in "Reflections on Economic Mobility and Policy," looks at additional indicators of the overall material circumstances of workers, including change in consumption as well as income.

One recurring policy topic throughout the conference was access to education. This is the theme of two chapters, "Helping Low-Wage Workers Persist in Education Programs: Lessons from Research on Welfare Training Programs and Two Promising Community College Strategies," by Lashawn Richburg-Hayes, and "Financial Aid and Older Workers: Supporting the Nontraditional Student," by Bridget Terry Long.

Spatial mismatch between residents of the inner city and areas with job growth remains a potential challenge when it comes to moving certain segments of workers in the labor market. Housing allowances and residential mobility programs help potential workers move outside areas of poverty concentration. James E. Rosenbaum addresses this subject in his chapter, "Can Residential Mobility Programs Improve Human Capital? Comparing Social Mechanisms in Two Different Programs." He discusses the results of impact evaluation of two programs, the Gautreaux program and the Moving to Opportunity (MTO) program.

Three subsequent chapters focus on policies and programs that provide employment training and assistance and that generally fall under the umbrella of workforce development. Collectively, those chapters offer a provocative look of the state and effectiveness of some major policies and programs.

Harry J. Holzer, in "What Might Improve the Employment and Advancement Prospects of the Poor?" proposes various potential alternatives and discusses the effectiveness of existing programs that have been targeted at three different groups: 1) the working poor, 2) disadvantaged youth, and 3) hard-to-employ ex-offenders.

Burt S. Barnow and Jeffrey A. Smith, in "What We Know about the Impacts of Workforce Investment Programs," discuss the state of knowledge of the effectiveness of various programs, including the Workforce Investment Act, Job Corps, and Worker Profiling and Reemployment Services (WPRS). Barnow and Smith also discuss employer-focused programs, which provide on-the job training (OJT), customized training, and sectoral training.

Continuing with the theme of worker training program evaluation but targeted at hard-to-employ/ex-offender populations, John H. Tyler and Jillian Berk discuss research results for programs designed to help ex-offenders reintegrate into mainstream society in their paper, "Correctional Programs in the Age of Mass Incarceration: What Do We Know about 'What Works'?"

Finally, Robert J. Lalonde discusses the inherent analytical and methodological problems and challenges associated with evaluating the impact of programs from small, community-based organizations and makes some recommendations as to what these organizations can do in his chapter, "Comparing Apples to Oranges When Evaluating Community-Based Programs and Services."

2

Bringing Together Policymakers, Researchers, and Practitioners to Discuss Strategies for Improving Economic Mobility

Maude Toussaint-Comeau
Federal Reserve Bank of Chicago

Three principles seem to be broadly accepted in our society: that economic opportunity should be as widely distributed and as equal as possible; that economic outcomes need not be equal but should be linked to the contributions each person makes to the economy; and that people should receive some insurance against the most adverse economic outcomes, especially those arising from events largely outside the person's control.

—Ben S. Bernanke (2007)

To be sure, Americans have not been obsessed with the distribution of income but have instead placed much greater emphasis on the need to provide equality of opportunity. But equal opportunity requires equal access to knowledge. We cannot expect everyone to be equally skilled. But we need to pursue equality of opportunity to ensure that our economic system works at maximum efficiency and is perceived as just in its distribution of rewards.

—Alan Greenspan (2004)

The issue of economic opportunity for the disadvantaged has grown in importance. It is well known that inequality in economic outcomes has increased. Those at the lowest end of the wage spectrum, with less education and fewer skills, have limited opportunities for economic mobility. These people may be working, but nonetheless they remain poor.

The adverse consequences of substandard wages and poverty on individuals, families, communities, and even the economy are numerous and interconnected. From a macroeconomic perspective, if increased inequality is accompanied by considerable decreases in consumption and in lifetime income for a growing segment of the population, this could lead to marginalization and welfare losses (Heathcote, Storesletten, and Violante 2004; Krugman 1994). Growing income inequality reinforces social ills, including class tensions and residential segregation along racial and income lines (Freeman 1998; Jencks 2002).

Poorer families generally have little in savings to deal with unanticipated events. That is, they have less of a cushion to absorb exogenous shocks and deal with adverse circumstances, such as a serious health problem. As noted in Bernanke (2006), based on the Survey of Consumer Finances, the median net worth for households in the lowest income quintile—the bottom fifth of the population—was only $7,500 in 2004 versus $93,000 for all families. These households are significantly less likely to maintain a checking or savings account: almost 25 percent of those families were "unbanked," compared with less than 10 percent of families in the other income quintiles. Low-income individuals without a relationship with the mainstream financial markets may be at a disadvantage, as it may prove more difficult for them to establish credit, obtain financing, and build equity.

Living in a poor family increases the chances of living in a poor neighborhood. For the year 2000, nationwide about 1 in 10 individuals below the poverty line lived in communities classified as "concentrated poverty," where at least 40 percent of the population is poor (Berube 2006). Forty-six of the nation's 50 largest cities contained at least one neighborhood that met the 40 percent concentrated poverty threshold. According to the same author there is a trend toward increased concentrated poverty. Although poverty became less concentrated in certain neighborhoods within cities during the 1990s, this progress appears to be threatened by recent dynamics (Berube 2007b).

Ethnic minorities are disproportionately affected by concentrated poverty in urban areas. While only 13 percent of the U.S. population is black, just over 65 percent of the population of the urban census tracts with the worst employment rates is black, and another 18 percent are members of other minority groups (Dickens 1999). Neighborhoods with concentrated poverty tend to lack adequate housing, jobs, business and financial services, and transportation infrastructure, and as a result residents tend to face higher local prices for goods and services. Also, living in distressed neighborhoods increases one's exposure to health hazards and violence (Berube 2006). Residents in areas that are characterized by concentrated poverty tend to experience higher unemployment. Some may not have the social networks necessary to find good jobs, a critical asset since informal referrals tend to be one of the most popular and potentially most effective ways to connect job seekers and employers in low-wage markets (Henly 2000). Being socially isolated, these residents may be more unfamiliar with the demands of employers. For example, they may not understand the importance of what William Julius Wilson, in his famous book *When Work Disappears: The World of the New Urban Poor*, refers to as soft skills (such as proper work attire) and a proper work ethic (such as arriving to work on time or notifying employers of absences), both of which could prevent low-skilled workers in areas of concentrated poverty from finding or keeping a job (Wilson 1996).

Alex Kotlowitz, the award-winning author and journalist who chronicled the lives of inner-city youth on Chicago's South Side, refers to the "unraveling" of these communities. He writes, "The number one reason for this unraveling of community has to do with the absence of work, because . . . work is the very thread that holds [the] social fabric together. And what we see in these communities where work has disappeared, are communities in which the very institutions that we take for granted are absent. Often there are no banks, there are no movie theaters, no libraries, no skating rinks or bowling alleys for the kids, there are few grocery stores . . . there are few restaurants. Again, these neighborhoods are devoid of the very private and public institutions which help create communities" (Kotlowitz 2008).[1] In his keynote address to the conference Kotlowitz shared the ways in which youth in these communities experience particular challenges as they confront violence, a lack of role models, low school quality, and lack of employment.

While the employment rates of poor single mothers improved quite dramatically in the 1990s, the labor force activity of less-educated black men has been declining for the past several decades (Holzer 2009). According to research, this lack of access can be attributed to lack of information, lack of informal contacts, transportation challenges, employer discrimination, and a variety of additional reasons. Consistent with Kotlowitz, Holzer notes that the research suggests these young men, growing up in poor and fatherless families and in highly segregated schools and neighborhoods, become disconnected from school at very early ages. Once this disconnection occurs, they often fail to obtain formal work experience. Furthermore, they also become more likely to engage in other detrimental behaviors, such as illegal activity and fathering children out of wedlock. Many among these young men will become incarcerated and also receive child support orders. Upon release from prison, their ex-offender status will further inhibit their labor market prospects, as employers are reluctant to hire them. These individuals are classified as the hard-to-employ.

From a labor market perspective, understanding what happens to the hard-to-employ is important (Tyler and Berk 2009). As of June 2007, roughly 1.5 million people are in the nation's federal and state prisons, and an additional 2.2 million in jail. Ninety-five percent of these people will be released from prison, the bulk of them into already distressed communities. About 650,000 people a year are released from incarceration into our communities and neighborhoods, and they tend to have low levels of education: 60 percent of the prisoners in state and federal prisons lack a high school diploma. The outcome of this situation is that very low-educated, very low-skilled individuals are being released into a high-skill economy.

How can we address the specific needs of low-wage workers and households in poor communities and help open the door to greater economic opportunity? This question was explored at the conference mentioned in the introduction, "Strategies for Improving Economic Mobility of Workers."[2] This chapter provides an overview of the research discussion at the conference and addresses the specific contributions of the papers included in this volume.[3] I conclude with an outline of the recurring themes of the chapters, drawing from some of the lessons learned from the diverse perspectives and identifying key challenges and opportunities.

TRENDS IN WORK, WAGES, AND POVERTY

Data suggest that a substantial percentage of American citizens are poor, and that the percentage has remained fairly constant over time. As shown in Figure 2.1, the percentage of individuals who are poor has seldom risen above 12 percent or dipped below 10 percent for the past 30 years. The figure also shows that from 1994 onward, more than half of the poor work during the whole year, and nearly one-quarter work full time the whole year.[4] They are the working poor.

What are the demographic characteristics of the working poor? Gleicher and Stevans (2005) find that blacks and Hispanics are twice as likely as whites to be among the working poor. Less-educated individuals also tend to be more likely to be among the working poor: of those in the labor force with a college degree, only 1.7 percent are members of the working poor, compared to 15.2 percent of those without

Figure 2.1 Percent of Population under the Poverty Level

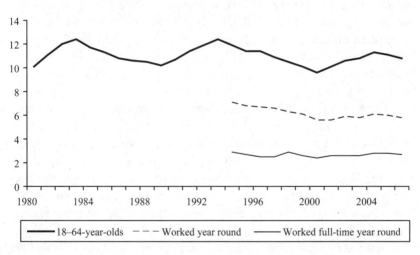

NOTE: Information on how the U.S. Census Bureau defines the poverty level can be found at http://www.census.gov/hhes/www/poverty/definitions.html (accessed April 24, 2009).
SOURCE: Haver Analytics and U.S. Census Bureau Annual Social and Economic Supplement Tables POV22.

a high school diploma. The working poor tend to have weaker labor market attachment (i.e., tend to work part time) and are in occupations or industries where the average pay is lower—namely, services, sales and office work, and production. Most of the former welfare recipients who entered the labor market as a result of changes in welfare policy in the late 1990s also entered low-wage occupations or industries and added to the pool of the working poor.

Arguably, the typical poor family appears to have fallen further behind the average family. Figure 2.2 shows the average real hourly wages for workers at different quartiles of the wage distribution over time. On average, workers at the bottom of the income distribution have not seen their wages grow as fast as those at the top. In fact, the average wage for those at the bottom is stagnating, indicating increased income inequality.

David Autor confirms that economic inequality has increased. In his chapter, "Past Trends and Projections in Wages, Work, and Occupations in the United States," he calculates that for 2005 the median real hourly wage rates for workers in service jobs working full time was approximately $20,000. He notes that while such an income level would exceed the poverty threshold of $19,350 for a family of two adults and two dependent children, this wage is probably insufficient for families to make optimal investments in child-rearing and education. This suggests that mobility over the lifetime of family members and across generations could be more limited for such families.

The extent to which families experience economic mobility remains somewhat unclear. Figure 2.2, since it is based on cross-sectional data, provides only a snapshot of all workers at different points in time. It does not convey the extent to which workers are actually experiencing mobility, that is, are moving up (or down) the income ladder over the course of their lifetimes or across generations. This is important to know in order to access the extent to which there is actual improvement in the economic well-being of people. Such a question is best answered with time-series and panel data that can trace the same individuals over an extended period of time. These data are more limited, which make the mobility question harder for researchers to address.

In general, families in the United States experience upward mobility over the life cycle and across generations (Bernanke 2005). However, Gottschalk and Danziger (1998) and Gottschalk (1997) examine the

Figure 2.2 Average Real Hourly Wages, 1979–2006 (2005 $)

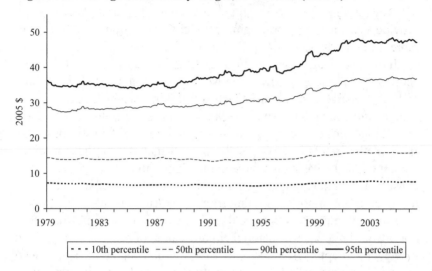

NOTE: The Current Population Survey (CPS) Outgoing Rotation Group Files represent the six-month moving average for the tenth, fiftieth, ninetieth, and ninety-fifth percentile hourly wages from 1979 through 2006 for workers more than 24 years old.

SOURCE: Author's construction using Current Population Survey Outgoing Rotations.

extent to which people change positions within the income distribution and found that mobility patterns have not changed in a way that would offset rising inequality. Other researchers find, not surprisingly, that mobility largely depends on the income and education level of the family to start with. Over the previous 25 years, a child born into a low-income family had a 20 to 25 percent chance of earning above median income as an adult and less than a 5 percent chance of moving into the highest fifth of the income distribution (Hertz 2007; Lee and Solon 2006). It has also been found that *within* generations, among families who started in the bottom fifth of the income distribution in 1988, more than half remained there in 1998, and fewer than one-quarter managed to achieve at least middle-income status by the end of the decade (Bradbury and Katz 2002).[5] Aaronson and Mazumder (2008) estimate trends in intergenerational economic mobility and find that mobility increased from 1950 to 1980 but has declined sharply since 1980. Their results suggest that earnings are regressing to the mean more slowly now than at any time since World War II, causing economic differences between families to become more persistent. These studies together provide evidence that some families in the population have relatively more limited prospects for upward economic mobility.

Individual wage data may not give us the full picture of the true economic conditions of low-wage workers since families share income and may receive income assistance and in-kind benefits, such as food stamps and Medicaid. Bruce D. Meyer makes the point in his chapter, "Reflections on Economic Mobility and Policy," that we must also think of the trends in terms of the overall material circumstances of workers. That is, we should have in mind not only wages, but also food consumption, housing quality, purchases of other goods, and access to health care. An important finding from his research is that if we look at consumption poverty numbers, there are causes to be somewhat more optimistic about the true material circumstances of people. As explained in Meyer's chapter, from 1988 to 2005 the percentage of people who are poor, as measured by "consumption poverty," actually has fallen consistently. Meyer notes that, similarly, the living standards of people in the United States over time have improved more than official measures suggest, once one accounts properly for inflation. For example, by 2004, while the official income poverty rate was close to 14 percent, if measured by consumption with an improved measure of price changes the rate was only 5 percent.

A similar message to Meyer's comes from Dahl (2007), who shows that income for low-income families (income including earnings and assistance such as the Earned Income Tax Credit [EITC], Social Security, child support, and public and subsidized housing) increased on average from $12,400 in 1991 to $16,800 by 2005. Following the same female-headed households as well as other types of families over a period of time (from 2001 to 2003), she finds that overall average income for the low-income families (those in the bottom twentieth percentile) increased. Averages of course mask differences in the actual experience of different families. Most of these households did experience improvement in their income: 60 percent of the low-income households with children experienced income growth from 2001 to 2003. However, 25 percent saw large declines, and 15 percent experienced no changes.

More research is needed to ascertain whether these income changes were sufficient to allow these low-income families to make optimal financial decisions and adequate investment in their children's future. We should also consider the extent to which families are able to leverage their resources and, if they are not able to, whether they accumulate more debt than they can afford. Evidence suggests that this can be the case. According to analysis of data from the 2004 Survey of Consumer Finances, lower-income households are less able than others to manage their debts. A greater fraction of these households had debt-to-income ratios of 40 percent or more or had a payment at least 60 days past due (Bernanke 2007).

Dahl's research shows that 25 percent of families over a two-year period experienced declines in earnings. We do not know the sources of these income variations and losses nor do we know the duration. Some journalistic reports suggest that families have been experiencing greater income risks and uncertainty.[6] For example, Gosselin and Zimmerman (2007) find a substantial increase in the transitory variance of family income over time. Admittedly, as Meyer noted in his chapter, it is unclear how to interpret trends in "volatility." There are many factors that can contribute to temporary variation in income that do not necessarily convey negative experiences, such as going back to school or taking time out to raise children. However, concerns arise in instances where volatility is due to circumstances that negatively affect workers, such as loss of jobs or job displacement. This could have some implications for the prospect of economic mobility. Displaced workers are more likely, in their new positions, to be downgraded relative to previous earning levels and job quality. They are more likely to suffer longtime earnings losses and standard of living declines. For society the loss of the productive capacity of these workers can be costly (Butcher and Hallock 2004, 2005).

Although Meyer's research and others', such as Dahl's, that has looked at overall economic resources of low-income households and has shown improvement over time is encouraging, it does not mean that there is no need for policy. On the contrary, as Meyer proposes, some of the policies and initiatives such as the EITC and welfare reform (along with past economic growth) have worked to some extent and should be maintained and extended.

LOW-INCOME ASSISTANCE POLICY

There have been tremendous changes in policy on income assistance for the poor in recent years, notably welfare reform and the expansion of the EITC. A good deal of research is being done to evaluate the impact of these programs for families, in particular for single women with children and for former welfare recipients. Sessions of the conference discussed these issues. To give a brief background, Aid to Families with Dependent Children (AFDC), part of the Social Security Act of 1935, provided cash assistance to low-income single mothers; this program was phased out in the 1990s. The Personal Responsibility and Work Opportunity Reconciliation Act (PRWORA) was enacted in 1996. Effective July 1, 1997, Temporary Assistance for Needy Families (TANF) replaced AFDC (as well as the Job Opportunities and Basic Skills [JOBS] training program of 1988). Welfare reform added a requirement for individuals to work as soon as they are job-ready or no later than two years after coming on assistance. It also imposed a lifetime limit of five years on benefits received from the federal government. The program is funded through block grants to states, so the states have some latitude in designing their own systems (e.g., Wisconsin Works, WorkFirst), although they have to meet some federal requirements.

EITC began in 1975 as a program designed to offset payroll taxes for low-income families with children. It is a refundable federal tax credit so that if the EITC exceeds the amount of taxes owed, it results in a tax refund to those who claim and are qualified for the credit. To become eligible one must have income below a specified amount. The program was expanded in the Tax Reform Act of 1986 (TRA86) and again through the Omnibus Reconciliation Acts of 1990 and 1993 (OBRA90, OBRA93).

Hilary Williamson Hoynes gives a brief history of the EITC and welfare reform and analyzes what they entail for trends in employment. In her chapter, "The Earned Income Tax Credit, Welfare Reform, and the Employment of Low-Skilled Single Mothers," she shows that employment (defined as any work over the prior calendar year) increased by 16 percentage points from 1992 to 1999 for single mothers and by 20 percentage points for single mothers with low education—who tend to be more affected by EITC and welfare reform. No such improvement occurred for any other groups. Hoynes argues that it is difficult to disentangle the effects of EITC, welfare reform, and an expanding economy, all three of which were happening over the period covered by her analysis, during which she observed increased employment and earnings. Empirical research by Meyer and Rosenbaum (2001) suggests that between 1992 and 1996, a period in which employment of single mothers increased by 8 percentage points, about one-third of those gains can be attributed directly to the EITC and another one-fifth to welfare reform. Over the longer period from 1984 to 1996, the EITC might have been responsible for about 60 percent of the increase in employment.

The implication of these studies is that the EITC has several positive effects. In fact, in his chapter, Bruce D. Meyer proposes expanding it. Currently the benefit structure is the same for those with three or more children as for those with two, he notes. He proposes that there should be a more generous schedule for those families with three or more children.

An important question concerns the types of employment former welfare recipients end up taking: are they the types of jobs that truly help them achieve economic mobility? Research suggests that many former welfare recipients end up in low-wage service jobs and part-time or temporary jobs. As Autor and Houseman (2007) report, in the Detroit WorkFirst program in Michigan, a disproportionate number of workers were placed in the temporary help sector (the authors note that this is also the case nationwide). While some may view the temporary help sector as providing a stepping stone toward more permanent and stable jobs, Houseman and Autor find that temporary placements do not help workers transition to direct-hire and more stable or regular jobs and, as such, may not improve long-term labor market outcomes for these workers.

To assess the effectiveness of work incentive programs, we should not only focus on impacts on employment and family income, we should extend our view to look at impacts on child outcomes and what is happening to parenting and child care arrangements. A number of income supplement programs and nonearning supplement employment programs have been evaluated for their effects on children, according to Greg Duncan.[7] The income supplement programs include, among others, the MDRC Welfare-to-Work policy evaluations, which drew data from information on about 30,000 children in various programs and was evaluated with random assignment; Minnesota's welfare reform program, called the Minnesota Family Investment Program (MFIP), which was also evaluated with random assignment; the Connecticut Jobs First program, a generous program but with a time limit; and the New Hope program, a Milwaukee program that had both income supplement and employment features. The employment programs include a Florida program mandating work and Los Angeles County's GAIN (Greater Avenues for Independence) program.

Duncan noted that programs that supplemented income were found to have impacts on mothers' earnings (of about $1,000) and on family income (of $2,000). The nonearnings supplement employment programs had a big impact on employment and, as expected, a smaller effect on earnings (about $720 in this case) and an insignificantly small effect on family income. The nonearnings supplement programs generally had an insignificant impact on young children. Both the earnings and the nonearnings supplement sets of programs had negative impacts on adolescents. The lesson to draw: it is not universally true that these programs were beneficial for kids.

According to Duncan, the more comprehensive approach of the New Hope program made it work better, particularly for children. New Hope was created and backed by a coalition of community activists, business leaders, and academics in Milwaukee. By the time it was launched in 1994, 1,400 low-income families had volunteered for a chance to participate. New Hope participants had to show they had worked 30 hours a week or more; then, they were entitled to a suite of benefits: an earnings supplement that raised income above the poverty line, a child care subsidy, and a health insurance subsidy. If they could not find work in the private sector to get up to the 30 hours a week, a temporary community services job that paid the minimum wage was available. The program was delivered by the New Hope staff in a very respectful and competent way. Furthermore, it was available to all adult men and women, not just mothers with kids; the idea was that anyone who was working full time and had a low income ought to be eligible for these kinds of support.

The earnings impact of New Hope was mixed, but it seems to have benefited single men and children in particular. For certain demographics the impact persisted beyond the three-year demonstration period.[8]

An important feature of the New Hope model was that it allowed people to select the benefits that would work best for their family. People were very strategic about taking up benefits. Most people didn't take up all the benefits all the time, but they picked and chose from the potential benefits that were available and put together a package that made the most sense for them; sometimes it involved working more, and sometimes it involved working less.

EDUCATION—LOW-INCOME ADULT STUDENT RETENTION PROGRAMS AND FINANCIAL AID

There is general agreement that investment in early childhood education is the most promising venue to enhance human capital. It has been found to yield very large personal, economic, and societal benefits (Carneiro and Heckman 2002; Karoly, Kilburn, and Cannon 2005; Sachs and Shatz 1996). Education is one of the cornerstones of American public policy. Among the education initiatives, the Head Start program, Project Upward Bound, and, more recently, the No Child Left Behind Act of 2001, are examples of federal programs that aim at redressing educational inequality. At the level of higher education, the Education Amendments of 1972 created the Basic Educational Opportunity Grants, renamed Pell Grants in 1980, which provide federal financial aid to undergraduates from low-income families.

Edward Lazear, chairman of the President's Council of Economic Advisers, in a keynote presentation, "Mobility of Factors of Production and Economic Growth," touched on the Bush II administration's education policy. He argued that the No Child Left Behind Act has been one of the greatest achievements of the administration, adding, "it made clear that it is unacceptable for schools to fail to provide the necessary skills to allow their graduates to compete in a modern society." Still, Lazear pointed out that a number of academic studies have found that the students are inadequately prepared from kindergarten through 12th grade and that the system is still in need of major improvement (Lazear 2008).

Although education is unanimously viewed as important, access to education by low-income students requires the availability of adequate financial aid. A report by the Commission on National Investment in Higher Education found that funding for educational programs has diminished sharply in recent years. For example, in 1975 Pell Grants covered about 80 percent of tuition costs. By 1999, that share had fallen to 40 percent (King 2000). At the same time, it is well known that the cost of a college education has risen significantly. Such trends would suggest a compounded problem of access and affordability for poorer students and those from moderate-income households at a time when the value of education in the job market is enhanced.

The question remains of how to promote education among adult low-wage workers whose skills may not be readily transferable or adaptable to the changing labor marketplace. What type of education is best for these workers, and how should it be provided? How do we design financial assistance that will help meet the needs of nontraditional students?

To address these questions, it is instructive to first understand some of the causes behind the trends in wages and income for low-skilled workers mentioned and their particular implications. David Autor discusses in his chapter the many factors behind the trends. One factor that merits attention is the skill-biased technological changes in today's marketplace.[9] Autor points to the fact that hourly wage growth from 1973 through 1989 did indeed fall at the bottom and grow modestly at the top. However, what is less well known, he observes, is that from 1989 through 2005 wage growth was in fact polarized, with high growth at the bottom and the top, and little growth between the thirtieth and the seventieth percentiles. Autor suggests that this trend can be explained by the growing use of computer technology, which tends to substitute for workers in accomplishing routine tasks (in the middle), and to complement workers in performing nonroutine, education-intensive, conceptual tasks (at the top).[10] Those two mechanisms of substitution and complementarity explain a preference in the job market for levels of education (and related job skills) beyond high school. At the same time, manual jobs are arguably not easily performed by computers; hence the growth in demand for manual, low-skilled jobs as well.

How should education policy respond to this challenge, Autor asks? He suggests that we should not necessarily pursue a bimodal human capital investment strategy of training for bottom jobs and providing high-level education for an elite group for top jobs. This is because although earnings *growth* in low-education jobs exceeds that in middle-education jobs, earnings levels are still considerably higher in middle-level education jobs than in low-level education jobs. Therefore, in his opinion, universal, high-quality education remains the best public investment that we can make to foster opportunity, raise earnings, and increase well-being.

The challenge is to equip workers with the training that will allow them to adapt to a changing global economy, according to Alan Blinder, in a keynote lecture delivered at the conference.[11] Blinder argued that with advances in information and communication technologies, the array of services that can be performed outside the United States continues to expand. Unfortunately, as he noted, we still do not have reliable data on what jobs and services will be offshored or which ones will remain. As a result, it remains a challenge to know what specific training should be provided. In the meantime, it is imperative that we have some kind of safety net for those workers who get displaced as a result of outsourcing.[12]

Community colleges can potentially help redress mismatch of skills with jobs. In "Helping Low-Wage Workers Persist in Education Programs: Lessons from Research in Welfare Training Programs and Two Promising Community College Strategies," Lashawn Richburg-Hayes argues that, indeed, community colleges play a critical role in American higher education, and most importantly for low-wage workers, who might need to upgrade their skills. But in reality many students, especially low-wage workers, who begin attending community colleges end up leaving prematurely. Family obligations, academic underpreparedness, and financial constraints may make this group particularly vulnerable to retention problems. Hayes describes various strategies, in particular the Opening Doors Demonstration by the MDRC, which are in place to improve persistence and retention of low-wage workers in community colleges.

An important policy topic is the access and affordability of education and training for low-income adult students. Bridget Terry Long makes the case in her chapter, "Financial Aid and Older Workers: Supporting the Nontraditional Student," that given the importance of education, particularly postsecondary education, larger percentages of older workers are returning to higher education than ever before. However, these nontraditional students confront a major hurdle with finances. Simply put, Long's research finds that the financial aid system is designed with the traditional-age college student in mind and fails to address the needs of older, nontraditional students. Nontraditional students are often displaced or unemployed workers, or welfare recipients, and often have dependent children. Financial aid is therefore particularly relevant for these groups. Yet, Long explains, the different ways in which the design elements of the current system work, such as how needs analysis is applied to the nontraditional students and the number of hours needed to meet enrollment requirements, do not cater to the circumstances of these students. Long suggests several creative ways to reform the financial aid system and support low-income workers. For example, states could expand their use of TANF dollars, which currently support only short-term training, to fund training longer than 12 months. Also, community colleges could create employment-linked programs that could be supported by the Workforce Investment Act (WIA), as opposed to the typically brief training programs generally supported by the WIA.

SPATIAL MISMATCH—MOVING TO OPPORTUNITY

Spatial mismatch between poor inner-city areas (where poor residents are concentrated) and other areas (where there is job growth) has been heavily documented. As a Brookings Institute report states, job growth in suburbs "in sectors most vital to low-skilled inner-city residents" increased at a much faster rate than central city job growth (Katz and Allen 1999). Transportation remains a problem for many low-income workers. According to a report by the Century Foundation, citing research from the Community Transit Association of America, 40 percent of the 10 million daily public transit riders are low-income. Low-skilled workers who rely on public transportation and who work evenings or night shifts may in particular confront limitations, as many of the public transportation systems do not have services during these odd hours. Those who have to drop off children in day care on their way to work and pick them up on their way from work may also find it particularly difficult to rely on public transportation (Rhodes and Malpani 2000). Housing and transportation mismatch remains an issue worth considering as part of a comprehensive strategy to address economic mobility.

Spatial economic disparities and concentrated poverty and their implications for poor residents in distressed communities threaded through the discussion at the conference. The concept of spatial mismatch can be traced back to a seminal paper by Kain (1968) that suggests that residential segregation (among blacks) in inner-city neighborhoods, combined with dispersal of low-skilled jobs from central cities to suburbs, could be responsible for higher rates of unemployment and low earnings of workers in inner cities. This so-called spatial mismatch between residents in poor inner-city communities and areas with job growth has captured the attention of researchers and policymakers alike.[13] As Kain (1992) explains, the genesis of the policy interest in the spatial mismatch problem began in response to sporadic violence in poverty-stricken neighborhoods throughout the United States that erupted in the 1960s. As a result, a number of studies were commissioned. The McCone Commission, which studied the causes of the Watts (Los Angeles) riots in 1965, as well as other studies, such as the National Advisory Commission on Civil Disorders (the Kerner Commission) in 1968, identified unemployment and lack of access to jobs as major problems for "isolated" inner-city residents. These kinds of mismatches were compounded by the fact that poor inner-city residents relied more on public transportation, and such transportation between the inner cities and the areas with job growth was often inadequate. These commission findings prompted a variety of policy suggestions among researchers and programs to address inner-city poverty and unemployment arising from spatial mismatch.[14]

Housing allowances help potential workers move outside areas of poverty concentration. These residential mobility programs, by moving individuals to better environments, create the potential for very quick changes in their lives, especially with regard to safety. James E. Rosenbaum addresses the subject in his chapter, "Can Residential Mobility Programs Improve Human Capital? Comparing Social Mechanisms in Two Different Programs," in which he analyzes the effects of two programs, the Gautreaux Assisted Housing Program and the Moving to Opportunity (MTO) program. The Gautreaux program was a court-ordered demonstration project in Chicago that moved low-income black families from housing projects to two different kinds of locations—white, middle-income suburbs or black, low-income urban neighborhoods. Rosenbaum reports that, compared to city moves, the suburban moves led children to have better educational outcomes, mothers to have better employment rates, and both to feel much safer.

The MTO program—a U.S. Department of Housing and Urban Development program that offers housing vouchers to families in public housing—is a random-assignment experiment that includes a control group that didn't move through MTO. So the MTO program is a more rigorously designed program than Gautreaux, according to Rosenbaum. Recent MTO studies have found that residential moves have a small impact on wages and employment, but have a significant impact on safety (Katz, Kling, and Liebman 2001). Rosenbaum argues that the differences in the economic outcomes of the two programs could be due to the differences in the programs themselves. For example, the Gautreaux program had real estate staff to help people identify units that are not in low-income enclaves and that are located some 25 miles away from participants' old addresses. In addition, participants received counseling advice on locations with better schools and better job opportunities. As a result, people's moves changed their social experiences—they were placed in different schools, different labor markets, and engaged in more positive social interactions with new neighbors. Rosenbaum draws the following conclusion: building best practices into the program delivery is as important as evaluating the outcome.

Daniel McMillen discussed the papers that were presented on spatial mismatch. Going back to the fundamentals of the premises of spatial mismatch and putting aside for a moment the problem of transportation, he asked, "Why aren't people simply moving to suburbs where the jobs are?" His answer: lack of affordable housing in suburbs. Then he raised the question of why developers weren't building more low-income housing in the suburbs. His answer: zoning regulations make it difficult to build multiple family housing in suburban areas.

"Now that cars are so readily available, why is it so difficult to get people to commute to work in the suburbs?" McMillen continued. He argued that either people have social networks in place and are reluctant to leave their neighborhoods, or they do not have the types of networks that would provide them with information about where job growth is taking place. In any case, McMillen said, the kind of (low-skilled) jobs that are often available may not be worth the fairly expensive and long commute. So the issue may have less to do with location than with the mismatch between jobs that pay well and the skills that people have. Commuting costs certainly make it harder to take a job in another location, McMillen said, but if the gains (in terms of the pay and the quality of the job) were big enough, people would move, as migration history has proven.

From a policy point of view, a clear implication is that one ought to have an encompassing approach, beyond transportation, to address the consequences of spatial mismatch, given the multifaceted aspects of the problem. McMillen proposes allowing more multiunit housing to be built in suburban locations (in the context of the Chicago housing market). As mentioned earlier, a goal of the conference was to align research with practice. Frank Beal, executive director of Chicago Metropolis 20/20, and Robin Snyderman, housing director for the Chicago Metropolitan Planning Council (CMPC), were asked to share their experiences in addressing spatial mismatch issues.

Beal explained that a few years ago his organization engaged in efforts that led to the drafting of legislation to mandate that Illinois develop a state housing plan. Now the state has a plan. "It isn't action," he said, "but at least we have policymakers sensitive to the issue and the Illinois House and Senate now have committees on housing, and they didn't 10 years ago." The state housing policy, Snyderman explained further, is a comprehensive plan that puts state resources to work on housing from different perspectives to advance five underserved populations—people who can't afford to live near their jobs, seniors, people with disabilities, people struggling with homelessness, and people living in housing that's at risk of becoming unaffordable to its current residents. Beal noted that there is also draft legislation to create a new regional planning agency with accountability for land use that, among other goals, would take into account the job/housing mismatch. Finally, working with the State Department of Commerce and Economic Opportunity, the Illinois legislature has passed a law that gives incentives to businesses that locate in job-poor neighborhoods. These organizations are also working to get more funding for public transit.

Snyderman gave some examples of action plans her organization is engaged in to respond to the challenge of spatial mismatch.[15] First, CMPC engaged business leaders as active participants and talked to them about the menu of options and ways they can get involved, either to help make accessible to people affordable housing that is out there already, or, more and more, to look at addressing supply-side issues. Snyderman said that as a result there were 66 or so other employers contracting with not-for-profit organizations that assist their employees with affordable housing, and about 1,300 employees had purchased homes with those employers' support. Now, Snyderman said, the organization has a tax-credit incentive for other employers who do this and matching funds for the employees themselves. Finally, Snyderman noted that the bills passed aren't all about workforce housing. The rental housing support bill that passed the Illinois state legislature in 2005 provides rent subsidies for people earning less than 30 percent of the median income for the area.

WORKFORCE DEVELOPMENT POLICY AND EVALUATION

Policies and programs that provide a job-centered approach to combating poverty and address specific needs of targeted disadvantaged individuals generally fall under the umbrella of workforce development. Some of the major programs started in the 1960s with the Manpower Development and Training Act (MDTA, 1962–1972), the Comprehensive Employment and Training Act (CETA, 1973–1982), and the Job Training Partnership Act (JTPA, 1982–1998). The JTPA was replaced in 2000 by the current Workforce Investment Act (WIA).

The current WIA operates like the JTPA, which it replaced, as a joint public/private federal/state/local program.[16] The federal government provides most of the money ($3 billion a year). The money is given in block grants to the states, which set up oversight and coordinating councils of various kinds. Local boards of private and public officials supervise the activities carried on by the public and private training and educational institutions that run the programs. One-third of the money is for adult training for the more disadvantaged. For example, in 2000, just under $1 billion was spent on 380,000 adults for training, support, and job placement.

The act provides for work experience and subsidized on-the-job training (OJT) arrangements. The act also provides for training to workers who were displaced by plant closings or outsourcing by assisting them with job search and relocation (in the year 2000, about $1.6 billion went to helping 840,000 displaced workers).

Critics of the WIA argue that the funding level is not enough and therefore the program does not cover many who are eligible. Moreover, the elimination of stipends to program participants, starting in 1982, caused serious retention problems for program trainees. Some say the training periods of these programs may be too short to make them effective (training usually lasts on average less than 20 weeks). Furthermore, some employers may be reluctant to train "less than desirable" workers for only small and temporary subsidies.

Three chapters in this volume focus on the state of research on employment and related workforce program evaluations, including major federal programs like the current WIA and ex-offender reentry programs such as the Center for Employment Opportunities.

Harry J. Holzer, in "What Might Improve the Employment and Advancement Prospects of the Poor?" proposes various potential alternatives and discusses the effectiveness of existing programs that have been targeted to three different groups: 1) the working poor, 2) disadvantaged youth, and 3) "hard to employ" ex-offenders. He suggests that the prospects of the more disadvantaged would be better served by a combination of further job training, job placement assistance, and other supports and services that would promote access to better jobs. One way this objective is being achieved is with labor market intermediaries (i.e., nonprofit community organizations, or educational institutions such as some community colleges) that help link workers to existing jobs and employers. These strategies may include sectoral training programs (in which training is targeted towards key high-demand sectors in the economy).

Holzer supports prisoner reentry programs, such as the Center for Employment Opportunity, which provides a paid but temporary transitional job for each participant. He also advocates legislative efforts to reduce the many legal barriers at the state level that limit employment options for ex-offenders. For disadvantaged youth, Holzer proposes strategies to improve early outcomes and prevent disconnection, such as youth development efforts aimed at adolescents (for example, Big Brothers/Big Sisters or the Harlem Children's Zone); creating "multiple pathways to success" in high schools, including high-quality Career and Technical Education (CTE) options (such as the Career Academies) and apprenticeships as well as those stressing direct access to higher education; "second chance" programs (like YouthBuild and the Youth Service and Conservation Corps) and dropout prevention or recovery efforts; and the resurrection of community-based models like the Youth Opportunity Program, which created employment centers in low-income neighborhoods that tracked at-risk youth and referred them to available services.

Burt S. Barnow and Jeffrey A. Smith focus on the bottom-line question: whether or not the programs have measurable and economically relevant impacts on labor market outcomes. In their chapter, "What We Know about the Impacts of Workforce Investment Programs," they discuss the state of knowledge based on more robust research evaluations of the effectiveness of various programs, including the WIA, Job Corps, and Worker Profiling and Reemployment Services (WPRS). Barnow and Smith also discuss employer-focused programs, which provide on-the-job training, customized training, and sectoral training.

The WIA currently has no published econometric evaluation, but in November 2007, the U.S. Department of Labor announced a random assignment evaluation of the WIA. As for what we know from various evaluations about the effectiveness of the programs that preceded the WIA—CETA and JTPA—these programs typically had either no effect or a very small positive effect. Generally, these employment and training programs work best for adult women and least well for males and youth.

Job Corps provides vocational and academic activities as well as support services to disadvantaged youth, ages 16–24. The first key finding is that removing disadvantaged young men from their local neighborhood dramatically reduces their criminal behavior in the short run. Second, there is a notable effect on educational attainment in the short run, as measured in terms of hours, literacy and numeracy, and General Educational Development (GED) and vocational certificate receipt. Third, the Job Corps program generates substantial sustained earnings impacts for 20–24 year old recipients, but not for younger recipients. Barnow and Smith argue that this program is fairly costly and may not pass cost/benefit tests, though it may be worth continuing on equity grounds.

The WPRS system assigns mandatory reemployment services to new Unemployment Insurance (UI) claimants predicted to have long spells of benefit receipt or high probabilities of benefit exhaustion. The research suggests that the WPRS system reduces UI usage without imposing a large cost on referred claimants through lower-quality job matches. The program also has a substantial effect relative to its (very small) cost, with that effect consisting largely of a deterrent effect— some claimants immediately find employment upon receiving notice of the requirement that they receive services.

On-the-job training (OJT) can be attractive to employers because it reduces their costs; they usually pay only about half the wages and they incur less risk: because the trainees are not real employees until after the OJT period is up, employers can dismiss them if they choose. Customized training programs are ones where the employer has a lot of input into the training. The employer approves and actually develops the curriculum for the training. The employer has the authority to establish the eligibility criteria in terms of who can go into the program, and there's generally a commitment by the employer to hire successful program completers. Case studies have indicated that the placement rates are 80 to 90 percent, as Barnow noted during his presentation. Similarly, sectoral training programs also involve customized training but aim at a whole industry, such as construction.

Barnow and Smith note that most evaluations suggest positive impacts of OJT on participant employment and earnings. But three qualifications should be noted: first, none of the OJT evaluations have used random assignment; second, it is expensive to set up these on-the-job training slots; and, third, on-the-job training can be abused—it can basically pay employers for what they would have done anyway. Barnow illustrated this in his presentation with a quick example: while visiting an OJT site, "an employer . . . pointed out that his program used to have a six-month dishwasher on-the-job training program," and clearly, he said, it does not take six months to learn to wash dishes. Barnow concludes, "We need to monitor [OJT programs] to make sure that [OJT] is not just welfare for the corporations."

Continuing with the theme of work training program evaluation but targeted to hard-to-employ and ex-offender populations, John H. Tyler and Jillian Berk discuss the research results on programs designed to help ex-offenders reintegrate into mainstream society. The programs include the Center for Employment Opportunities (CEO) program and the Serious and Violent Offender Reentry Initiative (SVORI). Their chapter, "Correctional Programs in the Age of Mass Incarceration: What Do We Know about What Works?" also discusses research findings on the effect of education and vocational programs on ex-offenders' earnings, based on administrative data from the state of Florida.

Berk and Tyler report the results of the first year after random assignment for the CEO evaluation. They qualify the results on employment as being "not impressive." The treatment group does not seem to do well past the transitional jobs in terms of enhanced probability of being employed. However, the CEO program seems to be more effective for offenders who come to the program and get employment assistance soon after release. Furthermore, early results of the CEO evaluation show that program participation reduces recidivism but has no employment effects. As for the SVORI program, it has smaller impacts. Tyler and Berk contend that the important lesson to be learned is that in reality there is a "paucity of programs in prison" (the prisoners do not really participate in the programs) and that this is not surprising, given that the institutional realities of prisons and prison life make it difficult to deliver rehabilitative programs as originally designed. The SVORI program has a small impact because the program is small. The actual services are far below what is needed: prerelease, only 39 percent of the treatment group and 24 percent of the comparison group had received any employment, education, or skill-building services. Postrelease, only 15 percent of the treatment group and 24 percent of the comparison group received any services.

Reinforcing Tyler and Berk's arguments, Kristin F. Butcher, who served as discussant for the session on research evaluation, said that we must ask whether in some cases there is in fact a program at all. Butcher explained that when she worked for the MacArthur Foundation and was looking into prison program funding, she visited a number of prisons in Illinois. In one prison she saw a huge machine for doing computer-aided design. "It looked hard to operate, and it looked really like something that took training to use," she said, "and that if you knew how to use that, you could get a real job, and that would be good." Butcher asked someone, "How do you select who gets trained on that machine?" The response was, "We train the lifers." "Why do you train the lifers?" she asked. "Because it takes a long time to train the people on the machine, and we don't want to train somebody and have them leave," the person said. Tyler and Berk note that when one looks at people who go into prison industries and compares them with those who do not, one may not see very big effects. Butcher said this could be explained by the fact that for most of the people who are getting out, even if they've participated in prison industries, there is no incentive for those prison industries to train them in the more skilled jobs.

On a broader sense, Butcher agrees that we must have more realistic goals concerning programs, especially since very often the expenditures (per participant) of typical programs are quite small. To illustrate, a Job Search Assistance program, the Louisville Work Incentive (WIN) laboratory experiment, which was rigorously evaluated, was found to have effects that exceeded its costs, but the costs of this program were pretty small—net cost was $223 per participant in 2007 dollars. The National Supported Work Demonstration was found to have a fairly big impact in terms of income, which exceeded its costs, but its net cost per participant was also much higher at $11,000 (LaLonde 1995). The implication is that with a federal poverty threshold of $20,516 for a family of four (in year 2006), the chances that a program like the Job Search Assistance program, with an expenditure of $223 per participant, would get somebody out of poverty are very low.

COMMUNITY-BASED PROGRAM SERVICES AND EVALUATION

Robert J. LaLonde provides a nuanced view of program evaluation. In "Comparing Apples to Oranges when Evaluating Community-Based Programs and Services," he discusses the inherent problems and challenges associated with evaluating the impact of programs from small, community-based organizations.

As he illustrated in his presentation at the conference, a government employment training program raises annual income by about $1,000 per year (according to research, for women that's a pretty fair assessment of what programs provide). These programs typically combine general skills, vocational skills, and also job-search assistance. Let's suppose that the cost of producing these programs is $5,000 per year (to give a high estimate of how much these programs really cost). Ignoring other indirect costs and what economists call opportunity costs, the question is, is this $1,000 impact per year permanent? Will earnings increase by $1,000 per year every year for the rest of the person's career? (Research has found that these programs typically have an impact for women who are about 30 years old, and this is the only group that, according to research, will work consistently for another 30 years.) One must think of this initial cost of providing the service to that woman as an investment, a stock, LaLonde says: if you go through the calculation, you will find that the real rate of that return is 25 percent, which is huge. It's far better than a year of schooling. So a $1,000 impact is quite a large impact, if it can persist.

But the problem, LaLonde points out, lies in trying to reach the point of being able to say that the program impact is going to be $1,000 a year and the program is therefore a good and effective program. Doing so is hard because of several analytical problems. First, there is the problem of missing data. One might ask, "Why is the program operating in community A—is it due to strong community leaders compared to community B, which does not have the program?" In such a case, one could expect their outcomes to differ even if the program had no impact on community A. The challenge then comes from the fact that the evaluation is unable to account for these decisions. Second, there is a selection problem among evaluators, which arises from the following two possibilities: 1) participants choose to participate in programs based on their own assessments of whether they will benefit from them, or 2) program operators select applicants that they believe will benefit from the program. In other words, as Butcher, the session discussant, noted, in evaluations we want to ask these questions: How do we know a program works? What is the counterfactual? Wouldn't the participant have made progress anyway? These are very difficult questions; nevertheless, they are important to address given that the programs entail spending public monies.

LaLonde's chapter recommends that small organizations should not focus on impact evaluation or cost-effectiveness, but simply on measuring and collecting data on program services. He argues this can provide valuable information about how the program operates or how services are delivered and the challenges that need to be overcome in order to affect recipients' outcomes. At the very least this information can improve program management. This information also is essential for considering whether it is appropriate and a good use of resources to initiate an impact evaluation of these programs and services.

As mentioned above, one goal of the conference was to align the interests of researchers and practitioners. We asked Edwin Meléndez, who has also been in positions where he spearheaded specific work development programs, to discuss program service delivery from a research and practice perspective. Meléndez noted that these programs vary tremendously not only in the resources they use but also in the practices they implement and how they actually think about the factors that affect outcomes. An example is labor market intermediaries. Intermediaries are in essence "firms" that mediate the collective actions of employers in the provision of general training. Some of them are very effective in bringing employers together to structure a training program. In terms of the practices they implement, some are too specific to be replicable in other industries. Many intermediaries are very context-dependent, and practices in one industry are likely to be ineffective in others. We have a highly disconnected system, Meléndez said: "Intermediaries have scrap money from all kinds of places."

The problem of coordination raised by Meléndez corroborates comments made by Bob Giloth, who talked about the problem of "multiple silos" in the workforce development field. Giloth illustrates the scope of the problem: "A few years ago, GAO counted a hundred different federal workforce programs. Pennsylvania alone had 49. In neighborhoods, you often see seven or eight public investors spending $8 million to $10 million with different, unrelated objectives, and different perceptions of the problem." He adds: "It is important to make these pieces work together, because it's not simply an inefficient use of money, it means that the transitions for a lot of the folks we work with are not well crafted."

One final challenge Meléndez noted is that we need more effort to create ongoing evaluation mechanisms, with practitioners thinking about the logic of the service model that affects outcomes for participants. Learning about effective program design and practices works best when these are embedded within the program and function on day-to-day operations. Practitioners have to be trained to be critical thinkers who can incorporate analysis, systematize data collection, implement effective practices, and reflect on what they do. Success depends on empowering the staff on the front line to assess and change the program as they implement it and to effect change in the services that they deliver.

CONCLUSION

Opportunities and Challenges

In conclusion, I outline below challenges and opportunities we face as we move forward in addressing the economic mobility of workers. I draw from the research findings as well as the more compelling examples of best practices, program evaluations, and social and institutional challenges illustrated by researchers and practitioners.

Educating and training workers to redress mismatch of skills with jobs

The chapter by David Autor highlights that job growth will be concentrated among both highly education-intensive "abstract" jobs and comparatively low-education "manual" jobs. This bifurcation presents both challenges and opportunities. As Autor says, the rising productivity of highly educated workers is good news. But the growing importance of manual and service tasks presents a challenge. As he points out, "the positive news about rising demand for in-person service occupations is that it will tend to increase the earnings of less-educated workers. The less favorable news is that wages for those at the bottom will remain low and will not be enough to ensure mobility for these workers. This result suggests that it is still important to improve economic opportunities for these workers.

From an education policy perspective, although earnings growth in low-education jobs exceeds that in middle-education jobs, earnings levels are still considerably higher in middle- than in low-education jobs. Such investment in high-quality universal education remains vital to endow future workers with better earnings prospects when they later enter the workplace. On an immediate basis, the question remains how to promote education among adult low-wage workers whose skills may not be readily transferable or adaptable to the changing labor market.

Advances in information and communication technology are changing the labor market in an unpredictable fashion. For example, the range of services that can be outsourced and performed outside the United States continues to expand, as Alan Blinder discussed. Consequently, many workers will become displaced. The effects of this are uncertain. To the extent that resources are reallocated to areas where we have comparative advantage, it is possible that the net effect on jobs in the future could still be positive. However, it is also possible that the loss of jobs, if not addressed, could lead to downward economic mobility of workers and large societal losses. It is challenging at best to predict what specific jobs in what industries and occupations will see rises or declines in the future, and when and how to equip workers with the training that will enable them to adapt to a changing economic landscape.

Vocational education opportunities, such as community college education and job training programs for adult workers and nontraditional students, must be part of a comprehensive strategy to address mismatches between job requirements and worker skills. The challenge remains to improve retention in educational programs and ensure accessibility and affordability for many low-wage working students and nontraditional students who could benefit most by enhancing their skills. Several creative suggestions, such as tying low-income assistance dollars (TANF and WIA) to longer community college training, have been offered.

Extending low-income assistance like the EITC and supporting work in a comprehensive manner

Programs such as the EITC that provide support and incentives for employment have been shown to increase earnings and employment. This result was particularly evident for former welfare recipients and single women with children when the economy was healthier. It remains a challenge for policymakers to structure income redistribution programs like the EITC in a way that retains incentives for productive work. Currently, researchers suggest the possibility that the EITC (which is available only to working taxpayers) could lead individuals who are in the phaseout region of the credit to reduce the number of hours worked. Even so, most experts agree that the EITC should be continued and even expanded. A number of groups, such as single men, single women, and some low-income married couples, do not benefit from the current EITC structure. Moreover, the current benefit structure is the same for a family with three or more children as it is for one with two children—although it has been found that the former have fewer resources to devote to food, housing, and other consumption items compared to single mothers with two or fewer children. The EITC should be expanded for these larger families. Indeed, it will be important to consider amounts by which the EITC should be expanded.

Earnings supplement programs (which encourage work by either directly subsidizing earnings or easing the benefit reductions from the welfare system) do not only affect a family's income, they have been found to have generally positive developmental effects for young children. Early childhood seems to be a particularly sensitive period, when a higher income can allow families to avail themselves of higher-quality child care and provide more learning tools at home. As such, earnings and employment programs that approach mobility in a broader sense—those that target intervention to match the various needs of low-income families to balance their lives, such as programs with child care components—remain possibly one of the best ways for society to allocate its scarce resources.

There are many promising and innovative for-profit and non-profit efforts and programs, which generally come under the umbrella of workforce development, that help connect low-wage workers and more disadvantaged workers, including hard-to-employ ex-offenders, to greater economic opportunities. Most practitioners agree that workforce development programs work best when they are woven into an overall strategy to address the multipronged issues that prevent employment and result in economic distress. A combination of simultaneous efforts is likely to work best. These efforts would include addressing transportation, housing, and child care needs, as well as an emphasis on early prevention, job training, and placements into high-quality jobs.

Addressing the spatial mismatch between inner cities and areas with job growth

Spatial mismatch between residents in the inner city and areas with job growth remains a potential problem. Housing allowances help potential workers move outside areas of minority and poverty concentration. These residential mobility programs, by moving individuals to better environments, create the potential for quick changes in their lives, especially with regard to heightened safety.

Attention must be given to how the housing voucher programs are crafted procedurally in order to ensure changes in labor market outcomes. One best practice noted is the necessity to incorporate counseling in service delivery.

Consideration must also be given to the supply side aspect of the housing mismatch problem, i.e., where people can afford to move and can be accepted. Efforts are needed to ensure greater affordability of housing in suburban job centers. Other possible responses include giving incentives to businesses to locate in poorer communities, and working with businesses to ensure affordable housing for their workers.

Evaluate the effectiveness of workforce development program and service delivery

While a number of employment and related workforce development programs have been evaluated, the cost-effectiveness of many programs has still not been established. Some programs may have high costs but still be viable on grounds of equity. Other programs have expenditures (per participant) that are quite small. Thus, even if they are effective, given the small level of funding, they may not be sufficient to lift people out of poverty. Policymakers must grapple with difficult choices, inherent in income redistributive initiatives, to ensure that they strike the right balance between upholding the right economic incentives for productive behaviors while providing insurance against economic and financial risks (Bernanke 2007).

Often community-based organizations are required by foundations and other entities that fund them to demonstrate a measurable impact of their programs. For example, an organization that is providing training to former welfare recipients may be called on to demonstrate the effectiveness of its training programs. With scarce resources on the line, it is reasonable to ask whether programs have measurable and economically relevant impacts. While this is a legitimate question, inherent problems with evaluation make it in some cases impractical for small, community-based organizations to engage in rigorous evaluation. For small, community organizations running workforce development programs, even if rigorous impact evaluation may not be feasible, measuring and collecting data on program services is still worthwhile. Practitioners trained and equipped to gather information can improve program management and help determine whether further assessment is necessary.

FINAL THOUGHTS

The conference "Strategies for Improving Economic Mobility of Workers," on which this book is based, was unique in that it brought together groups of researchers and practitioners, individuals who too often do not come together, yet have a lot in common. The mixing of perspectives can be extremely helpful and enlightening, yet few opportunities exist to capture these diverse points of view. In the short term, these exchanges may have generated more questions than answers. However, I hope that the information in this book will spur more research on this important topic, and, even more importantly, will encourage more mutually beneficial interactions among researchers, practitioners, and policymakers.

Appendix 2A

Conference Agenda

DAY 1

Welcoming remarks by:
Charles L. Evans, president and chief executive officer,
Federal Reserve Bank of Chicago
Randall W. Eberts, president, W.E. Upjohn Institute
for Employment Research

Session I: Setting the Stage–Trends in Work, Wages, and Poverty
Chair: Maude Toussaint-Comeau, Federal Reserve Bank of Chicago

Presentations by:
David Autor, Massachusetts Institute of Technology
Alan Berube, Brookings Institution
Peter Gosselin, *Los Angeles Times*

**Session II: Spatial Mismatch—Moving to Work,
Networks, Business Incentives**
Chair: William Testa, Federal Reserve Bank of Chicago

Presentations by:
James E. Rosenbaum, Northwestern University
William Spriggs, Howard University
Frank Beal, Chicago Metropolis 2020
Robin Snyderman, Metropolitan Planning Council

Discussant: Daniel McMillen, University of Illinois at Chicago

Session III: Income Support, EITC, Welfare-to-Work
Chair: Bhashkar Mazumder, Federal Reserve Bank of Chicago

Presentations by:
Molly Dahl, Congressional Budget Office
Hilary Williamson Hoynes, University of California, Davis
Susan Houseman, W.E. Upjohn Institute for Employment Research

Discussant: Thomas DeLeire, University of Wisconsin–Madison

Session IV: Workforce Development—The Power of Public/Private Partnerships
Chair: Maria Hibbs, The Partnership for New Communities

Panelists:
Evelyn Diaz, Mayor's Office, City of Chicago
Donald Sykes, Mayor's Office, City of Milwaukee
Robert Straits, W.E. Upjohn Institute for Employment Research
Brenda Palms-Barber, North Lawndale Employment Network
Bob Giloth, Annie E. Casey Foundation

Keynote address: Alex Kotlowitz
Keynote lecture: Alan S. Blinder, Princeton University

DAY 2

Welcoming remarks by: Daniel Sullivan, senior vice president
and director of economic research, Federal Reserve Bank of Chicago

Session I: Evaluations of Training and Vocational Programs
Chair: Alicia Williams, Federal Reserve Bank of Chicago

Presentations by:
Robert J. LaLonde, University of Chicago
Burt S. Barnow, Johns Hopkins University
John H. Tyler, Brown University

Discussant: Kristin F. Butcher, Wellesley College

Session II: Financial Aid, Education, Employment Prospects
Chair: Lisa Barrow, Federal Reserve Bank of Chicago

Presentations by:
Harry J. Holzer, Georgetown University
Bridget Terry Long, Harvard University
Lashawn Richburg-Hayes, MDRC

Session III: Where to Go from Here—Policy Panel
Chair: Unmi Song, Lloyd A. Fry Foundation

Panelists:
Bruce D. Meyer, University of Chicago
Greg Duncan, Northwestern University
Edwin Meléndez, New School University

Keynote address: Edward Lazear, chairman,
President's Council of Economic Advisers

Notes

The views expressed are the author's and do not necessarily reflect those of the Federal Reserve Bank of Chicago or the Board of Governors of the Federal Reserve System. I thank Ludovic Comeau Jr. for planting the seed of the idea of the conference in my mind and for valuable assistance. I thank Alicia Williams, Dan Aaronson, and Bruce D. Meyer for valuable comments and suggestions.

1. Kotlowitz's essay can be found in its entirety in the September 2008 issue of *Profitwise News and Views*, a newsletter published by the Federal Reserve Bank of Chicago's Consumer and Community Affairs Division.
2. For the conference agenda, see Appendix 2A.
3. This chapter makes specific mention of and reviews presentations that were given in a formal manner. Although not discussed in this chapter, a panel of practitioners at the conference talked about their programs in a less structured format. They include Evelyn Diaz, deputy chief of staff to Mayor Daley; Bob Giloth, director of Family Economic Success at the Annie E. Casey Foundation; Don Sykes, president and CEO of the Milwaukee Area Workforce Investment Board; Bob Straits, administrator of the W.E. Upjohn Institute and director of the Kalamazoo County and St. Joseph County Michigan Works Area; Brenda Palms-Barber, CEO of the North Lawndale Employment Network in Chicago; and Maria Hibbs, executive director of the Partnership for New Communities, who served as moderator for the practitioner panel. See Toussaint-Comeau (2008) for a detailed description of their programs and related comments.
4. A low-wage worker, or a member of the working poor, is defined as one who works at least 37 weeks a year but whose total annual family income falls below the federal poverty level (an annual threshold based on census data). In 2005, this figure was $15,735 for a family of three.
5. Cited in Berube (2007a).
6. See, for example, Hacker (2006) and Gosselin (2005).
7. Greg Duncan made these comments at the "Strategies for Improving Economic Mobility of Workers" conference as one of the panelists (along with Bruce D. Meyer and Edwin Meléndez) in the last session, "Where to Go from Here— Policy Panel." This panel helped synthesize the messages from the papers and presentations.
8. Greg Duncan led the evaluation of the program. See Duncan, Huston, and Weisner (2007).
9. Debates about causes of the trends in wage inequality are plentiful. More recent trends in wage inequality have been linked to a number of factors. To mention a few, Pierce (2001) suggests that nonwage compensation patterns contribute to increased inequality in total compensation. That is, nonwage income and benefits, which primarily go to high-wage workers, have increased with such significance in recent decades that they also are contributors to the spread between top and bottom wage levels. Other arguments point to institutional factors instead, such as

decrease in unionization. For example, Card, Lemieux, and Riddell (2003) suggest that the deceleration of unionization rates in the 1970s and 1980s has negatively impacted earnings equality. Various aspects of globalization have also been reported to be linked to wage inequality (Sachs and Shatz 1996). Interestingly, the lack of uniformity in wage distributions has been traced as far back as the beginning of the twentieth century (Steelman and Weinberg 2005). In the 1900s wage inequality widened because of the introduction and increased use of electricity and new machineries, which decreased the demand for ordinary laborers. However, by the middle part of the century, demand- and supply-side factors (e.g., increases in the supply of college-educated workers and an upsurge in the demand for labor-intensive skills) depressed wages at the top and caused "compression" in the wage structure, thus reducing inequality. The trend towards wage dispersion resumed only around the 1970s, when information technology started spreading.

10. Some authors suggest that the increase in the wage gap in the 1980s may have been a temporary shock. They point to the fact that the 1990s experienced more modest growth in wage inequality despite the fact that there was strong technological progress (Card and DiNardo 2002; Lemieux 2006). Another argument that challenges the skill-biased technological growth idea is the occurrence of residual inequality, that is, inequality within groups with similar education or experience. For example, people with the same level of education may have differences in wages—although some might argue that these differences may be due to unobservable characteristics, such as school quality or motivation of workers.

11. The keynote presentation was based on two Princeton University Center for Economic Policy Studies working papers: "How Many U.S. Jobs Might Be Offshorable?" (Blinder 2007a) and "Offshoring: Big Deal or Business as Usual?" (Blinder 2007b).

12. Trade adjustment assistance and unemployment insurance are ways to address workers' displacement. Title III of the Workforce Investment Act provides for the Dislocated Worker and Employment and Training activities, which allocate about $1 billion a year to helping workers who are displaced by plant closings or outsourcing. It does this by providing them with job search and relocation allowances and trade adjustment allowances after their unemployment insurance has run out, so long as the individuals show proof of continuing certified training (Page and Simmons 2002).

13. A comprehensive summary of the academic literature on the spatial mismatch hypothesis is provided in Kain (1992).

14. For example, Hughes (1989) outlines the following six mobility strategies to combat spatial mismatch: 1) provision of job training to the would-be workers for suburban labor market–specific jobs in retail, back office, etc.; 2) creation of a job information system to match the residents to suburban employers; 3) restructuring the transportation system; 4) provision of day care facilities and subsidies to parents of young children; 5) increasing the level of earned income tax credit for the low-income in entry-level jobs; and 6) modifying policing and correctional practices to protect residents in the ghetto from predatory criminals in

their midst. Some of Hughes' policy prescriptions were also offered by Kain and Persky (1969) much earlier. In addition, Kain in various publications recommended some more entrenched measures. In the area of schooling, Kain proposed various strategies to ensure increased integration of schools, including busing and giving generous federal or state subsidies that pay participating suburban communities significantly more than the marginal costs of educating minority children from the central cities. In the area of housing he advocated the following: aggressive enforcement of federal, state, and local fair-housing statues and strong enforcement of HUD affirmative marketing plans for federally assisted rental housing; continued efforts to provide scattered-site public housing and a prohibition on the construction of new subsidized units in minority neighborhoods; and a housing allowance that would allow minorities to move outside of areas of minority concentration to reduce racial segregation.

15. The Metropolitan Planning Council is a regional policy-advocacy and technical-assistance organization that broadly focuses on the issues of sensible growth, economic competitiveness, and equity of opportunity. Created in 1934, it was originally called the Metropolitan Housing Council.

16. The description of the WIA in this section is drawn from Page and Simmons (2002).

References

Aaronson, Daniel, and Bhashkar Mazumder. 2008. "Intergenerational Economic Mobility in the United States, 1940 to 2000." *Journal of Human Resources* 43(1): 139–172.

Autor, David H., and Susan N. Houseman. 2007. "Do Temporary Help Jobs Improve Labor Market Outcomes for Low-Skilled Workers?" PowerPoint Presentation at the Chicago Federal Reserve and Upjohn Institute conference "Strategies for Improving Economic Mobility of Workers," held in Chicago, IL, November 15–16. http://www.chicagofed.org/community_development/files/11_2007_houseman_ppt_pres_session3.pdf (accessed April 28, 2009).

Bernanke, Ben S. 2005. "Economic Opportunity." Speech given at the National Economists Club, Washington, DC, October 11. http://cssp.us/pdf/Bernanke on Economic Opportunity.pdf (accessed February 3, 2009).

———. 2006. "Increasing Economic Opportunity: Challenges and Strategies." Speech, Fifth Regional Issues Conference of the Fifteenth Congressional District of Texas, Washington, DC, June 13. http://www.federalreserve.gov/newsevents/speech/Bernanke20060613a.htm (accessed February 3, 2009).

———. 2007. "The Level and Distribution of Economic Well-Being."

Speech given before the Greater Omaha Chamber of Commerce, Omaha, NE, February 6. http://www.federalreserve.gov/newsevents/speech/bernanke20070206a.htm (accessed February 3, 2009).

Berube, Alan. 2006. "Metropolitan Poverty in the United States." Presentation at the Cambridge-MIT Institute's "Poverty and Place Workshop," Cambridge, UK, September 28. http://www.brookings.edu/speeches/20060928metropolitanpolicy_berube.aspx?rssid=welfare (accessed February 4, 2009).

———. 2007a. "The Geography of U.S. Poverty and Its Implications." Testimony before the Committee on Ways and Means, Subcommittee on Income Security and Family Support. U.S. Congress. House of Representatives. 110th Cong., 1st sess. http://www.brookings.edu/testimony/2007/0213childrenfamilies_berube.aspx (accessed April 1, 2009).

———. 2007b. "Geographic Dynamics in Income and Poverty: Recent U.S. Trends." PowerPoint presentation at the Chicago Fed and Upjohn Institute conference "Strategies for Improving Economic Mobility of Workers," held in Chicago, IL, November 15–16. http://www.chicagofed.org/community_development/files/11_2007_berube_ppt_pres_session1.pdf (accessed April 1, 2009).

Blinder, Alan S. 2007a. "How Many U.S. Jobs Might Be Offshorable?" CEPS Working Paper No. 142. Princeton, NJ: Princeton University. http://www.princeton.edu/~blinder/papers/07ceps142.pdf (accessed April 28, 2009).

———. 2007b. "Offshoring: Big Deal, or Business as Usual?" CEPS Working Paper No. 149. Princeton, NJ: Princeton University. http://www.princeton.edu/~blinder/papers/07juneCEPSwp149.pdf (accessed April 2, 2009).

Bradbury, Katharine L., and Jane Katz. 2002. "Women's Labor Market Involvement and Family Income Mobility When Marriages End." *New England Economic Review* 2002(4): 41–74.

Butcher, Kristin F., and Kevin F. Hallock. 2004. "Job Loss: Causes, Consequences, and Policy Responses." *Chicago Fed Letter* 2004(207): 1–4.

———. 2005. "Bringing Together Policymakers, Researchers, and Practitioners to Discuss Job Loss." *Economic Perspectives* 2005(2): 2–12.

Card, David, and John E. DiNardo. 2002. "Skill-Biased Technological Change and Rising Wage Inequality: Some Problems and Puzzles." *Journal of Labor Economics* 20(4): 733–783.

Card, David, Thomas Lemieux, and W. Craig Riddell. 2003. "Unionization and Wage Inequality: A Comparative Study of the U.S., the U.K., and Canada." NBER Working Paper 9473. Cambridge, MA: National Bureau of Economic Research.

Carneiro, Pedro, and James J. Heckman. 2002. "The Evidence on Credit Constraints in Post-Secondary Schooling," NBER Working Paper 9055. Cambridge, MA: National Bureau of Economic Research.

Dahl, Molly W. 2007. "Changes in the Economic Resources of Low-Income Households with Children." PowerPoint presentation at the Chicago Federal Reserve and Upjohn Institute conference "Strategies for Improving Economic Mobility of Workers," held in Chicago, IL, November 15–16. http://www.chicagofed.org/community_development/files/11_2007_dahl_ ppt_pres_session3.pdf (accessed April 24, 2009).

Dickens, William T. 1999. "Rebuilding Urban Labor Markets: What Community Development Can Accomplish." In *Urban Problems and Community Development*, Ronald F. Ferguson and William T. Dickens, eds. Washington, DC: Brookings Institution Press, pp. 381–436.

Duncan, Greg J., Aletha C. Huston, and Thomas S. Weisner. 2007. *Higher Ground: New Hope for the Working Poor and Their Children*. New York: Russell Sage Foundation.

Freeman, Richard B. 1998. "Is the New Income Inequality the Achilles' Heel of the American Economy?" In *The Inequality Paradox: Growth of Income Disparity*, James A. Auerbach and Richard S. Belous, eds. Washington, DC: National Policy Association, pp. 219–229.

Gleicher, David, and Lonnie K. Stevans. 2005. "A Comprehensive Profile of the Working Poor." *Labour* 19(3): 517–529.

Gosselin, Peter G. 2005. "How Bedrock Promises of Security Have Fractured across America: Companies Are Discarding Traditional Pensions—or Making Government Foot the Bill." *Los Angeles Times*, December 30, A:1.

Gosselin, Peter G., and Seth Zimmerman. 2007. "Trends in Income Volatility and Risk, 1970–2004." PowerPoint presentation at the Chicago Federal Reserve and Upjohn Institute conference "Strategies for Improving Economic Mobility of Workers," held in Chicago, IL, November 15–16. http://www.chicagofed.org/community_development/files/11_2007_gosselin_ ppt_pres_session1.pdf (accessed April 27, 2009).

Gottschalk, Peter. 1997. "Inequality, Income Growth and Mobility: The Basic Facts." *Journal of Economic Perspectives* 11(2): 21–40.

Gottschalk, Peter, and Sheldon Danziger. 1998. "Family Income Mobility—How Much Is There, and Has It Changed?" In *The Inequality Paradox: Growth of Income Disparity*, James A. Auerbach and Richard S. Belous, eds. Washington, DC: National Policy Association, pp. 92–111.

Greenspan, Alan. 2004. "The Critical Role of Education in the Nation's Economy." Remarks by the Chairman of the Board of Governors of the U.S. Federal Reserve System at the Greater Omaha Chamber of Commerce 2004 Annual Meeting, held in Omaha, NE, February 20.

Hacker, Jacob S. 2006. *The Great Risk Shift: The Assault on American Jobs,*

Families, Health Care and Retirement, and How You Can Fight Back. New York: Oxford University Press.

Heathcote, Jonathan, Kjetil Storesletten, and Giovanni L. Violante. 2004. "The Macroeconomic Implications of Rising Wage Inequality in the United States." New York University working paper. New York: New York University. http://www.econ.nyu.edu/user/violante/Workingpapers/hsv_final.pdf (accessed April 27, 2009).

Henly, Julia R. 2000. "Mismatch in the Low-Wage Labor Market: Job Search Perspective." In *The Low-Wage Labor Market: Challenges and Opportunities for Economic Self-Sufficiency*, Kelleen Kaye and Demetra Smith Nightingale, eds. Washington, DC: Urban Institute, pp. 145–168. http://www.urban.org/publications/309642.html (accessed April 27, 2009).

Hertz, Tom. 2007. "Trends in the Intergenerational Elasticity of Family Income in the United States." *Industrial Relations* 46(1): 22–50.

Holzer, Harry J. 2009. "What Might Improve the Employment and Advancement Prospects of the Poor?" In *Strategies for Improving Economic Mobility of Workers: Bridging Research and Practice*, Maude Toussaint-Comeau and Bruce D. Meyer, eds. Kalamazoo, MI: W.E. Upjohn Institute for Employment Research, pp. 149–160.

Hughes, Mark Alan. 1989. *Fighting Poverty in Cities: Transportation Programs as Bridges to Opportunity*. Washington, DC: National League of Cities.

Jencks, Christopher. 2002. "Does Inequality Matter?" *Daedalus* 131(1): 49–65.

Kain, John F. 1968. "Housing Segregation, Negro Employment, and Metropolitan Decentralization." *Quarterly Journal of Economics* 82(2): 175–197.

———. 1992. "The Spatial Mismatch Hypothesis: Three Decades Later." *Housing Policy Debate* 3(2): 371–392.

Kain, John F., and Joseph J. Persky. 1969. "Alternatives to the Guilded Ghetto." *Public Interest* 14(Winter): 74–87.

Karoly, Lynn A., M. Rebecca Kilburn, and Jill S. Cannon. 2005. *Early Childhood Interventions: Proven Results, Future Promise*. Santa Monica, CA: RAND Corporation.

Katz, Bruce, and Katherine Allen. 1999. "Help Wanted: Connecting Inner-City Job Seekers with Suburban Jobs." *Brookings Review* 17(4): 31–35.

Katz, Lawrence F., Jeffrey R. Kling, and Jeffrey B. Liebman. 2001. "Moving to Opportunity in Boston: Early Results of a Randomized Mobility Experiment." *Quarterly Journal of Economics* 116(2): 607–654.

King, Jacqueline E. 2000. *2000 Status Report on the Pell Grant Program*. Washington, DC: American Council on Education.

Kotlowitz, Alex. 2008. "Strategies for Improving Economic Mobility of Workers Conference: Keynote Speech." *Profitwise News and Views* (September): 3–5. http://www.chicagofed.org/community_development/files/PNV_Sep2008_ReEd_FINAL_WEB.pdf (accessed April 28, 2009).

Krugman, Paul. 1994. "Past and Prospective Causes of High Unemployment." *Federal Reserve Bank of Kansas City Economic Review* 79(4): 23–43.

LaLonde, Robert J. 1995. "The Promise of Public Sector–Sponsored Training Programs." *Journal of Economic Perspectives* 9(2): 149–168.

Lazear, Edward. 2008. "Mobility of Factors of Production and Economic Growth." Keynote address at the Chicago Federal Reserve and Upjohn Institute conference "Strategies for Improving Economic Mobility of Workers," held in Chicago, IL, November 15–16.

Lee, Chul-In, and Gary Solon. 2006. "Trends in Intergenerational Income Mobility." NBER Working Paper No. 12007. Cambridge, MA: National Bureau of Economic Research.

Lemieux, Thomas. 2006. "Increasing Residual Wage Inequality: Composition Effects, Noisy Data, or Rising Demand for Skill?" *American Economic Review* 96(3): pp. 461–498.

Meyer, Bruce D., and Dan T. Rosenbaum. 2001. "Welfare, the Earned Income Tax Credit, and the Labor Supply of Single Mothers." *Quarterly Journal of Economics* 116(3): 1063–1114.

Page, Benjamin I., and James R. Simmons. 2002. *What Government Can Do: Dealing with Poverty and Inequality*. Chicago: University of Chicago Press.

Pierce, Brooks. 2001. "Compensation Inequality." *Quarterly Journal of Economics* 116(4): 1493–1525.

Rhodes, Eric, and Sonal Malpani. 2000. "A Metropolitan Approach to Workforce Development." New Ideas for a New Century Idea Brief No. 17. New York: Century Foundation. http://www.tcf.org//Publications/EconomicsInequality/WorkforceDevelopment.pdf (accessed April 27, 2009).

Sachs, Jeffrey D., and Howard J. Shatz. 1996. "U.S. Trade with Developing Countries and Wage Inequality." *American Economic Review* 86(2): 234–239.

Steelman, Aaron, and John A. Weinberg. 2005. "What's Driving Wage Inequality?" *Federal Reserve Bank of Richmond Economic Quarterly* 91(3): 1–17.

Toussaint-Comeau, Maude. 2008. "Strategies for Improving Economic Mobility of Workers: A Conference Report." *Profitwise News and Views* 2008 (September): 1–10. http://www.chicagofed.org/community_development/files/PNV_Sep2008_ReEd_FINAL_WEB.pdf (accessed April 28, 2009).

Tyler, John H., and Jillian Berk. 2009. "Correctional Programs in the Age of Mass Incarceration: What Do We Know about 'What Works'?" In *Strategies for Improving Economic Mobility of Workers: Bridging Research and*

Practice, Maude Toussaint-Comeau and Bruce D. Meyer, eds. Kalamazoo, MI: W.E. Upjohn Institute for Employment Research, pp. 175–194.

Wilson, William Julius. 1996. *When Work Disappears: The World of the New Urban Poor*. New York: Alfred A. Knopf.

Part 2

Trends, Policies, and Programs Affecting the Poor

3

Past Trends and Projections in Wages, Work, and Occupations in the United States

David Autor

Massachusetts Institute of Technology and NBER

It is widely recognized that inequality of labor market earnings in the United States has increased dramatically in recent decades. This may be seen in Figure 3.1, adapted from Autor, Katz, and Kearney (2008), which plots the growth of real hourly wages of U.S. workers (both male and female) by earnings percentile for the years 1973 through 2005. Over the course of more than three decades, wage growth was weak to nonexistent at the bottom of the distribution, strong at the top of the distribution, and modest in the middle. While real hourly earnings of workers within the bottom 30 percent of the earnings distribution rose by no more than 10 percentage points, earnings of workers at the nineti-eth percentile and above rose by more than 40 percentage points.

What is less widely known, however, is that this smooth, monotonic growth of wage inequality is a feature of a specific time period—and that this time period has passed.[1] Figure 3.2, adapted from Autor, Katz, and Kearney (2006), shows that, consistent with common perceptions, the growth of wage inequality between 1973 and 1989 was strikingly linear in wage percentiles, with sharp drops in real wages at the bottom of the distribution and modest increases at the top.[2] Yet, starting in the late 1980s, the growth of wages became polarized, as wages experienced strong, ongoing growth in the top of the earnings distribution (at or above the seventieth percentile) and modest growth in the lower tail of the distribution (at or below the thirtieth percentile). Notably, the portion of the wage distribution that saw the least real earnings growth between 1989 and 2005 was the middle, roughly the group of earners between the thirtieth and seventieth percentiles of the distribution.[3]

Figure 3.1 Changes in Real Male and Female Hourly Wages by Percentile, 1973–2005

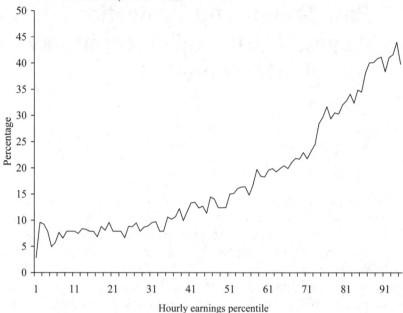

Hourly earnings percentile

NOTE: Figure represents March CPS data for earnings years 1963–2005, full-time, full-year workers ages 16 to 64 with 0 to 39 years of potential experience whose class of work in their longest job was private or government wage/salary employment. Full-time, full-year workers are those who usually worked 35-plus hours per week and worked 40-plus weeks in the previous year. Weekly earnings are calculated as annual earnings divided by weeks worked. Calculations are weighted by CPS sampling weights and are deflated using the personal consumption expenditure deflator. Earnings of below $67/week in 1982 dollars ($112/week in 2000 dollars) are dropped. Allocated earnings observations are excluded in earnings years 1967 forward using either family earnings allocation flags (1967–1974) or individual earnings allocation flags (1975 earnings year forward).
SOURCE: Autor, Katz, and Kearney (2008).

Thus, the periods of 1973–1989 and 1989–2005 present two distinct periods of rising inequality: one of diverging wages throughout the distribution, a second of polarizing wage growth.

What explains the polarization since 1990?[4] It is fair to say that the question has not yet received an entirely satisfactory answer. One potentially promising—though surely incomplete—explanation lies in

**Figure 3.2 Change in Real Male and Female Hourly Wages by
Percentile, 1973–1989 and 1989–2005**

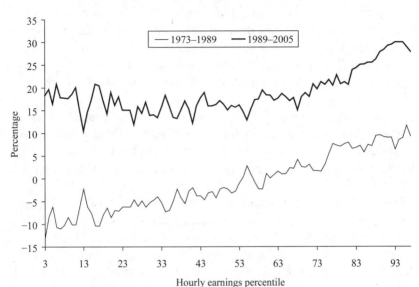

SOURCE: Autor, Katz, and Kearney (2006), and author's calculations based on data
from the U.S. Census Bureau's Current Population Survey, produced by Unicon
Research Corporation.

the changing demand for job tasks spurred by the remarkable spread of
computerization. The price of computer power has fallen by roughly
one-third to one-half each year for several decades (Berndt and Rappaport 2001). Processing tasks that were unthinkably expensive 30 years
ago, such as searching the full text of a university's library for a single
quotation, are now so cheap that the expense is trivial. This rapid, sec-
ular price decline creates enormous economic incentives for employers to substitute cheap computers for expensive labor in performing
workplace tasks. Simultaneously, it creates significant advantages for
workers whose skills become increasingly productive as computerization advances.

But what *are* the tasks that computers perform?[5] One is immediately tempted to answer, "Everything." Indeed, it is hard to think of
a quotidian activity—from checking the weather forecast to investing
our retirement savings—that doesn't involve using a computer in one

way or another. Yet, although computers are everywhere, they don't do everything—far from it. In fact, computers have a very specific set of capabilities and limitations. Ultimately, the ability of a computer to accomplish a task is dependent upon the ability of a programmer to write a set of procedures ("rules") that directs what the machine does at each possible contingency. This means that computers are "good" at the things that people can program them to do—and inept at everything else.

For example, computer programs can play an unbeatable game of checkers and a nearly unbeatable game of chess. These games follow well-described rules and so are reasonably straightforward to program. In the workplace, computers accomplish countless data processing and clerical activities such as sorting, filing, calculating, storing, retrieving, and manipulating information. Similarly, computers now handle many of the repetitive assembly and monitoring tasks on the factory floor. I refer to these procedural, rule-based activities as "routine" tasks.

Yet there are many essential tasks that workers perform daily for which programmers and engineers do not know "the rules." One such set of tasks is abstract thinking—for example, developing a hypothesis, making a persuasive argument, creating a new idea or product, or motivating and managing a group of workers. These abstract thinking tasks require creativity, intuition, and insight. Though all of us have ideas and insights, the science of programming computers to do likewise is still in its infancy. Thus, for the moment, abstract thinking tasks require educated, creative, and clever people. Moreover, computerization likely raises the productivity of workers performing abstract tasks. For example, lawyers accomplish faster and more thorough case research by tapping into legal databases. Engineers develop products more quickly when assisted by computer-aided design tools. Financial professionals using powerful machines handle much larger volumes of client money than was feasible in the paper-based era. There is abundant evidence that the demand for highly educated "abstract" workers has increased in the computer era, and it is likely that the complementarity between computerization and abstract work is part of the explanation.

But education-intensive, abstract tasks are not unique in their (partial) immunity from automation. A second group of tasks that have proved remarkably hard to computerize are so-called manual tasks. These are tasks that require on-the-spot flexibility and adaptability. Driving a truck through city traffic, waiting tables at a restaurant, checking passengers' IDs at the airport—these are all tasks that are easy for people but "hard" for computers. Why? Because they require complex and rapid interactions with unpredictable factors—erratic traffic, hungry restaurant patrons, and unfamiliar faces. Notably, these manual tasks do not require high levels of formal education.

One can glimpse the impact that computerization—more recently complemented by international outsourcing—is having on job tasks by considering the changing occupational structure of U.S. employment.[6] Table 3.1, adapted from Autor and Dorn (2008), reports the educational level and employment shares in six major occupational groups covering all of U.S. employment: 1) managerial and professional specialties; 2) technicians, sales, and administrative support; 3) precision production, craft, and repair; 4) service occupations; 5) operators, fabricators, and laborers; and 6) farming, fishing, and forestry occupations. The highest skilled of these occupational categories is managerial and professional specialty occupations, followed (at some distance) by technicians, sales, and administrative support. The four remaining categories—each averaging half the size of the first two—are demonstrably less education-intensive. Whereas in the year 2000 high school dropouts made up 2.2 percent of employment in professional and managerial jobs and 6.7 percent of employment in technical, sales, and administrative support jobs, they composed 20-plus percent of employment in the four remaining categories.

Growth has not been uniform across these six categories. Figure 3.3 shows that managerial and professional specialty occupations—the highest-skilled category—experienced consistent, rapid growth between 1980 and 2005, gaining 7.1 percentage points as a share of overall employment over those 25 years, a 30 percent increase. In contrast, employment in the "middle skill" group of technical, sales, and administrative support occupations showed an inverse U-shaped pattern over this period, expanding in the 1980s and then contracting to below its initial 1980 level over the next 15 years (consistent with the growing substitution of technology for routine tasks). Most strikingly, employment shares in three of the four low-skill occupations fell sharply in each decade.[7] For the entire period of 1980–2005, farming, forestry, and fishery occupations contracted by more than 50 percent as a share of employment; operators, fabricators, and laborers contracted

Table 3.1 Descriptive Statistics for Main Census Occupation Groups in 2000

	Employment share	Median hourly wage ($)	% high school dropout	% no college	% female	% nonwhite	% foreign-born
All occupations	100.0	13.58	12.1	39.3	42.1	21.6	14.2
Service occupations	13.4	9.40	21.3	55.1	51.3	30.8	19.7
All occupations except service occupations	86.6	14.42	10.7	36.8	40.8	20.1	13.3
Managerial and professional specialty occupations	30.2	19.23	2.2	11.4	46.5	16.2	11.8
Technicians, sales, and administrative support	28.8	12.50	6.7	35.0	58.8	20.8	11.6
Farming, forestry, and fishery occupations	1.3	7.50	33.0	67.2	14.9	20.6	22.3
Precision production, craft, and repair occupations	12.3	14.40	19.9	60.4	8.6	18.7	14.3
Operators, fabricators, and laborers	14.0	11.49	27.3	71.9	22.2	28.3	18.6

NOTE: Statistics are calculated from census IPUMS 2000, 5 percent sample. All calculations are weighted by hours of annual labor supply and exclude those under age 18 or over age 65.
SOURCE: Autor and Dorn (2008).

Figure 3.3   Employment Share of Major Census Occupation Groups, 1980, 1990, 2000, and 2005

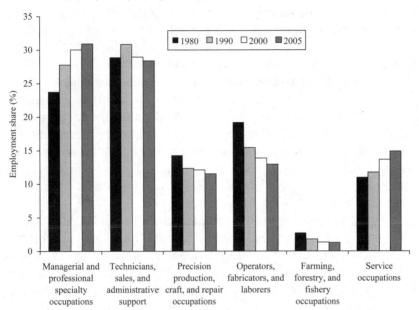

SOURCE: Autor and Dorn (2008), and author's calculations based on data from the University of Minnesota, Minnesota Population Center, Integrated Public Use Microdata Series.

by 33 percent; and precision production, craft, and repair occupations contracted by 19 percent.

Standing in sharp contrast to these patterns of declining employment, however, is the experience of service occupations.[8] Despite being among the least educated and lowest paid occupations in the U.S. economy, service occupations had an employment that expanded in each decade between 1980 and 2005, rising from 11.0 percent of employment in 1980 to 11.8 percent in 1990, to 13.7 percent in 2000, and to 14.9 percent in 2005. Overall, employment in service occupations gained 35 percent, which is 6 percentage points more than the gain in employment shares of managerial and professional occupations during the same period. In fact, service occupations constitute the only major occupational category that is growing among noncollege workers (that is, those with high school or lower education).

Why should service occupations be the exception? Table 3.2 lists the major service occupations, the largest of which are food preparation and service, health service support (a group that excludes registered nurses and other skilled medical personnel), and buildings and grounds cleaning and maintenance. These are low-paying jobs; in 2005, 75 percent had hourly wages below the overall hourly median. However, from the perspective of our conceptual framework, what distinguishes these occupations is that each is highly intensive in "nonroutine manual" tasks—activities requiring interpersonal and environmental adaptability yet little in the way of formal education. These are precisely the job tasks that are difficult to automate with current technology because they are nonroutine. Moreover, these jobs are difficult to outsource because, in large part, they must (at least at the moment) be produced and performed in person.

Employment projections from the Bureau of Labor Statistics' (BLS) *Occupational Outlook Handbook, 2006–2007* (BLS 2006) support the view that low-education service jobs are likely to be a major contributor to U.S. employment growth going forward. The BLS forecasts that employment in service occupations will increase by 5.3 million, or 19 percent, between 2004 and 2014.[9] The only major occupational category with greater projected growth is professional occupations, which are predicted to add six million jobs, a 21.2 percent increase.[10] Like all forecasts, these should be treated as tentative. Historically, the BLS has underpredicted the growing demand for professional and managerial occupations (Bishop and Carter 1991; Freeman 2006).

This process of employment polarization—in which job growth is concentrated among both highly education-intensive, abstract jobs and comparatively low-education, manual jobs—presents both challenges and opportunities for the United States, as well as for other industrialized economies. The rising productivity of highly educated workers is good news; the return on investments in higher education has perhaps never been greater. But the growing importance of manual and service tasks presents a challenge. The positive news about rising demand for in-person service occupations is that it will tend to increase the earnings of less-educated workers. The less favorable news is that, even given rising demand, labor supply to services may be sufficiently elastic that wages stay low. Median real hourly wages in service jobs were $8.86 in 1980, $9.01 in 1990, $10.24 in 2000, and $10.28 in 2005 (all expressed

Table 3.2 Descriptive Statistics for Service Occupations in 2005, and Employment Growth Rates for 1980–2005

	Employment share in 2005	Median hourly wage in 2005 ($)	% female in 2005	% nonwhite in 2005	% foreign-born in 2005	% employment growth 1980–1990	% employment growth 1990–2000	% employment growth 2000–2005
All service occupations	14.9	9.07	51.9	32.2	23.4	6.7	16.2	17.8
Housekeeping, cleaning, laundry	0.9	7.09	82.1	43.9	48.2	–11.0	2.5	12.0
Protective service	2.3	15.55	20.1	27.0	77.0	16.1	8.7	12.3
Food preparation and service	4.0	7.21	53.5	31.5	27.5	4.7	11.6	14.4
Health service support	3.0	9.93	75.0	34.7	17.8	4.5	65.0	21.6
Building/grounds cleaning/maintenance	2.6	9.09	19.7	32.5	31.3	9.1	–7.9	31.7
Personal appearance	0.7	8.64	82.0	34.2	26.6	5.4	0.0	20.3
Child care	0.8	6.91	94.4	32.0	19.8	8.9	59.2	–5.1
Recreation and hospitality	0.4	10.37	47.9	29.6	18.0	17.6	85.0	10.8
Other personal service	0.4	10.80	57.8	20.3	15.5	17.2	0.0	47.1

NOTE: All calculations are weighted by hours of annual labor supply and exclude those under age 18 or over age 65.
SOURCE: Autor and Dorn (2008), calculated from census IPUMS of 1980, 1990, and 2005, 5 percent sample, and from the American Community Survey 2005, 1 percent sample.

in 2005 dollars). These hourly wage rates imply annual, full-time earnings of approximately $20,000 a year (of course, many service jobs do not provide full-time, full-year earnings). This income level exceeds the poverty threshold for the year 2000 of $19,350 for a family of two adults and two dependent children. Yet this is probably insufficient for families to make optimal investments in child-rearing and education.

How should education policy respond to this challenge? One might be tempted to reason that if earnings growth is concentrated among the most- and least-educated workers, educators should pursue a bimodal human capital investment policy: equipping all students with a solid foundation in basic skills while reserving high levels of preparation (leading to college and graduate education) for an elite. For a number of reasons, this argument is unattractive. First, as stressed above, the returns to human capital investments are quite high. In the late 1990s, the college wage differential stood at a near-historic level, and it has risen further in the subsequent decade (see Goldin and Katz [2008]), so that it now stands at an all-time high.[11] Second, though earnings *growth* in low-education jobs exceeds that in middle-education jobs, earnings levels themselves are considerably higher in middle- than in low-education jobs—and this ranking is unlikely to reverse itself any time soon. Finally, universal, high-quality education is perhaps the only public investment proven to reliably foster opportunity, raise earnings, and increase well-being over the life cycle.[12] Thus, while it appears to be a legitimate worry that the polarization of earnings levels among U.S. households may serve to thwart economic mobility, the best insurance policy we have against this undesirable outcome is equipping citizens with skills that permit them to take full advantage of the opportunities that the future offers. It is not an overstatement to say that the case for extensive, universal investments in human capital is as strong at the outset of the twenty-first century as it has been at any time in the last century.

Notes

1. This observation was, to my knowledge, first offered by Mishel, Bernstein, and Boushey (2003).
2. The public-use Current Population Survey and Census of Populations data analyzed here do not cover the top several percentiles of the earnings distribution, where the most dramatic increases in real earnings have occurred during these decades (see Piketty and Saez [2003]). Including these top percentiles would reveal even greater growth at the top throughout the years studied.
3. It bears noting, however, that all percentiles of the distribution fared better in the second half of the time period (1989–2005) than in the first (1973–1989), reflecting the acceleration of U.S. productivity growth commencing in the mid-1990s.
4. To my knowledge, Goos and Manning (2007) were the first to refer to the simultaneous growth of low- and high-skill jobs (at the expense of the middle) as a "polarization" of employment, thus coining that usage of the term to describe this phenomenon.
5. The "task view" of computerization presented here is formalized by Autor, Levy, and Murnane (2003) and elaborated on and advanced by Autor, Katz, and Kearney (2006, 2008); Dustmann, Ludsteck, and Schönberg (2007); Goos and Manning (2007); Levy and Murnane (2004); and Spitz-Oener (2006). Bartel, Ichniowski, and Shaw (2007) present detailed, representative evidence on the relationship between computerization, work organization, and productivity. Goldin and Katz (2008) provide a longer-term historical perspective on the relationship between technical change, work organization, and skill demand.
6. There is vast uncertainty about the degree to which international outsourcing will ultimately affect domestic labor demand. At present, most quantitative assessments of these potential impacts are preliminary or impressionistic (Blinder 2007; Kletzer 2006). Levy and Murnane (2005) consider the relationship between computerization and outsourcing through the lens of the "task" framework exposited above.
7. Operator, fabricator, and laborer occupations fell from 19.2 percent of employment in 1980 to 14.5 percent in 1990, to 13.9 percent in 2000, and to 13.0 percent in 2005. Production, craft, and repair occupations fell from 14.3 percent of employment in 1980 to 12.4 percent in 1990, to 12.1 percent in 2000, and to 11.6 percent in 2005. Farming, forestry, and fishery occupations fell from 2.8 percent of employment in 1980 to 1.8 percent in 1990, to 1.3 percent in 2000, and to 1.3 percent in 2005. The sources for these calculations are the census Integrated Public Use Microdata Series (IPUMS) files for 1980, 1990, and 2000, and the American Community Survey for 2005.
8. It is important to distinguish service *occupations*, a relatively narrow group of low-education occupations composing 13.4 percent of employment in 2000 (author's calculation from the census IPUMS), from the service *sector*, a broad category of industries including everything from health care to communications to real estate and constituting 81 percent of nonfarm employment in 2000 (BLS 2009).
9. The service employment measure used by the Bureau of Labor Statistics' *Occu-*

pational Outlook Handbook, 2006–2007 (BLS 2006) indicates a service employment share that is several percentage points higher than our calculations given in note 8 (17.7 percent versus 13.4 percent). The discrepancy stems from three factors: unlike our calculations, which are based on household data from the census, the BLS numbers use Current Employment Statistics (CES) data. The CES, as an establishment survey, double-counts workers who hold multiple jobs; our census-based numbers are weighted by hours of labor supply, and so part-time jobs (common in service occupations) are weighted down, whereas the CES data count all jobs equally. Furthermore, our census calculations exclude workers younger than 18, whereas the CES data include workers ages 16 and above. The service occupation in which the census and CES data are most different is in food preparation and service, where our data show a 3.5 percent employment share and the CES data show a 7.4 percent employment share. Despite these discrepancies in levels, we have no reason to believe that the qualitative employment trends in the census and CES data are at odds with each other.

10. The BLS category of professional occupations excludes managerial occupations and so is more disaggregated than the census category of professional and managerial occupations. Combined growth in professional and managerial jobs is projected at 8.2 million jobs, or 18.8 percent.

11. The college wage differential is at its highest level since 1915, which is as far back as representative U.S. data are available.

12. Recent work by Kopczuk, Saez, and Song (2007) finds little change in mobility over the course of a career among U.S. cohorts born between 1920 and 1950. However, these data do not speak to economic mobility across generations—in particular, to how likely children of low-income households are to reach higher echelons of the earnings distribution during their careers.

References

Autor, David H., and David Dorn. 2008. "Inequality and Specialization: The Growth of Low-Skill Service Jobs in the United States." MIT mimeograph. Cambridge, MA: Massachusetts Institute of Technology.

Autor, David H., Lawrence F. Katz, and Melissa S. Kearney. 2006. "The Polarization of the U.S. Labor Market." *American Economic Review* 96(2): 189–194.

———. 2008. "Trends in U.S. Wage Inequality: Revising the Revisionists." *Review of Economics and Statistics* 90(2): 300–323.

Autor, David H., Frank Levy, and Richard J. Murnane. 2003. "The Skill Content of Recent Technological Change: An Empirical Exploration." *Quarterly Journal of Economics* 118(4): 1279–1333.

Bartel, Ann P., Casey Ichniowski, and Kathryn L. Shaw. 2007. "How Does Information Technology Affect Productivity? Plant-Level Comparisons of

Product Innovation, Process Improvement and Worker Skills." *Quarterly Journal of Economics* 122(4): 1721–1758.

Berndt, Ernst R., and Neal J. Rappaport. 2001. "Price and Quality of Desktop and Mobile Personal Computers: A Quarter-Century Historical Overview." *American Economic Review* 91(2): 268–273.

Bishop, John H., and Shani Carter. 1991. "How Accurate are Recent BLS Occupational Projections?" *Monthly Labor Review* 114(10): 37–43.

Blinder, Alan S. 2007. "How Many U.S. Jobs Might Be Offshorable?" CEPS Working Paper No. 142. Princeton, NJ: Princeton University Center for Economic Policy Studies.

Bureau of Labor Statistics (BLS). 2006. *Occupational Outlook Handbook, 2006–2007.* Indianapolis: JIST Publishing.

———. 2009. *Industries at a Glance.* Washington, DC: Bureau of Labor Statistics. http://www.bls.gov/iag/tgs/iag07.htm (accessed March 12, 2009).

Dustmann, Christian, Johannes Ludsteck, and Uta Schönberg. 2007. "Revisiting the German Wage Structure." IZA Discussion Paper No. 2685. Bonn, Germany: Institute for the Study of Labor.

Freeman, Richard B. 2006. "Is a Great Labor Shortage Coming? Replacement Demand in the Global Economy." NBER Working Paper No. 12541. Cambridge, MA: Nationa Bureau of Economic Research.

Goldin, Claudia, and Lawrence F. Katz. 2008. *The Race between Education and Technology.* Cambridge, MA: Belknap Press.

Goos, Maarten, and Alan Manning. 2007. "Lousy and Lovely Jobs: The Rising Polarization of Work in Britain." *Review of Economics and Statistics* 89(1): 118–133.

Kletzer, Lori G. 2006. "The Scope of Tradable Services and the Task Content of Offshorable Services Jobs." UC Santa Cruz mimeograph. Santa Cruz, CA: University of California, Santa Cruz.

Kopczuk, Wojciech, Emmanuel Saez, and Jae Song. 2007. "Uncovering the American Dream: Inequality and Mobility in Social Security Earnings Data since 1937." NBER Working Paper No. 13345. Cambridge, MA: National Bureau of Economic Research.

Levy, Frank, and Richard J. Murnane. 2004. *The New Division of Labor: How Computers Are Creating the Next Job Market.* Princeton, NJ: Princeton University Press.

———. 2005. "How Computerized Work and Globalization Shape Human Skill Demands." MIT-IPC Working Paper 05-006. Cambridge, MA: Massachusetts Institute of Technology, Industrial Performance Center.

Mishel, Lawrence, Jared Bernstein, and Heather Boushey. 2003. *The State of Working America, 2002/2003.* Ithaca, NY: ILR Press.

Piketty, Thomas, and Emmanuel Saez. 2003. "Income Inequality in the United States, 1913–1998." *Quarterly Journal of Economics* 118(1): 1–39.

Spitz-Oener, Alexandra. 2006. "Technical Change, Job Tasks, and Rising Educational Demands: Looking Outside the Wage Structure." *Journal of Labor Economics* 24(2): 235–270.

4

The Earned Income Tax Credit, Welfare Reform, and the Employment of Low-Skilled Single Mothers

Hilary Williamson Hoynes
University of California, Davis

Cash assistance for low-income families with children underwent tremendous change in the 1990s. Welfare reform led to a dramatic reduction in the generosity of state cash assistance and an elimination of the Aid to Families with Dependent Children (AFDC) program. At the same time, cash assistance through the tax system, in the form of the Earned Income Tax Credit (EITC), increased substantially. In fact, the EITC is now the largest federal cash transfer program for lower-income families, generating a total cost (in 2005) of $34 billion, compared with $24 billion in Temporary Assistance for Needy Families (TANF) expenditures.

This shift in the structure of cash assistance for low-income families, away from welfare and toward tax-based assistance, is the outcome of a long-standing criticism that traditional welfare programs generate adverse incentives for work and family. Importantly, the policy changes to welfare and the EITC in the 1990s both provided incentives (financial and otherwise) for single mothers with children to increase their employment. Indeed, employment rates of single mothers with children rose 11 percentage points over a 20-year period, from 73 percent in 1987 to 84 percent in 2006. Even more striking is the 16-percentage-point change (from 72 to 88 percent) that occurred between 1992 and 1999. During this span, gains were even larger for single mothers without a high school diploma; among this group, employment rates increased by 20 percentage points between 1992 and 1999. No other group of women (single women without children, married women with or without children) or men experienced such a dramatic increase in employment. In this chapter, I describe these important policies, as well as present trends in employment for single mothers, and I summarize what is known about how the changes in welfare and the EITC have affected employment.

WELFARE REFORM AND THE EARNED INCOME TAX CREDIT

The AFDC program provided cash assistance to low-income single mothers with children from the 1930s to the 1990s. The program was designed to provide an income transfer for needy families in an era when women with children had minimal labor-market attachment. Consequently, AFDC benefits were phased out at a very high rate: after a small disregard, benefits were reduced by one dollar for every additional dollar in earned income. This, by design, created a targeting of benefits to those with the lowest income levels, but it also inadvertently created a disincentive to enter the labor force because the increase in earnings was offset by a reduction in the cash transfer.

Concerns about the labor supply disincentives in the AFDC program had an important impact on welfare reform at the state and federal level. Beginning in the early 1990s, many states were granted waivers to change their AFDC programs, and by 1995 about half of the states had implemented some sort of welfare waiver. On the heels of this state experimentation, the Personal Responsibility and Work Opportunity Reconciliation Act (PRWORA) was enacted in 1996, replacing AFDC with TANF. The key elements of reform in the state waivers and TANF legislation include work requirements, lifetime time limits, financial sanctions, and enhanced earnings disregards. These changes were designed to increase work and reduce welfare participation. Figure 4.1 shows the dramatic decline in welfare caseloads that occurred during this period.

The EITC began in 1975 as a modest program aimed at offsetting Social Security payroll taxes for low-income families with children. It was the outcome of a vigorous policy debate surrounding the efficacy of a negative income tax (NIT) as a means of reducing poverty. The con-

Figure 4.1 AFDC/TANF Caseload, 1970–2006

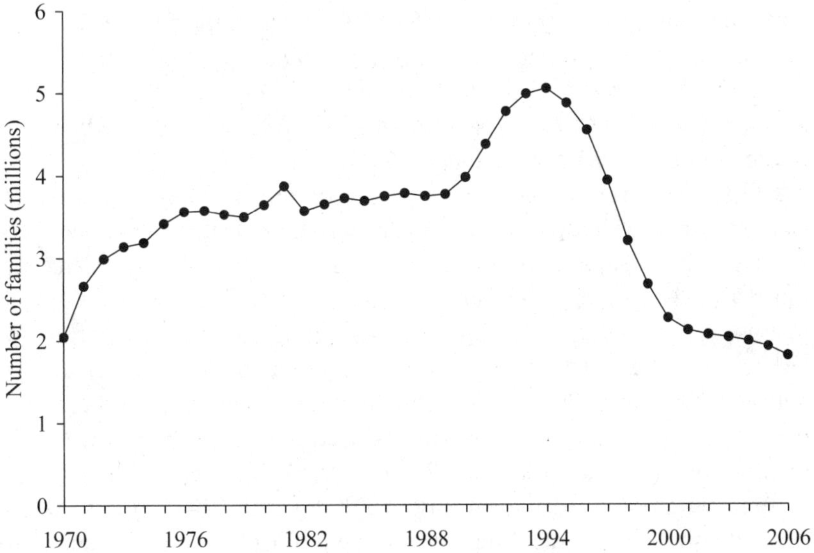

SOURCE: U.S. Department of Health and Human Services (2008).

cern was that the NIT would discourage labor market activity as it was gradually phased out. Ultimately the EITC was born out of a desire to reward work. The EITC provides a cash transfer to low-income working families through the tax system. The EITC is refundable so that a taxpayer with no federal tax liability, for example, would receive a tax refund from the government for the full amount of the credit. Eligibility for the credit requires one to have positive earned income and also requires one's adjusted gross income and earned income to be below a specified amount; in 2007, the maximum allowable income for a single taxpayer with one child was $33,241 ($37,783 with two or more children).[1]

The amount of the credit to which a taxpayer is entitled depends on the taxpayer's earned income, adjusted gross income, and, since 1991, the number of EITC-eligible children in the household. There are three regions in the credit schedule: the phase-in region, the flat region, and the phase-out region. The credit for those in the phase-in region is equal to the subsidy rate times their earnings. The subsidy rate is quite high—

34 percent for taxpayers with one child and 40 percent for taxpayers with two or more children. In the flat region, the family receives the maximum credit (in 2007 it was $2,853 for one child and $4,716 for more), whereas in the phase-out region the credit is discontinued at the phase-out rate (16 and 21 percent). As shown in Figure 4.2, the program expanded under the Tax Reform Act of 1986 (TRA86) and the Omnibus Reconciliation Acts of 1990 and 1993 (OBRA90 and OBRA93). Figure 4.2 illustrates these expansions in the program by plotting the (real) EITC payment schedule by (real) earnings for selected years between 1984 and 2006, separately for families with one child (Panel A) and for those with two or more children (Panel B).[2] The figure clearly shows that not only was the 1993 expansion the largest of the three but that it was much larger for families with two or more children. For example, between 1993 and 2006, single mothers with two children and earning between $15,000 and $25,000 (in 2006 dollars) experienced a more-than-doubling of their real transfer from the EITC. In contrast, single mothers with one child and earning $15,000 (in real 2006 dollars) experienced about a 40 percent increase in the real EITC, while those earning $25,000 experienced about a 25 percent increase in the real EITC.

These expansions have led to a dramatic increase in the total cost of the EITC in recent years. Figure 4.3 plots the number of EITC recipients (taxpaying units or families) and the total tax cost of the EITC (in 2006 dollars) over the period from 1975 to 2005. The figure clearly shows the rising expenditures and number of recipients associated with the 1986, 1990, and 1993 tax acts. Importantly, between 1990 and 1996, real EITC costs increased more than threefold.[3]

Finally, Figure 4.4 contrasts the aggregate cost of the EITC with the cost of AFDC/TANF from 1975 to 2005. In a very short time, the EITC has overtaken AFDC/TANF and become the largest cash transfer program for low-income families.

POLICY CHANGES AND EXPECTED IMPACTS ON EMPLOYMENT

Labor supply theory suggests that welfare reform and EITC expansions should increase employment of low-income single mothers.[4] Vir-

Figure 4.2 Real EITC Schedule for Single Mothers, by Real Earnings

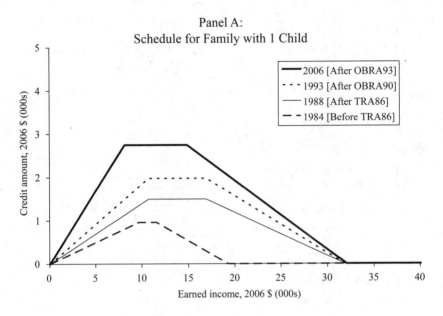

Panel A:
Schedule for Family with 1 Child

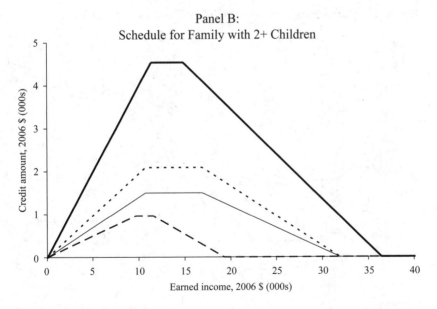

Panel B:
Schedule for Family with 2+ Children

SOURCE: Author's tabulations.

Figure 4.3 EITC Recipients and Expenditures, 1975–2005

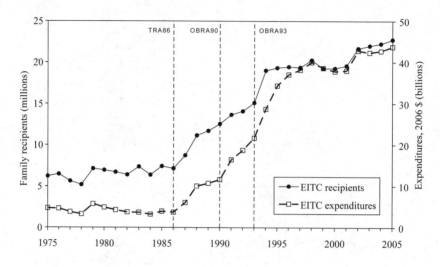

SOURCE: Tax Policy Center (2007).

Figure 4.4 Comparing Cost of AFDC/TANF to EITC, 1975–2005

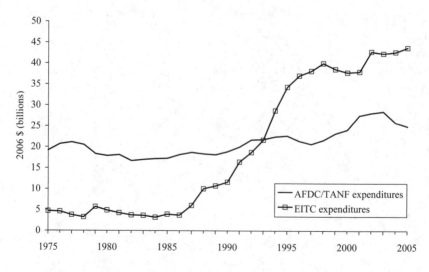

SOURCE: AFDC/TANF expenditures from the Office of Management and Budget (2007). EITC expenditures from the Tax Policy Center (2007).

tually all of the provisions implemented in the state and federal welfare reform should lead to more employment through removing the entitlement nature of welfare (time limits), increasing the costs of participation in welfare (work requirements, financial sanctions), and reducing the financial work disincentives (reducing the phase-out rate, increasing work disregards).

The expansions in the EITC also are expected to lead to more employment among single mothers. Because the EITC is available only to taxpayers with earned income, standard labor supply theory predicts that the EITC will encourage labor force participation. While this effect is not the focus of this paper, the EITC is expected to reduce hours worked for those women already working whose earnings are in the flat and phase-out regions of the credit.[5]

TRENDS IN EMPLOYMENT OF SINGLE MOTHERS

Figure 4.5 presents annual employment rates for women aged 19–44 between 1983 and 2006.[6] We show the employment rates for four groups: 1) single women with children, 2) single women without children, 3) married women with children, and 4) married women without children. These groups are chosen to illustrate the dramatic changes particular to single women with children—the group most affected by welfare reform and the EITC.

The figure shows the dramatic increase in employment rates for single women with children during this period. For example, between 1983 and 2006 employment rates of single mothers increased by 13 percentage points—from 71 percent in 1983 to 84 percent in 2006. Most of this change occurred between 1992 and 1999, when employment rates increased by an amazing 16 percentage points (from 72 to 88 percent). This coincided with the largest expansion in the history of the EITC and the dramatic reform of the welfare system. Of course, not all the gains can be attributed to the EITC's growth and welfare reform; they also happened during the strong 1990s economic expansion—a time of rising wages and falling unemployment rates. However, it is clear from this simple figure that the gains in employment experienced by single mothers were not shared by all demographic groups.

Figure 4.5 Annual Employment Rates for Women Aged 19–44, by Marital Status and Presence of Children

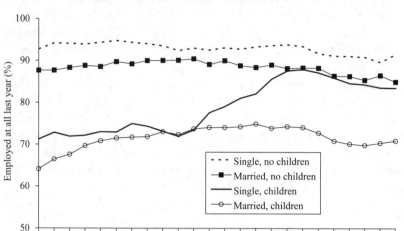

SOURCE: Author's tabulation of the 1984–2007 March Current Population Surveys.

To refine the analysis, and recognizing that EITC recipients are more likely to have lower skill and education levels, Figure 4.6 presents the annual employment rates when limiting the sample to women with 12 or fewer years of education. While employment rates are lower among less-educated women, the same pattern is evident—large gains in employment for single mothers over the period, as shown by a tremendous increase of 20 percentage points between 1992 and 1999.

The last figure, Figure 4.7, shows the employment rates for single women by number of children (none, one, or two or more). Breaking down the data in this way reveals that the increases in employment were concentrated among single women with two or more children.

Figure 4.6 Annual Employment Rates for Women Aged 19–44 with a High School Education or Less, by Marital Status and Presence of Children

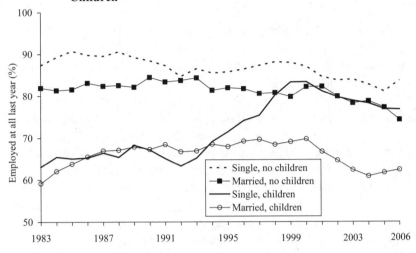

SOURCE: Author's tabulation of the 1984–2007 March Current Population Surveys.

Figure 4.7 Annual Employment Rates for Single Women Aged 19–44, by Number of Children

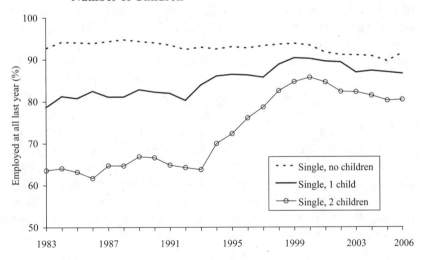

SOURCE: Author's tabulation of the 1984–2007 March Current Population Surveys.

DID WELFARE REFORM AND THE EITC CONTRIBUTE TO THE INCREASES IN EMPLOYMENT?

Separately identifying the impact of welfare reform, the EITC, and the strong economy on single women is a challenge, as the three factors were all at play in the mid- to late 1990s. The literature on the subject documents many approaches that have been taken in an attempt to disentangle the impacts. One approach is to take advantage of the variation across states in welfare reform, the business cycle, and the state EITCs. A second approach uses comparison groups. Yet another approach parameterizes the gains to work and utilizes variation in gains to work for women over time, across states, and in different skill groups. From all of these approaches, there is strong evidence that welfare reform, the EITC, and the strong economy all played a role in the rising employment rates experienced by single mothers in the 1990s. This section provides a brief summary of the large literature on the impact that the EITC and welfare reform have had on the labor supply of single mothers.[7]

Much of the work in this area concentrates on the impact of either welfare reform or the EITC. In the EITC literature, the studies suggest a strong positive relationship between the EITC and employment rates of single women with children. Furthermore, the results are remarkably consistent across different policy expansions, different control groups, and different methodologies. Several studies (Ellwood 2000; Meyer and Rosenbaum 2000; Rothstein 2005) find that groups with the most to gain from EITC expansions (e.g., single women and women with lower wages, lower education levels, and more children) experienced larger gains in employment rates. The welfare reform studies also find positive impacts on employment, with magnitudes somewhat smaller and less statistically significant than those of the EITC studies.

Few studies provide a direct comparison of welfare reform and the EITC. Meyer and Rosenbaum (2001) is an important exception. Their analysis examines the impact of taxes, welfare generosity, welfare reform, other policies (minimum wages, in-kind transfer programs), and demographics on the employment of single mothers. They find that of the 12-percentage-point increase in employment rates of single mothers between 1984 and 1996, fully 60 percent of the increase was attributable to the EITC and other tax changes, and 15 percent was attributable to welfare reform. The results on the relative importance of EITC versus welfare reform are sensitive to the particular time period analyzed. For the period from 1992 to 1996, however, Meyer and Rosenbaum find that the importance of welfare reform rose relative to that of the EITC—specifically, 35 percent of the increase in employment was linked to the EITC and other tax changes, and 20 percent was linked to welfare reform.

CONCLUSION

The 1990s were a period of tremendous change in policies affecting single mothers with children. The expansion of the Earned Income Tax Credit and welfare reform both raised the financial rewards to welfare recipients for moving into the labor force. Furthermore, the gains in employment for single mothers during this period were sizable, and no such gains were experienced by other groups of workers. There is an extensive body of research that looks at these facts and, using a wide variety of methodologies, concludes that these changes in taxes and transfers contributed in an important way to these increases in employment. The research suggests that the expansions in the EITC were the most important contributor to these changes.

Notes

1. There is also a small credit for childless taxpayers. We ignore that here and focus on the main recipients, families with children.
2. Figure 4.2 plots the EITC schedule that applies to single taxpayers. Beginning in 2002, the flat and phaseout regions were expanded modestly (by $1,000 from 2002 to 2004, by $2,000 from 2005 to 2007, and by $3,000 from 2008 onwards) for married filers.
3. In addition to the federal EITC, an increasing number of states offer state EITCs. As of 2004, a total of 18 states had introduced state EITCs that supplement the federal credit. Almost all states structure their credits as a share of the federal credit, ranging between 5 percent (Illinois) and more than 40 percent (Minnesota and Wisconsin), and almost all make the credit refundable like the federal credit (Llobrera and Zahradnik 2004).

4. The focus in this chapter is on single mothers, who represent the vast majority of AFDC/TANF recipients and over 75 percent of EITC claims (Eissa and Hoynes 2006a). The labor supply impacts of the EITC expansion on married couples are more complicated and are likely to lead to reductions in employment for some married women (Eissa and Hoynes 2004, 2006a,b).

5. In the phase-in region, the EITC has an ambiguous impact on hours worked because of the negative income effect and positive substitution effect. In the flat region, the EITC produces a negative income effect, leading to an unambiguous reduction in hours worked. In the phase-out region, the EITC produces a negative income and negative substitution effect, leading again to an unambiguous reduction in hours worked. Eissa and Hoynes (2006a) show that about three-quarters of single EITC recipients have earnings in the flat and phase-out regions of the credit—thus, the expectation is that the EITC will reduce the number of hours worked by most eligible single taxpayers already in the labor force.

6. These tabulations are calculated using the 1984–2007 March Current Population Surveys. The sample includes all women aged 19–44 who are neither in school nor disabled. We also drop the relatively small number of women who report working positive hours but have zero earnings or report positive earnings but zero hours. For these calculations, employment is defined as any work done over the previous calendar year.

7. Individual papers are cited where particularly relevant. The interested reader should consult the recent and comprehensive reviews of this literature by Blank (2002), Eissa and Hoynes (2006a), Grogger and Karoly (2005), and Hotz and Scholz (2003).

References

Blank, Rebecca M. 2002. "Evaluating Welfare Reform in the United States." *Journal of Economic Literature* 40(4): 1105–1166.

Eissa, Nada, and Hilary Williamson Hoynes. 2004. "Taxes and the Labor Market Participation of Married Couples: The Earned Income Tax Credit." *Journal of Public Economics* 88(9–10): 1931–1958.

———. 2006a. "Behavioral Responses to Taxes: Lessons from the EITC and Labor Supply." In *Tax Policy and the Economy*, James M. Poterba, ed. Vol. 20. Cambridge, MA: MIT Press, pp. 74–110.

———. 2006b. "The Hours of Work Response of Married Couples: Taxes and the Earned Income Tax Credit." In *Tax Policy and Labor Market Performance*, Jonas Agell and Peter Birch Sørensen, eds. CES/ifo Seminar Series. Cambridge, MA: MIT Press, pp. 187–228.

Ellwood, David T. 2000. "The Impact of the Earned Income Tax Credit and Social Policy Reforms on Work, Marriage, and Living Arrangements." *National Tax Journal* 53(4): 1063–1106.

Grogger, Jeffrey, and Lynn A. Karoly. 2005. *Welfare Reform: Effects of a Decade of Change*. Cambridge, MA: Harvard University Press.

Hotz, V. Joseph, and John Karl Scholz. 2003. "The Earned Income Tax Credit." In *Means-Tested Transfer Programs in the United States*, Robert A. Moffitt, ed. Chicago: University of Chicago Press, pp. 141–198.

Llobrera, Joseph, and Bob Zahradnik. 2004. "A Hand Up: How State Earned Income Tax Credits Help Working Families Escape Poverty in 2004." Washington, DC: Center on Budget and Policy Priorities.

Meyer, Bruce D., and Dan T. Rosenbaum. 2000. "Making Single Mothers Work: Recent Tax and Welfare Policy and Its Effects." *National Tax Journal* 53(4): 1027–1062.

———. 2001. "Welfare, the Earned Income Tax Credit, and the Labor Supply of Single Mothers." *Quarterly Journal of Economics* 116(3): 1063–1114.

Office of Management and Budget. 2007. "Table 8.5—Outlays for Mandatory and Related Programs: 1962–2012." In *Historical Tables: Budget of the United States Government, Fiscal Year 2008*. Washington, DC: Office of Management and Budget.

Rothstein, Jesse. 2005. "The Mid-1990s EITC Expansion: Aggregate Labor Supply Effects and Economic Incidence." Industrial Relations Section Working Paper No. 504. Princeton, NJ: Princeton University, Department of Economics.

Tax Policy Center. 2007. *Tax Facts: Historical EITC Recipients*. Washington, DC: Urban Institute and Brookings Institution.

U.S. Department of Health and Human Services (HHS). 2008. *Data and Reports: TANF Caseload Data—Number of Families and Recipients*. Washington, DC: U.S. Department of Health and Human Services, Administration for Children and Families. http://www.acf.hhs.gov/programs/ofa/data-reports/index.htm (accessed February 24, 2009).

5
Reflections on Economic Mobility and Policy

Bruce D. Meyer
University of Chicago and NBER

This chapter comments on presentations from the "Strategies for Improving Economic Mobility of Workers" conference and discusses trends in the material circumstances of Americans. I will also briefly discuss some policies that have been used to equalize the distribution of resources.

In looking at trends over the past 30 years in the material circumstances of U.S. residents (I am defining "material circumstances" to include wages, income, and poverty, as well as food consumption, purchases of other goods, housing quality, and access to health care), there are two main patterns one should keep in mind. The two patterns are 1) increased inequality in income and consumption and 2) improvements at almost all points of the distribution of material circumstances, when properly measured. These patterns may not be apparent in all measures of material circumstances, but they are the general tendency. Often only one of these patterns is emphasized by researchers or pundits, but the two patterns really should be discussed together because each one by itself gives a distorted impression of how the economy has changed.

A third pattern I am going to mention, increased income volatility, is different. It is not clear whether volatility has increased in recent years, since there is conflicting evidence. Moreover, if income volatility is indeed increasing, what that means for the well-being of the population is not clear at all.

Regarding the first pattern, increased inequality, Autor (2009) has shown in the first chapter of this book that hourly wage growth from 1973 through 1989 was remarkably linear across the various percentiles. In other words, wages fell somewhat at the bottom, changed little in the middle, and grew modestly at the top. From 1989 through 2005, in contrast, wage growth was polarized, with high growth at the bottom and the top and little growth between the thirtieth and the seventieth percentiles. Autor suggests that the growing use of computers and the changing demand for job tasks form a large part of the explanation for this pattern. He suggests that policies should encourage investment in human capital to take advantage of likely future growth in education-intensive "abstract" jobs.

Berube (2007) emphasizes that regional growth in productivity and employment and regional changes in poverty have been uneven. While cities continue to have higher poverty rates than suburbs, suburban growth has meant that slightly more than half of the poor now reside in suburbs. He notes that when poverty rises, it seems to rise more for children. He also notes that although poverty became less concentrated in particular neighborhoods within cities during the 1990s, this pattern appears to have reversed so far during the current decade.

Gosselin and Zimmerman (2007) examine trends in income volatility and risk. They find a substantial increase in the transitory variance of family income over time in data from the Panel Study of Income Dynamics (PSID). This pattern of increased variance seems to be much more pronounced in the PSID than in the alternative data set they examine, the Survey of Income and Program Participation (SIPP).

The PSID data indicate a large increase in the likelihood of a 50 percent drop in family income over two years. This increase comes not through a greater likelihood of a bad event occurring (such as unemployment or disability), but through a greater likelihood that a bad event will be associated with a 50 percent drop in family income.

On this issue of volatility, I do not believe that the facts are clear; nor is it clear how any trends should be interpreted. First, what are the facts? As mentioned, there is some conflicting evidence on the trends in income variability. In contrast to Gosselin and Zimmerman (2007), Dahl, DeLeire, and Schwabish (2007), in a Congressional Budget Office report, examine Social Security records and find a decline in income variability in recent years. Their evidence is at the individual level, rather than the family level, which clouds the interpretation. Another research team that uses a version of the same data, Kopczuk, Saez, and Song (2007), finds the same pattern. Thus, there is a question as to what have been the changes over time in income variability (also see the recent working paper by Shin and Solon [2008], who find little change in volatility since 1980 until an upward trend in the last few years).

Leaving aside this puzzle, a deeper question is whether these measures of volatility are good measures of people's material circumstances. The Kopczuk, Saez, and Song (2007) paper argues that more variability is good. The authors say such variability makes possible the American dream of upward mobility. On the other hand, Gosselin and Zimmerman (2007) argue that trends in family income volatility reflect increased economic risk and are thus bad.

To better understand the two ways of looking at volatility, consider the situation in which the share of people in poverty is roughly constant over time. In fact, the official income poverty measure (pretax money income, which is similar to the Gosselin and Zimmerman [2007] income measure) was exactly the same in 1970 and 2005 (and has fallen only slightly since). If the level of poverty is roughly constant, then if more people are falling into poverty, more people must be leaving. Gosselin and Zimmerman emphasize the former, while Kopczuk, Saez, and Song (2007) emphasize the latter. The patterns are merely opposite sides of the same coin.

It should be clear from this discussion that for research and policy we probably should focus on changes in the distribution of resources over time, rather than on volatility or mobility measures. We know that if the bottom of the resource distribution shifts down but the remainder of the distribution is unchanged, society is worse off. Similarly, if the entire distribution shifts up, we know society is better off. Volatility measures are of secondary or tertiary importance because their interpretation is unclear. This discussion also suggests that we might be better off looking at the frequency with which people have extended periods of poverty.

In any case, if we are examining severe drops in income, their interpretation depends on whether or not the decrease in income means families are hungry, ill-housed, or suffering from other types of material deprivation. Families have many ways to shield their standard of living as their income falls. These ways include obtaining resources from government programs, borrowing money for the short term, and drawing down savings. While it is difficult to examine some of these patterns directly, researchers and policy analysts can study the consumption patterns of families. As I will describe in greater detail below, consumption measures show a decline in poverty overall, with the decline being especially large for measures of severe poverty.

Dahl (2007) shows that the incomes of households with children have grown over time. Low-income households with children (i.e., the bottom 20 percent) have had increases in income over the past 15 years. Single-mother households have seen their incomes rise noticeably over the past 15 years, mostly because of increases in earnings and to a lesser extent because of the Earned Income Tax Credit (EITC). The growth in earnings in percentage terms has been greatest in the bottom 20 percent of households with children (but it started at a low level). Dahl notes that she is not able to account for the effects of the Food Stamp Program and public health insurance coverage in her calculations. I should also mention that her measure excludes public and subsidized housing benefits.

I am more upbeat about the living standards of most people than even Dahl. Most researchers rely on government income statistics that overadjust for inflation. This overadjustment makes it seem that living standards have not improved. The official government adjustment for price changes does not adequately account for new goods, does not consider lower prices at discount stores such as Wal-Mart, and misses much of the quality improvements in existing goods. It also does not fully account for the fact that when the price of one good rises relative to similar goods, people move away from purchasing it, substituting cheaper alternatives in its place.

The Boskin Commission (Boskin et al. 1996), a group of eminent economists appointed by the Senate Finance Committee, concluded that the official government price measure is biased upward by 1.3 percentage points per year. Subsequent research has mostly supported this conclusion. The implication of this mismeasurement of inflation is that median family incomes have actually risen faster than reported by the Census Bureau (Meyer and Sullivan 2007). Figure 5.1 shows the evolution of median income using better measures of inflation and accounting for taxes and noncash benefits. In addition, many other factors affecting measurement suggest we are better off than official reports indicate. Measures of income-based poverty that account for taxes and transfers have fallen sharply since 1980. Measures of poverty based on what people are able to purchase in food and housing—i.e., consumption poverty measures—have fallen even faster, as can be seen

Figure 5.1   Real Median Family Income, 1980–2004

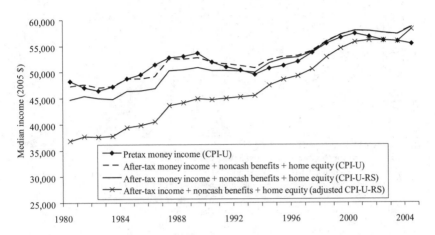

NOTE: Medians are reported for the individually weighted, scale-adjusted distribution of family income for each measure of income. We use the National Academy of Sciences (NAS)–recommended equivalence scale. After-tax income + noncash benefits + home equity includes taxes and credits, capital gains and losses, food stamps, Current Population Survey (CPS)–imputed measures of housing and school lunch subsidies, the fungible value of Medicaid and Medicare, the value of employer health benefits, and the value of the net return on home equity. See Meyer and Sullivan (2007) for details.

in Figure 5.2. The fraction of those with consumption below half of the poverty line, so-called deep poverty, has fallen faster yet (Meyer and Sullivan 2009).

All of these trends in material circumstances provide the background for policy to address the situation of workers today. Better-measured numbers indicate that we are not as badly off as official statistics and news reports suggest. One might conclude from this that there is less need for policy. On the contrary—the numbers show that some past policies have been successful and suggest that additional policies might be able to build on that success. Two types of policies that come up repeatedly are 1) education or other human capital building and 2) work subsidies, such as the EITC.

Just as Autor (2009) and Berube (2007) propose investing in human capital, Blinder (2007) contends that we need to think about how to educate the next generation of workers. Both Autor and Blinder acknowl-

Figure 5.2 Consumption and Income Poverty Rates, 1972–2005

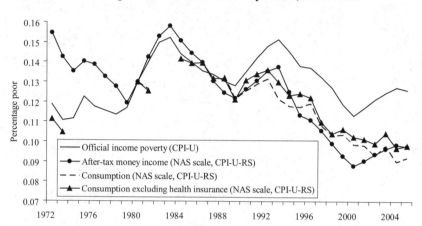

NOTE: Rates anchored at 1980. All poverty rates are at the person level. Consumption data are from the Consumer Expenditure Survey (CE), and income data are from the Current Population Survey's Annual Social and Economic Supplement (CPS-ASEC), formerly know as the Annual Demographic Survey (ADS). CE survey data are not available for the years 1974–1979 and 1982–1983. Also, consumption data are not available for the years 1984–1987 for measures that include health insurance. See Meyer and Sullivan (2009) for details.

edge that it is hard to predict which industries and occupations will see employment increases, which will see declines, and when these changes will occur. They make general predictions but provide few specifics. There remain tough decisions to be made about whose human capital should be enhanced and what skills these people need. We have little guidance from research to date on these questions.

   Both Dahl (2007) and Berube (2007) discuss how the EITC is targeted to families with children; Holzer (2009) suggests expanding the EITC; and Hoynes (2009) addresses the impact of the EITC. Hoynes notes that the tax credit sharply increased the employment of single mothers in the 1990s, and for much of the recent period it had perhaps as big a role in employment changes as welfare reform. She, like Holzer, suggests that we should consider expanding the EITC, since there are groups that do not especially benefit from the current EITC, such as childless men and women and some groups of low-income married couples.

In thinking about these possible expansions in the EITC, we should keep a couple of points in mind. First, by expanding the credit to reach more people, our policy could encourage work while transferring resources to low-income individuals. Second, the EITC likely was successful in increasing the employment of single mothers because they had a low employment rate to start with and because, before the EITC, their net financial reward for work was low since working often meant losing welfare, food stamps, and other benefits. Neither of these conditions will be as true for other groups, such as childless men and women. Thus, while such a reform may have favorable distribution effects, it should not be expected to increase employment sharply.

Hoynes (2009) suggests that we should consider raising the maximum EITC amount and raising the implicit tax rate over the phaseout portion of the credit (such a change could be revenue-neutral). This suggestion is based on the repeated finding that the credit has little effect on the hours worked by those already working (Eissa and Hoynes 2006; Meyer 2007). While I believe this idea has substantial merit, I have concerns that in the long run individuals will come to understand the structure of the credit, in particular the very high penalty on additional earnings that this change would create. In general, it is good for credit recipients to understand the tax rules, but we should be aware that such an understanding in this case might very well lead to a negative response on their part in terms of the number of hours worked.

I would like to offer one addition to the list of possible EITC reforms. The current benefit structure is the same for those with three or more children as for those with two. A more generous schedule for those with three or more children would help to support families that appear to be particularly needy. As can be seen in Table 5.1, those with three or more children have fewer resources to devote to food, housing, and other consumption than single mothers with one or two children.

Overall, the evidence suggests that while we have seen a sharp increase in inequality in recent years, those at the bottom are still much better off than they were 30 years ago. This improvement in well-being can be taken as either of two things: 1) an indication that poverty is less of a problem than advertised or 2) evidence that past policy efforts (and economic growth) have been successful and should be expanded. We have several options for expanding earnings subsidies such as the EITC. Besides this, a common suggestion for improving the earnings

Table 5.1 Percentiles of Annual Income ($) of Single Mothers, by Number of Children, 2001–2003

Income percentile	1 child	2 children	3+ children
Fifth	3,567	3,558	3,675
Tenth	5,593	5,949	6,186
Twentieth	9,025	9,874	8,843
Thirtieth	12,374	12,207	11,406
Fortieth	15,366	15,151	13,464
Fiftieth	19,351	19,353	16,394
Ninetieth	41,246	47,637	36,291

SOURCE: Author's calculations using Consumer Expenditure Survey data. See Meyer (2007) for details.

of the worst-off is improved education and training. We need more evidence on what type of education would be most effective and for what type of person targeted efforts would prove most beneficial.

References

Autor, David. 2009. "Past Trends and Projections in Wages, Work, and Occupations in the United States." In *Strategies for Improving Economic Mobility of Workers*, Maude Toussaint-Comeau and Bruce D. Meyer, eds. Kalamazoo, MI: W.E. Upjohn Institute for Employment Research, pp. 47–60.

Berube, Alan. 2007. "Geographic Dynamics in Income and Poverty: Recent U.S. Trends." PowerPoint presentation at the Federal Reserve Bank of Chicago and W.E. Upjohn Institute for Employment Research conference "Strategies for Improving Economic Mobility of Workers," held in Chicago, IL, November 15–16. http://www.chicagofed.org/community_development/files/11_2007_berube_ppt_pres_session1.pdf (accessed January 5, 2009).

Blinder, Alan S. 2007. "How Many U.S. Jobs Might Be Offshorable?" CEPS Working Paper No. 142. Princeton, NJ: Center for Economic Policy Studies. http://www.princeton.edu/~blinder/papers/07ceps142.pdf (accessed January 9, 2009).

Boskin, Michael J., Ellen R. Dulberger, Robert J. Gordon, Zvi Griliches, and Dale Jorgensen. 1996. *Toward a More Accurate Measure of the Cost of Living*. Final report to the Senate Finance Committee from the Advisory Commission to Study the Consumer Price Index. http://www.ssa.gov/history/reports/boskinrpt.html (accessed March 17, 2009).

Dahl, Molly W. 2007. "Changes in the Economic Resources of Low-Income Households with Children." PowerPoint presentation at the Federal Reserve Bank of Chicago and W.E. Upjohn Institute for Employment Research conference "Strategies for Improving Economic Mobility of Workers," held in Chicago, IL, November 15–16. http://www.chicagofed.org/community_development/files/11_2007_dahl_ppt_pres_session3.pdf (accessed March 17, 2009).

Dahl, Molly W., Thomas DeLeire, and Jonathan Schwabish. 2007. *Trends in Earnings Variability over the Past 20 Years*. Washington, DC: Congressional Budget Office.

Eissa, Nada, and Hilary Williamson Hoynes. 2006. "Behavioral Responses to Taxes: Lessons from the EITC and Labor Supply." *Tax Policy and the Economy* 20(2006): 73–110.

Gosselin, Peter, and Seth Zimmerman. 2007. "Trends in Income Volatility and Risk, 1970–2004." PowerPoint presentation at the Federal Reserve Bank of Chicago and W.E. Upjohn Institute for Employment Research conference "Strategies for Improving Economic Mobility of Workers," held in Chicago, IL, November 15–16.

Hoynes, Hilary Williamson. 2009. "The Earned Income Tax Credit, Welfare Reform, and the Employment of Low-Skilled Single Mothers." In *Strategies for Improving Economic Mobility of Workers*, Maude Toussaint-Comeau and Bruce D. Meyer, eds. Kalamazoo, MI: W.E. Upjohn Institute for Employment Research, pp. 61–74.

Holzer, Harry J. 2009. "What Might Improve the Employment and Advancement Prospects of the Poor?" In *Strategies for Improving Economic Mobility of Workers*, Maude Toussaint-Comeau and Bruce D. Meyer, eds. Kalamazoo, MI: W.E. Upjohn Institute for Employment Research, pp. 149–160.

Kopczuk, Wojciech, Emmanuel Saez, and Jae Song. 2007. "Uncovering the American Dream: Inequality and Mobility in Social Security Earnings Data since 1937." Unpublished manuscript. Columbia University, New York.

Meyer, Bruce D. 2007. "The U.S. Earned Income Tax Credit, Its Effects, and Possible Reforms." *Swedish Economic Policy Review* 14(2): 55–80.

Meyer, Bruce D., and James X. Sullivan. 2007. "The Material Well-Being of the Poor and the Middle Class since 1980." Unpublished manuscript. University of Chicago, Chicago, IL.

———. 2009. "Five Decades of Consumption and Income Poverty." NBER Working Paper No. 14827. Cambridge, MA: National Bureau of Economic Research.

Shin, Donggyun, and Gary Solon. 2008. "Trends in Men's Earnings Volatility: What Does the Panel Study of Income Dynamics Show?" NBER Working Paper No. W14075. Cambridge, MA: National Bureau of Economic Research.

6

Helping Low-Wage Workers Persist in Education Programs

Lessons from Research on Welfare Training Programs and Two Promising Community College Strategies

Lashawn Richburg-Hayes
MDRC

THE POLICY CONTEXT

Employment has long been held to be an important deterrent against poverty, and work is at the heart of a range of federal efforts to improve the economic well-being of low-income families. However, full-time, stable work alone is not sufficient to alleviate poverty: more than half of the families, with children, that have income below 200 percent of the poverty line (a standard commonly used to define low income) do have at least one full-time, year-round worker, implying that low wages are a problem for many. One study that followed prime-age workers who earned less than $12,000 a year for three consecutive years found that most of these low earners enjoyed earnings growth in subsequent years, but only about a fourth consistently earned more than $15,000 a year at the end of the period—a figure that still placed them firmly in poverty (Andersson, Holzer, and Lane 2005).

While there is some debate about the relative effect on the labor market of factors such as globalization, technological change, declining union membership, and immigration, most agree that the dominant labor market trends have been quite unfavorable for less-skilled workers. One of the clearest trends is that real wages have risen much more for workers with more education, resulting in a growing disparity in hourly wages between workers with and without postsecondary education. For example, between 1979 and 2005, real hourly wages for people with advanced degrees rose by 28 percent, wages for college graduates rose by 22 percent, wages for high school graduates remained stagnant, and wages for high school dropouts fell by 16 percent (Mishel, Bernstein, and Allegretto 2007). This is particularly damaging for low-income workers in families with children, since fewer than a third have more than a high school degree and about a third are high school dropouts (Acs and Nichols 2007).

This chapter summarizes what is known from evaluations of worker postsecondary education programs about the effectiveness of education acquisition to advance the earnings and careers of low-wage workers. The chapter then reviews several popular community college strategies intended to increase academic success among low-wage workers. Finally, the chapter presents findings from two random assignment evaluations of interventions intended to increase the success of such students and concludes with a discussion of new strategies and their implications for future studies to advance knowledge of what works for this population.

WHAT IS KNOWN ABOUT EDUCATION ACQUISITION AMONG LOW-WAGE WORKERS

There is compelling evidence that additional years of schooling and advanced education credentials are associated with higher earnings. Students who complete an associate's degree or certificate program earn more than those with a high school diploma or General Educational Development (GED) certificate (Grubb 1999), and those having about a year of college study appear to reap increased earnings, although not as much as with the completion of a degree (Grubb 1999; Kane and Rouse 1995).

Yet evaluations of education and basic skills training programs have yielded mixed results concerning their ability to increase earnings. In the welfare context, the National Evaluation of Welfare to Work Strategies—a random assignment demonstration—showed that "education first" programs, which require people to initially participate in education or training (typically, remedial reading and math, GED exam preparation, or English as a Second Language [ESL] classes), did not increase the likelihood of their becoming employed in "good" jobs or produce more earnings growth when compared with "job search–first" programs, which emphasize getting people into jobs as quickly as possible (Hamilton 2002). However, the program that had the largest effect on stable employment and earnings growth in this study was one that allowed some individuals to participate in short-term training or education before they searched for work. Nevertheless, in most cases, recipients dropped out of education programs quickly.

One site in the Employment Retention and Advancement Demonstration Project, another random assignment study, is currently testing two strategies for promoting participation in education and training among welfare recipients who are employed. Thus far, the results show that neither approach has been able to induce many people to enroll in education or training who would not have enrolled on their own (Navarro, Freedman, and Hamilton 2007). New Visions, a community college bridge program that sought to increase the job retention and advancement of welfare recipients in California, also had difficulty increasing college enrollment above the levels of the control group and ensuring program participation. After a two-and-a-half-year period, this program resulted in slightly higher college-going (6 percentage points) but reduced total earnings (about $2,300) relative to a control group that attended other employment and training services (Fein and Beecroft 2006).

Other studies that examine voluntary education and training programs outside the welfare system have found similarly mixed results. The National Job Training Partnership Act Study found some modest earnings impacts for adult women, with on-the-job training producing larger gains than classroom training (Orr et al. 1996). Similarly, a meta-analysis of voluntary training programs found larger effects for women than for men or youth, particularly for classroom skills training, on-the-job training, and mixed classroom and workplace training (Greenberg, Michalopoulos, and Robins 2003). Another project that tested voluntary training, the Minority Female Single Parent Demonstration, found positive results at one of four sites, the Center for Employment Training (CET), which was known for integrating vocational and basic-skills instruction and maintaining tight links to employers (Burghardt et al. 1992). However, the evaluation of a multisite replication of CET's model found few positive effects (Miller et al. 2005).

In sum, while the link between skills and wages suggests education and skills training may offer the best hope for substantial wage growth, encouraging people to enroll in education and training, to persist in it, and to complete it may be a key component. Furthermore, to enable education to lead to advancement for low-wage workers, several barriers to higher education will need to be addressed: access to postsecondary education, affordability, and academic success (Clymer, Roberts, and Strawn 2001; McSwain and Davis 2007). Of all higher education institution types, community colleges may be best situated to address the diverse barriers of low-wage workers (Jobs for the Future 2007).

THE ROLE OF COMMUNITY COLLEGES

Community colleges play a critical role in American higher education. According to the U.S. Department of Education, nearly half of all students who begin postsecondary education start at a community college (U.S. Department of Education 2002). Because community colleges have open admissions policies and relatively low tuition and fees, they are particularly important to the millions of adults who may lack preparation or may otherwise be unable to afford college. In addition, their flexible schedules and long history as sponsors of employment and training programs targeting both disadvantaged populations and local industries make them a key player in the development of a more skilled workforce (Meléndez et al. 2004).

Despite the accessibility and relative affordability of community colleges, however, many students who begin programs at community colleges end their formal education prematurely. One study of adult undergraduates who work found that 62 percent of students who considered themselves workers first and students second had not completed a certificate or degree and were no longer enrolled, compared with 39 percent of adults who described themselves as being students first and working only to cover minor expenses (Berker, Horn, and Carroll 2003). Longitudinal studies of postsecondary student populations indicate that 46 percent of those who begin at community colleges do not complete a degree or enroll elsewhere within a six-year time frame (U.S. Department of Education 2002). Clearly, persistence and retention are not issues isolated to low-wage workers pursuing advanced education. However, characteristics of jobs (absence of paid leave, lack of flexible work hours, unpredictability of hours or shift work), in addition to the limited financial aid for independent persons with dependents, academic underpreparedness, and family obligations, all contribute to this group's low enrollment and completion (Golonka and Matus-Grossman 2001; Levin-Epstein 2007; Matus-Grossman and Gooden 2001).

In recent years, several notable programs have been designed at community colleges to serve the unique needs of low-wage workers—with mixed success. For example, the New Visions program discussed above was codesigned and operated by Riverside (Calif.) Community College and Riverside County's Department of Public Social Services to build on earlier welfare reform approaches that had resulted in increased employment and earnings. As noted, this program did not meet its intended goals, perhaps because the intervention was less beneficial than other education and training programs available. Another example is the ACCESS Project at Hamilton College in Clinton, New York, which serves welfare-eligible single mothers. This program has reported student retention levels in excess of 90 percent and completion rates comparable to rates of the college's traditional students; moreover, ACCESS students have achieved these rates while working (Adair 2003). Findings from the Parents as Scholars program in Maine suggest that the program increased wages among TANF-eligible students who graduated (Butler, Deprez, and Smith 2003). There are similar findings from other programs in Boston and California (Polakow et al. 2004). While these findings suggest that targeted programs with wraparound services work, most programs are very small and not rigorously evaluated, so one cannot interpret the causality of these positive associations.

STRATEGIES TO IMPROVE PERSISTENCE AND RETENTION

MDRC launched the Opening Doors demonstration to learn how community colleges can implement reforms that may help greater numbers of students achieve their goals, particularly their academic and career goals, and that may lead to longer-term success in the labor market and in life for those students (Brock and LeBlanc 2005). Specifically, the demonstration is examining various programs or interventions that represent enhancements to community college teaching, student services, and financial aid to determine their effects on student persistence and other outcomes, including degree attainment, labor market experiences, and personal and social well-being. Opening Doors measured the effects of these enhancements by randomly assigning students who participate in the research either to a program group that receives the enhanced services or to a comparison group that receives the standard services offered by the college. By comparing the experiences of both groups over a period of several years, MDRC is able to measure the difference, or impact, that the interventions make in students' lives, in both the short and long term.

The Opening Doors project evaluates four popular strategies (two of which are widely implemented in community colleges) that are intended to increase student success and retention. These consist of 1) learning communities, 2) enhanced counseling with a small scholarship, 3) an incentive-based scholarship, and 4) enhanced student services. Table 6.1 provides a summary of the interventions and the target populations. The evaluations of the enhanced student services and the incentive scholarship are particularly relevant to the concern about low-wage workers and persistence, or success, in academic course work at community colleges.

Enhanced Student Services

The Opening Doors project comprising Lorain County Community College and Owens Community College in Ohio targeted new and continuing students who had completed fewer than 13 credits.[1] The linchpin of the program was an adviser with whom students were expected to meet at least once a month for two semesters to discuss academic progress and any other issues that might be affecting their schooling. Advisers carried a caseload of no more than 160 students, which stood in sharp contrast to the academic advising services available to students in the comparison group, where the ratio of counseling staff to students not enrolled in Opening Doors was about 1 to 1,000. In addition, designated staff members from other student service departments—including

Table 6.1 Opening Doors Interventions and Students' Eligibility Determinants, by Community College

	Kingsborough (NY)	Lorain County and Owens (OH)	Delgado and Louisiana Tech–West Jefferson (LA)	Chaffey College (CA)
Intervention	Learning communities and a book voucher: groups of students were assigned to take three linked credit courses together; students received enhanced advising and tutoring and vouchers to pay for textbooks.	Enhanced student services and a modest scholarship: students were assigned to a dedicated adviser with whom they had to meet frequently; students eligible for $150 scholarship for each of two semesters after meetings with adviser.	Incentive scholarship: students were eligible for a $1,000 scholarship for each of two semesters; scholarship tied to maintaining at least half-time enrollment and a grade point average of 2.0 (a "C" average).	College survival skills and enhanced student services: students assigned to a two-semester guidance course that provided instructional support as well as advising; students required to visit the college's success centers for extra academic support.
Criteria				
Age	17–34	18–34	18–34	18–34
Household income	Not screened.[a]	Below 250 percent of federal poverty level.	Below 200 percent of federal poverty level.	Below 250 percent of federal poverty level.
Other	Only new freshmen. English as a Second Language (ESL) students are excluded.	Continuing students must not have completed more than 12 credits; must have shown indications of academic difficulty (as determined by low grades or withdrawal from courses).	Must be a parent of at least one dependent under age 19. Must have a high school diploma or GED or have passed a college entrance exam. Must not have an occupational certificate or college degree.	Only continuing students. Students must be on probation for having a grade point average below 2.0 or for completing less than half of their attempted credits.

NOTE: See Bloom and Sommo (2005); Richburg-Hayes, Visher, and Bloom (2008); and Scrivener et al. (2008) for more information on the Opening Doors program at Kingsborough Community College. See Scrivener, Sommo, and Collado (2009) for more information about the Opening Doors program at Chaffey College.

[a] The majority of students enrolled at Kingsborough were low-income, so the Opening Doors study did not impose additional income screening.

financial aid and career services—functioned as a team, so that at least one staff member from each department served as a point person for the Opening Doors program. While students in the comparison group could access these same departments, they generally would have had to initiate such contact on their own rather than through a direct referral. Finally, students in the Opening Doors group were given a $150 scholarship for each of two consecutive semesters that they could use for any purpose. The scholarship payments were approved by the academic adviser and were made at the beginning and middle of the semester as a way of making sure that students stayed in contact with the adviser. Students in the comparison group did not receive these scholarships.

Even though academic guidance and counseling may arguably be the most important student service, most students receive minimal help. Nationally, the average community college employs one adviser for approximately every 1,000 students (Grubb 2001). While colleges differ in how their advisers deliver services and the topics they cover, the necessity of working with many students tends to drive them toward a traditional problem-solving approach in which a student presents an issue and the adviser offers a quick response. The National Academic Advising Association urges community colleges and four-year colleges and universities to provide sufficient staffing, so that students and advisers can have ongoing, interactive relationships. The association also urges these institutions to adopt a developmental approach whereby advisers help students clarify personal goals and objectives rather than simply approving their choice of courses (Gordon and Habley 2000). Research suggests that this is even more important for low-wage workers, who may need more help than their younger counterparts in navigating their way to a credential (Jobs for the Future 2007).

Incentive Scholarship

The Opening Doors project at Delgado Community College and the Louisiana Technical College–West Jefferson campus in Louisiana offered a $1,000 scholarship for each of two semesters (for a total of up to $2,000) to parents with children under age 19 whose family incomes were below 200 percent of the federal poverty level.[2] The scholarship was tied to academic performance: an initial payment of $250 was made after students enrolled at least half-time; a second payment of

$250 was made after midterms for students who remained enrolled at least half-time and earned at least a C average; and a final payment of $500 was made after students passed all their courses with a grade of C or better. The scholarship was paid in addition to any other financial aid students received. Each student was assigned to a counselor, and counselors monitored the students' grades, arranged tutoring or other help as needed, and approved scholarship disbursements.

This intervention developed out of focus groups with low-income parents who were attending or wanted to attend community college; it also sprang from interest among Louisiana state officials in a financial incentive plan similar to those implemented to move welfare recipients into employment (Brock and Richburg-Hayes 2006; Richburg-Hayes et al. 2009). Many of the focus-group students worried about the cost of tuition, books, and child care (Matus-Grossman and Gooden 2002). While most students may have qualified for the federal Pell Grant program (the primary need-based financial aid program for college students in the United States) and loan programs, worries about how to pay for college inevitably led some students to reduce their hours of attendance (thereby increasing the time it takes to earn a degree) or to drop out altogether. Given the high cost of attending college, many Pell Grant recipients have a significant amount of unmet need, especially those recipients who are independent and working (Mercer 2005). The incentive-based scholarship was intended to meet some of those needs while still being accessible to a large group typically missed by scholarship programs.

Findings

Table 6.2 presents some background characteristics of the students in each community college sample. The table shows that the samples consist largely of women and older adults, an outcome that mirrors the community college population more than the target criteria, since adults over the age of 24 make up close to 45 percent of all undergraduate enrollments (Berker, Horn, and Carroll 2003). A large proportion of the sample were parents and low-wage workers at the point of random assignment, and more than half of the students who worked earned about $8 an hour—in fact, more than 80 percent worked at least half-time in the preceding 12 months (not shown). Again, this mirrors

Table 6.2 Characteristics of Community College Sample Members at Baseline for Selected Opening Doors Sites

	Owens Community College (OH)	Lorain County Community College (OH)	Delgado Community College (LA)	Louisiana Technical–West Jefferson (LA)
Male[a]	28.1	20.5	5.5	15.8
Age				
18–20 years old	38.0	16.1	19.8	10.4
21–25 years old	32.4	39.6	37.6	28.2
26–30 years old	19.5	27.9	29.1	35.1
31 and older	10.2	16.4	13.5	26.2
Average age (years)	23.3	25.4	24.9	27.0
Number of children				
None	48.7	17.8	—	38.8
One	24.4	36.7	53.9	30.8
Two	15.3	24.1	26.3	30.8
Three or more	11.6	21.4	19.8	30.3
Among sample members with children:				
Age of youngest child (years)	3.0	3.3	3.0	3.6
Financially dependent on parents	23.4	10.3	17.9	14.4
Currently employed	57.1	54.0	51.4	52.5
Among those currently employed:[b]				
Number of hours worked per week in current job				
1–10 hours	5.1	4.6	4.8	4.9
11–20 hours	22.7	21.9	16.8	15.5
21–30 hours	29.4	26.9	25.6	20.4

31–40 hours	32.6	33.1	47.0	51.5
More than 40 hours	10.2	13.6	5.8	7.8
Average hourly wage at current job ($)	8.10	8.60	8.00	7.10
Highest grade completed				
8th grade or lower	1.3	1.1	0.6	1.5
9th grade	3.3	4.6	3.2	1.5
10th grade	5.0	6.7	4.9	4.5
11th grade	6.6	12.2	7.6	5.5
12th grade	83.8	75.5	83.7	87.1
Date of high school graduation/GED receipt				
During the past year	27.8	13.5	11.7	6.8
Between 1 and 5 years ago	32.8	30.8	33.7	23.4
Between 5 and 10 years ago	23.9	29.5	33.7	31.3
More than 10 years ago	15.5	26.2	20.9	38.5
Main reason for enrolling in college[c]				
To complete a certificate program	8.9	11.1	10.8	24.5
To obtain an associate's degree	44.0	55.7	60.4	39.5
To transfer to a four-year college/university	27.5	20.7	17.9	6.0
To obtain/update job skills	14.3	9.8	9.7	28.0
Other	8.4	4.8	5.7	7.5
Sample size	1,214	477	817	202

NOTE: Distributions may not add to 100 percent because of rounding or because subcategories are not mutually exclusive. — = data not available.

[a] All categories, including this one, are in percentages unless otherwise noted.

[b] Figures for this category are calculated for a proportion of the full sample.

[c] Distributions may not add to 100 percent because categories are not mutually exclusive.

SOURCE: MDRC calculations using data from a baseline information survey.

the population of community college students nationally, as close to 80 percent balance their studies with full-time or part-time work (Phillippe and Patton 2000). Most of the students in the samples are financially independent, and more than half received their high school diploma or GED five or more years prior to the study. In short, the sample may be representative of the pool of low-wage workers discussed at the beginning of this chapter.

Table 6.3 shows selected impacts for the two interventions during the first three semesters since random assignment. Each entry shows the difference in outcomes, or the impact, between the treatment group and the control group (which represents what would have happened in the absence of the intervention). The asterisks show the statistical significance of the differences between the two groups—in other words, whether the difference was a result of the program.

The first panel (Panel A) shows outcomes in the first Opening Doors semester. The first row shows no difference in registration rates in any of the samples. This result was expected given that random assignment was conducted for those students who had already matriculated at the college or showed considerable interest in enrolling. While there are no differences in the remaining outcomes for the enhanced student services intervention in Ohio, the performance-based scholarship intervention in Louisiana resulted in treatment group students passing slightly more courses (0.4 of a course more), earning more total credits (1.1 more), and withdrawing from courses at lower rates (6.9 percentage points lower).

The second panel (Panel B) shows academic performance for the second Opening Doors semester. Encouragingly, the Opening Doors program had a positive effect on student retention at two of the three sites. While the proportion registering for college courses dropped somewhat among both Opening Doors students and the control group (not shown), the Opening Doors program resulted in a 5.6-percentage-point increase (over a control-group base of 57.2 percent) in registrants at Owens Community College and an 18.2-percentage-point increase (over a control-group base of 57.5 percent) at the two community colleges in Louisiana. This latter result is quite large, and effects of this magnitude are seldom seen in program evaluations that use rigorous random assignment designs. In addition to registration gains, Opening Doors students are more likely than their control group counterparts to attempt more courses (and thus register for more credits) and earn more developmental credits at one Ohio site and at both of the Louisiana sites. In Louisiana, Opening Doors students also passed more courses and earned more regular credits (latter outcome not shown in table).

The third panel (Panel C) shows a few results from the first post-program semester, or the first semester that the intervention was not in place. The first two columns show small, insignificant impacts, which indicate that the outcomes for the treatment group largely mirror those for the control group. In contrast, the last column shows continued effects for the incentive scholarship intervention.

Overall, the interventions seem to have affected outcomes related to academic success in the semesters in which they operated. With the exception of the performance-based scholarship, the impacts appear to fade after the program ends. Nevertheless, there may still be delayed effects in subsequent semesters, and future work will examine these in addition to other outcomes that may be affected by education acquisition in the longer term, such as social and psychological outcomes, health behaviors, and labor market outcomes.

IMPLICATIONS FOR FUTURE WORK

In light of the long-term labor market trends that have resulted in stagnant wage growth for those in the lowest quintile of the income distribution because of global competition, declining union membership, and increased immigration, it appears that most low-wage workers will need to increase their skill levels in order to raise their earnings substantially. While results from previous studies of education and training programs for adults have been mixed at best, several new strategies emerging in the field offer the possibility of better results. For example, there are several promising efforts to provide employer-focused training to low earners that, in some cases, operate on a large scale (Martinson 2007). These include incumbent worker training programs (state grants to businesses for collaborating with training providers on training existing workers) and sectoral initiatives (providing training to a cluster of employers in one segment of the labor market).

Table 6.3 Impacts on Academic Performance during the First Three Semesters since Random Assignment in Selected Opening Doors Sites

	Owens Community College (OH)	Lorain County C.C. (OH)	Delgado C.C. & Louisiana Technical–West Jefferson
Panel A			
First Opening Doors semester			
Registered for any courses (%)	0.7	1.7	4.5
Number of courses attempted	0.1	0.0	0.2
Number of courses passed	0.1	0.1	0.4***
Total credits registered for (regular + developmental)	0.3	0.2	0.4
Total credits earned (regular + developmental)	0.3	0.2	1.1***
Developmental credits earned	0.2	0.3	0.2
Withdrew from one or more courses (%)	3.5	6.4	6.9*
Panel B			
Second Opening Doors semester			
Registered for any courses (%)	5.6***	10.5	18.2***
Number of courses attempted	0.2**	0.4	0.5****
Number of courses passed	0.1	0.2	0.4****
Total credits registered for (regular + developmental)	0.7***	1.4	1.4***
Total credits earned (regular + developmental)	0.4	0.7	1.2***
Developmental credits earned	0.2*	0.3	0.4****
Withdrew from one or more courses (%)	3.8***	5.3	4.3

Panel C

First postprogram semester			
Registered for any courses (%)	3.2	3.6	11.2***
Number of courses attempted	0.2	0.1	0.5***
Total credits registered for (regular + developmental)	0.5	0.4	1.4***
Summary outcomes			
Total number of semesters enrolled	0.1	0.3***	0.3***
Total credits earned (regular + developmental)	0.7	1.1	3.3***
Sample size	1,241	478	537

NOTE: Data from the Ohio sites use all observations. Data from the Louisiana sites consist of the two earliest cohorts, which represent 53 percent of the full sample of 1,019 students. Each column entry represents the regression-adjusted difference in treatment and control means for the specified outcome. A two-tailed *t*-test was applied to differences between the research groups. Statistical significance levels are indicated as follows: *significant at the 0.10 level; **significant at the 0.05 level; ***significant at the 0.01 level.

SOURCE: MDRC calculations from college transcript data.

While it is far too early to conclude that the Opening Doors program in Louisiana is an unequivocal success, the early results are large and compelling. For example, the third-semester retention impact of 11.2 percentage points is larger than most nonexperimental analyses of other scholarship programs would have predicted.[3] Clearly, the Louisiana results suggest that a performance-based scholarship can have a large positive effect on academic achievement among a predominantly female, single-parent student population that faces multiple barriers to completing college.

Nonexperimental research has also associated student aid programs with higher enrollment in postsecondary education (Abraham and Clark 2003; Turner 2007). However, the existing research is far from definitive, and more tests are needed. Several states have developed innovative financial assistance programs for nontraditional students (such as those without a high school diploma or those attending part time) who pursue postsecondary education or skills training (Martinson and Holcomb 2007).

The research to date clearly shows that the success of employer training programs or community college–based programs largely depends on addressing the barriers to education acquisition faced by low-wage adults. The current system of instruction and financial aid is largely based on "traditional" students—those entering postsecondary education out of high school, for whom work is of secondary importance. Future research in this area will need to examine the implications of relaxing some of the barriers the current system imposes.

Notes

I would like to thank Thomas Brock for reviewing an early draft of this chapter. I would also like to acknowledge the work of the Employment and Self-Sufficiency Strategies team for background on the evaluation of education initiatives. All errors and omissions remain my own.

1. See Scrivener and Au (2007) and Scrivener and Pih (2007), respectively, for more detail on the study at Lorain County Community College and Owens Community College.
2. The students did not need to be receiving welfare benefits.
3. While his results are not directly comparable to this retention estimate, Bettinger (2004) finds that a $1,000 increase in Pell Grant eligibility increases persistence

between the first and second year of college attendance by 2 to 4 percentage points. Dynarski (2005) finds that merit aid of about $3,000 increases the probability of persistence by 5 to 11 percentage points among those who would still have gone to college in the absence of the financial aid.

References

Abraham, Katharine G., and Melissa A. Clark. 2003. "Financial Aid and Students' College Decisions: Evidence from the District of Columbia's Tuition Assistance Grant Program." Working Paper No. 2. Princeton, NJ: Princeton University, Education Research Section.

Acs, Gregory, and Austin Nichols. 2007. *Low-Income Workers and Their Employers: Characteristics and Challenges*. Washington, DC: Urban Institute.

Adair, Vivyan C. 2003. *The ACCESS Project at Hamilton College: Year End Report, 2003*. Clinton, NY: Hamilton College. http://my.hamilton.edu/college/access/2003Report.pdf (accessed December 4, 2008).

Andersson, Fredrik, Harry J. Holzer, and Julia I. Lane. 2005. *Moving Up or Moving On: Who Advances in the Low-Wage Labor Market*. New York: Russell Sage Foundation.

Berker, Ali, Laura Horn, and C. Dennis Carroll. 2003. *Work First, Study Second: Adult Undergraduates Who Combine Employment and Postsecondary Enrollment*. Postsecondary Education Descriptive Analysis Reports. Washington, DC: U.S. Department of Education, National Center for Education Statistics.

Bettinger, Eric. 2004. "How Financial Aid Affects Persistence." In *College Choices: The Economics of Where to Go, When to Go, and How to Pay for It*, Caroline M. Hoxby, ed. Chicago: University of Chicago Press, pp. 207–238.

Bloom, Dan, and Colleen Sommo. 2005. *Building Learning Communities: Early Results from the Opening Doors Demonstration at Kingsborough Community College*. New York: MDRC.

Brock, Thomas, and Allen LeBlanc. 2005. *Promoting Student Success in Community College and Beyond: The Opening Doors Demonstration*. New York: MDRC.

Brock, Thomas, and Lashawn Richburg-Hayes. 2006. *Paying for Persistence: Early Results of a Louisiana Scholarship Program for Low-Income Parents Attending Community College*. New York: MDRC.

Burghardt, John, Anu Rangarajan, Anne Gordon, and Ellen Kisker. 1992. *Evaluation of the Minority Female Single Parent Demonstration: Vol. 1, Summary Report*. Princeton, NJ: Mathematica Policy Research.

Butler, Sandra S., Luisa Stormer Deprez, and Rebekah J. Smith. 2003. "Parents as Scholars: A Model Post-Secondary Education Program for Low-Income Women in the New Welfare Landscape." Paper presented at IWPR's Seventh International Women's Policy Research Conference, "Women Working to Make a Difference," held in Washington, DC, June 22–24. http://www.iwpr.org/pdf/Butler_Deprez_Smith.pdf (accessed December 3, 2008).

Clymer, Carol, Brandon Roberts, and Julie Strawn. 2001. *States of Change: Policies and Programs to Promote Low-Wage Workers' Steady Employment and Advancement.* Field Report Series. New York: Public/Private Ventures.

Dynarski, Susan. 2005. "Finishing College: The Role of State Policy in Degree Attainment." Working paper. Cambridge, MA: Harvard University, John F. Kennedy School of Government.

Fein, David J., and Erik Beecroft. 2006. *College as a Job Advancement Strategy: Final Report on the New Visions Self-Sufficiency and Lifelong Learning Project.* Bethesda, MD: Abt Associates.

Golonka, Susan, and Lisa Matus-Grossman 2001. *Opening Doors: Expanding Educational Opportunities for Low-Income Workers.* New York: MDRC.

Gordon, Virginia N., and Wesley R. Habley, eds. 2000. *Academic Advising: A Comprehensive Handbook.* San Francisco: Jossey-Bass.

Greenberg, David H., Charles Michalopoulos, and Philip K. Robins. 2003. "A Meta-Analysis of Government-Sponsored Training Programs." *Industrial and Labor Relations Review* 57(1): 31–53.

Grubb, W. Norton. 1999. *Honored But Invisible: An Inside Look at Teaching in Community Colleges.* New York: Routledge.

———. 2001. "'Getting into the World': Guidance and Counseling in Community Colleges." Working Paper No. 1. New York: Community College Research Center.

Hamilton, Gayle. 2002. *Moving People from Welfare to Work: Lessons from the National Evaluation of Welfare-to-Work Strategies.* Submitted to the U.S. Department of Health and Human Services and the U.S. Department of Education. New York: MDRC.

Jobs for the Future. 2007. *Adult Learners in Higher Education: Barriers to Success and Strategies to Improve Results.* Employment and Training Administration Occasional Paper 2007-03. Boston, MA: Jobs for the Future.

Kane, Thomas J., and Cecilia Elena Rouse. 1995. "Labor Market Returns to Two- and Four-Year Colleges: Is a Credit a Credit and Do Degrees Matter?" *American Economic Review* 85(3): 600–614.

Levin-Epstein, Jodie. 2007. "Responsive Workplaces: The Business Case for Employment that Values Fairness and Families." Special Report: Work and Family. *American Prospect* 18(3): A16–A17.

Martinson, Karin. 2007. *Building Skills and Promoting Job Advancement: The Promise of Employer-Focused Strategies.* Washington, DC: Urban Institute.

Martinson, Karin, and Pamela Holcomb. 2007. *Innovative Employment Approaches and Programs for Low-Income Families.* Washington, DC: Urban Institute.

Matus-Grossman, Lisa, and Susan Tinsley Gooden. 2001. *Opening Doors to Earning Credentials: Impressions of Community College Access and Retention from Low-Wage Workers.* New York: MDRC.

———. 2002. *Opening Doors: Students' Perspectives on Juggling Work, Family, and College.* New York: MDRC.

McSwain, Courtney, and Ryan Davis. 2007. *College Access for the Working Poor: Overcoming Burdens to Succeed In Higher Education.* Washington, DC: Institute for Higher Education Policy.

Meléndez, Edwin, Luis M. Falcón, Carlos Suárez-Boulangger, Lynn McCormick, and Alexandra de Montrichard. 2004. "Community Colleges, Welfare Reform, and Workforce Development." In *Communities and Workforce Development*, Edwin Meléndez, ed. Kalamazoo, MI: W.E. Upjohn Institute for Employment Research, pp. 293–330.

Mercer, Charmaine. 2005. *Federal Pell Grants: Implications of Increasing the Maximum Award.* CRS Report for Congress. Washington, DC: Congressional Research Service, Library of Congress.

Miller, Cynthia, Johannes M. Bos, Kristin E. Porter, Fannie M. Tseng, and Yasuyo Abe. 2005. *The Challenge of Repeating Success in a Changing World: Final Report on the Center for Employment Training Replication Sites.* New York: MDRC.

Mishel, Lawrence, Jared Bernstein, and Sylvia Allegretto. 2007. *The State of Working America, 2006/2007.* An Economic Policy Institute Book. Ithaca, NY: Cornell University Press.

Navarro, David, Stephen Freedman, and Gayle Hamilton. 2007. *The Employment Retention and Advancement Project: Results from Two Education and Training Models for Employed Welfare Recipients in Riverside, California.* New York: MDRC.

Orr, Larry L., Howard S. Bloom, Stephen H. Bell, Fred Doolittle, Winston Lin, and George Cave. 1996. *Does Training for the Disadvantaged Work? Evidence from the National JTPA Study.* Washington, DC: Urban Institute.

Phillippe, Kent A., and Madeline Patton. 2000. *National Profile of Community Colleges: Trends and Statistics.* 3rd ed. Washington, DC: American Association of Community Colleges.

Polakow, Valerie, Sandra S. Butler, Luisa Stormer Deprez, and Peggy Kahn, eds. 2004. *Shut Out: Low-Income Mothers and Higher Education in Post-Welfare America.* Albany, NY: State University of New York Press.

Richburg-Hayes, Lashawn, Thomas Brock, Allen LeBlanc, Christina Paxson, Cecilia Elena Rouse, and Lisa Barrow. 2009. *Rewarding Persistence: Effects of a Performance-Based Scholarship Program for Low-Income Parents*. New York: MDRC.

Richburg-Hayes, Lashawn, Mary G. Visher, and Dan Bloom. 2008. "Do Learning Communities Effect Academic Outcomes? Evidence from an Experiment in a Community College." *Journal of Research on Educational Effectiveness* 1(1): 33–65.

Scrivener, Susan, and Jenny Au. 2007. *Enhancing Student Services at Lorain County Community College: Early Results from the Opening Doors Demonstration in Ohio*. New York: MDRC.

Scrivener, Susan, Dan Bloom, Allen LeBlanc, Christina Paxson, Cecilia Elena Rouse, and Colleen Sommo. 2008. *A Good Start: Two-Year Effects of a Freshmen Learning Community Program at Kingsborough Community College*. New York: MDRC.

Scrivener, Susan, and Michael Pih. 2007. *Enhancing Student Services at Owens Community College: Early Results from the Opening Doors Demonstration in Ohio*. New York: MDRC.

Scrivener, Susan, Colleen Sommo, and Herbert Collado. 2009. *Getting Back on Track: Effects of a Community College Program for Probationary Students*. New York: MDRC.

Turner, Sarah E. 2007. "Higher Education: Policies Generating the 21st Century Workforce." In *Reshaping the American Workforce in a Changing Economy*, Harry J. Holzer and Demetra Smith Nightingale, eds. Washington, DC: Urban Institute, pp. 91–116.

U.S. Department of Education. 2002. *Descriptive Summary of 1995–96 Beginning Postsecondary Students: Six Years Later*. Washington, DC: U.S. Department of Education, National Center for Education Statistics.

7

Financial Aid and Older Workers

Supporting the Nontraditional Student

Bridget Terry Long
Harvard University

THE INCREASING ROLE OF NONTRADITIONAL
STUDENTS IN HIGHER EDUCATION

Educational trends increasingly highlight the growing numbers of older students who are seeking postsecondary training. According to figures from the *2006 Digest of Education Statistics* (National Center for Education Statistics 2007), only 28 percent of the college population was age 25 or above in 1970. However, by 1995, this had risen to 43 percent of students; currently 39 percent of students are age 25 or above. These trends mirror an important need in the country: changes in the labor market suggest that employers are demanding more-educated workers with different types of skills. Therefore, it has become important for many older workers to "retool." Workers are increasingly expected to utilize a broad base of knowledge in their jobs, as well as handle multiple responsibilities and changing procedures (Stuart and Dahm 1999). Voorhees and Lingenfelter (2003) estimate that currently 56 percent of American workers need education beyond a high school degree to do their jobs, and this proportion will most certainly increase in the future. Voorhees and Lingenfelter highlight studies that suggest 8 out of 10 new jobs created over the next two decades will require some postsecondary education. For workers without these skills, the punishment is severe. As noted by Acs, Phillips, and McKenzie (2000), working full time at a low-wage job will not lead to long-term economic well-being. They estimate that 80 percent of families who are part of the working poor would be low-income even if all able-bodied adult members worked full time.

The potential role of education, particularly postsecondary training, to improve outcomes for families is significant, as the returns to college attendance are likely large for older workers. Leigh and Gill (1997) find that the returns to associate degree and nondegree community college programs are not only positive but, for returning adults, similar to the returns for recent high school graduates. In the same vein, Jacobson, LaLonde, and Sullivan (2005) conclude that the impact of a year of community college schooling increases long-term earnings by 7 percent for men and 10 percent for women. Carnevale and Desrochers (1999), focusing on welfare recipients with basic skills equal to a high school diploma, estimate that an additional 200 hours of education and training could lead to jobs that pay $5,000 to $10,000 more. This is equivalent to a semester of postsecondary courses.

Beyond trends in the labor market, demographic change related to the aging of the baby boomers also explains part of the increase in nontraditional, older students. Because this group now forms a larger cohort, even if its members were to attend college at the same rates as older students have in the past, the proportion of college students who are older would have increased. However, it is also clear that larger percentages of older workers are returning to higher education than ever before. Pent-up demand for higher education may also explain increased enrollments among older working women and racial minorities. Some suggest that opportunities for college attendance were more limited when these groups were of traditional college age, but as norms have changed, these workers are now better able to access postsecondary training (Goldin, Katz, and Kuziemko 2006). Changes in social policies such as welfare may also explain some of the fluctuation in trends.

However, the financial concerns of nontraditional students are a serious issue. Research suggests that the financial aid system, originally designed to meet the needs of traditional-age college students, does a poor job of addressing the circumstances of older, nontraditional students. Particularly with such a diverse population in terms of background, situations, and goals, a key issue is whether one set of financial aid policies can meet all students' needs. The following sections detail how the financial aid system currently works and the ways it does or does not address the needs of nontraditional students. First, however, the rest of this section gives additional background on the characteristics and enrollment patterns of nontraditional students.

Defining the "Nontraditional" Student

While age captures much of what is considered to define a nontraditional student, the definition has become much more nuanced with the growth of such a diverse population. In contrast to "nontraditional" students, researchers and practitioners often refer to "traditional" students as those who earn a regular high school diploma, enroll in college full-time immediately after graduation, depend on their parents for financial support, and either do not work during the school year or only work part-time. Therefore, the definition of nontraditional has become much more inclusive of students who do not fit the traditional mold. Using a much broader definition, Choy (2002) defines a nontraditional undergraduate as one who fits any of the following criteria:

- delays enrollment after high school
- attends part time
- works full time while enrolled
- is considered financially independent
- has dependents other than a spouse
- does not have a regular high school diploma (i.e., has a GED or other certificate)
- is a displaced worker or unemployed
- is a welfare recipient
- is an immigrant

By her calculations, nearly three-fourths of undergraduates are nontraditional. This would include working adults, parents, welfare recipients, immigrants, displaced workers and the unemployed, and single, financially independent students.

In terms of financial aid, this last group of financially independent students is the most relevant. Independent students are treated differently in the calculation of need for government aid sources. Students can qualify for this designation in one of several ways. First, students age 24 or above are automatically considered independent. However, students who are married, have dependents, or are veterans also qualify as independent. Students whose parents are deceased or who were wards of the court before the age of 18 are likewise automatically considered independent.

Another category of nontraditional students are those who engage in training outside of formal programs, such as individuals who take particular courses for job-related skills. In 2002–2003 approximately 68.5 million people took courses or training that was not part of a traditional degree, certificate, or apprenticeship program for reasons related to their job or career (O'Donnell 2005). These courses included seminars, training sessions, or workshops offered by businesses, unions, and government agencies, as well as classes taken at colleges or universities that were not part of a degree program. Most (90 percent) of these workers did so to maintain or improve skills they already had. Employers often required or recommended participation in the courses for those who were already employed. A fifth of participants took courses to secure a pay raise or promotion (DeBell and Mulligan 2005). Voorhees and Lingenfelter (2003) estimate that by the end of the current decade more than half of American adults will take advantage of formal learning opportunities at some point in their lives.

A DESCRIPTION OF AID RESOURCES FOR NONTRADITIONAL STUDENTS

Need Analysis and the Nontraditional Student

The financial aid process begins with the Free Application for Federal Student Aid (FAFSA). The FAFSA collects information on family income and assets in order to determine the Expected Family Contribution (EFC), the amount the federal government determines a family is able to contribute to higher education expenses. Other information that affects this calculation is the size of the family, the number of family members in college, and the age of the older head of household (assuming two parents in the household), as well as information on the student's earnings and assets. To calculate a student's financial need, the government subtracts the EFC from the total cost of attendance.[1] A student's financial need, in combination with his or her EFC, determines whether he or she is eligible for certain grants and loans. For example, students who have a low EFC and financial need are eligible for federal need-based aid, like a Pell Grant. While the FAFSA is the federal application, it is also used by most states and institutions likely to enroll nontraditional students.

Being an independent (i.e., nontraditional) student affects the aid calculation in one important way. Because independent students may have their own dependents and are not expected to rely on parental contributions, the federal system does not expect them to contribute as much as the families of dependent students. Therefore, their EFCs tend to be lower. However, the amount an independent student is expected to contribute can be substantial, and it can vary substantially with only small changes in income. A single adult with two children who made an income at the poverty threshold ($16,242) would not be expected to contribute anything to his or her postsecondary training. However, at 150 percent of the poverty level ($24,363), the EFC would be $401, and at 200 percent of the poverty level ($32,484), the amount would be $2,116 (FinAid 2008).[2] Meanwhile, a married adult with two children who made an income at 150 percent of the poverty level ($30,666) would be expected to contribute $718; the amount would be $2,877 at 200 percent of the poverty level ($40,888). Therefore, as also noted by Choitz and Widom (2003), although there is not much difference between 150 and 200 percent of the federal poverty line, the difference in EFC can be large.

There are several major criticisms of the way federal need analysis is applied to nontraditional students. Foremost is that the system was designed with a traditional, dependent student in mind. Therefore, it assumes that the earnings of the potential student are relatively minor (i.e., the result of a summer job) and a large proportion of the student's earnings should be used to cover college expenses. Moreover, the calculation assumes that the parents' income, the main source of support for the child, will continue even while the student is in college and should be used to help cover expenses. In contrast, independent students do not have other major sources of support to rely upon. Most nontraditional students are formally engaged in the labor market when applying for financial aid, and while the government assumes this income level will remain the same even after college enrollment, the nontraditional student is actually likely to experience a reduction in earnings while pursuing a degree. Therefore, assumptions about the amount of earnings available to that person while in school are incorrect. As an extension of this, the EFC for many nontraditional students may be too high, as they are penalized for their earnings the year before starting school.

Beyond the EFC and need calculation, independence is not a major consideration in the award of financial aid. However, other criteria can disproportionally reduce aid eligibility for nontraditional students. For example, some programs require students to be enrolled at least part time or even full time. Because nontraditional students often attend part time or less than half time, this excludes them from qualifying for some aid. Nontraditional students are also less likely to be enrolled in a degree program and more likely to pursue a particular skill without the goal of completing a certificate or other credential. They are therefore excluded from programs requiring students to be enrolled in a degree program. Finally, some programs require a regular high school diploma, whereas many nontraditional students instead have a GED or other certificate (Bosworth and Choitz 2002). The next section describes several of the major financial aid programs and how they apply to nontraditional students.

Federal Financial Aid Programs and Nontraditional Students

The Pell Grant is the largest U.S. need-based aid program and serves as the foundation for other aid. This means that if students are eligible, the Pell Grant is awarded first. The majority of Pell recipients come from families with incomes in the lowest economic quartile; families earning between $30,000 and $40,000 begin to be phased out of Pell eligibility. The Pell Grant has been a particularly important program for nontraditional students. In 2006–2007, 59 percent of Pell Grants went to independent students (College Board 2007). However, students are required to attend at least part-time to receive a Pell Grant, and this excludes many working adults. According to analysis by FutureWorks, few working parents who had an income of less than 200 percent of the federal poverty level received a Pell Grant (Bosworth and Choitz 2004). Additionally, students must be enrolled in an institution eligible for federal Title IV funds in order to receive aid such as the Pell Grant. Students with financial need may also be eligible for federal work-study funds, which subsidize the wages of students employed in on-campus jobs. However, these awards rarely go to nontraditional students.

Students with higher EFCs usually will not qualify for Pell Grants or work-study funds, but they are eligible for government loan programs. The federal government sponsors several major loan programs. The largest is the Federal Stafford Loan Program, which offers subsidized and unsubsidized loans. Interest on subsidized loans, available only to needy students as determined by the FAFSA, is paid by the government while the students are in college. During their first year of undergraduate education, students may receive up to $3,500; the limit increases in subsequent years and is higher for independent students. However, many community colleges, a common destination for nontraditional students, do not participate in the federal loan program because of penalties that would be incurred if their students had high default rates. The Perkins Loan Program is another federal program, and it is distributed by campuses on the basis of financial need. Finally, the Federal PLUS Loan Program (Parent Loans for Undergraduate Students) is available to the parents of dependent college students as well as to independent students themselves. PLUS loans have no annual or aggregate limit, except that one may not borrow more than the cost of attendance, net of other financial aid. All of the federal loan programs require repayment after the student stops attending college, regardless of whether or not he or she has completed a degree.

In addition to grant, loan, and work-study programs, the federal government offers aid through the tax code. The Hope and Lifetime Learning Tax Credits provide a benefit to families who pay tuition expenses and incur tax liability (Long 2004). Relative to the Pell Grant, the higher education tax credits maintain a much higher level of income eligibility, phasing out at an adjusted gross income of $90,000 to $110,000 for joint filers, or $45,000 to $55,000 for single filers (Internal Revenue Service 2006). The Lifetime Learning Tax Credit (LLTC) is particularly relevant for nontraditional students. It was designed for adults in their later years of postsecondary study and for those returning to school to upgrade their skills or prepare for a new career. The student does not need to be enrolled in a particular degree program. The LLTC targets postsecondary study after the first two years of college and is equal to 20 percent of tuition expenditures up to a tax credit of $2,000. However, the tax credits are not refundable, and therefore lower-income workers without tax liability are not eligible for a benefit. Additionally, the more generous Hope Tax Credit requires at least part-time attendance and was designed to meet the needs of more traditional-age students during their first two years of college.

There are also a number of tax benefits for families who save for college, such as 529 Plans and Coverdell Savings Accounts. The government does not tax investment gains in these accounts if they are used to pay for tuition. Finally, there are several federal programs that indirectly target nontraditional students. Among them are veteran's and military benefits and job training programs, such as the Workforce Investment Act (WIA). The WIA is the primary national workforce development program, and it focuses on employment services and basic training for the unemployed. While much of the funding is targeted for job search assistance for unemployed adults, there is also a little support for the training of current workers (Bosworth and Choitz 2004).

State Financial Aid Programs and Nontraditional Students

Most state financial aid programs have eligibility requirements similar to those of federal programs. This in turn often makes them less accessible to nontraditional students for the reasons mentioned above: EFC cutoffs and enrollment requirements, such as attending at least part time and in a particular educational program. Additionally, many state programs are explicitly designed for students who recently graduated from high school, which means they favor traditional students. However, according to Choitz and Widom (2003), approximately 15 states have programs or policies that provide special funding to students who are enrolled less than half time or do not exclude students at any enrollment intensity level (including less than half time). According to Choitz and Widom's survey, for example, Illinois and Minnesota allow less-than-half-time students to participate in the state's main need-based student grant program. Georgia, Ohio, Oregon, Washington, and West Virginia also have tuition-assistance programs for less-than-half-time students. Other states such as Louisiana allow the use of Temporary Assistance for Needy Families (TANF) dollars for postsecondary training.

Golonka and Matus-Grossman (2001) note additional examples of innovative state models. California has used multiple aid sources to provide comprehensive financial support for students. The state's "75/25" work-study program combines state work-study funds for TANF students with employer and college contributions. Employers must pay at least 25 percent of students' off-campus work-study wages while colleges pay the rest. The work-study earnings are excluded from income when calculating TANF eligibility. Unfortunately, while food stamps, Medicaid, and other federal programs do not count federal work-study income in determining eligibility, the same is not true for this state-created work-study program. Washington is an example of a state that has developed a program for working parents interested in job training. The Work-Based Learning Tuition Assistance Program gives aid to students who have one or more children and are TANF-eligible or have a family income at or below 175 percent of poverty level. The aid can be applied to any job-related vocational training or continuing education program.

The Role of Employers in Supporting the Training of Working Adults

Many question whether employers have incentives to invest in the training of their workers. Economic theory suggests that firms will not bear the costs of general training because of the risk of losing the worker without reaping the benefits of the human capital investment (Becker 1964). However, in many cases firms catering to working adults with little education do provide free skills training (Autor 2001; Autor, Levy, and Murnane 1999). Stokes (2006), citing *Training* magazine, notes that American corporations spent more than $51 billion on training in 2004. According to other estimates, 7 out of 10 businesses provide some form of formal employee training, and between 35 and 65 percent of all workers participate (Lerman, McKernan, and Riegg 2001). While the authors find training to be more common among workers with higher earnings and levels of education, the training appears to be more intensive for younger, part-time, and less-experienced workers.

Although the majority of this $51 billion in training dollars went to the salaries of internal training staff, more than $13 billion was devoted to purchasing services from third-party providers (Stokes 2006). These include commercial training companies, government agencies, and professional associations. Colleges and universities had only a 5 percent share of these expenditures, according to estimates from Eduventures, a consulting firm for higher education. Stokes suggests these institutions could therefore do much more to support older students by taking on this mission more seriously.

RESEARCH ON AID AND NONTRADITIONAL STUDENTS

Does the Aid System Serve the Needs of Nontraditional Students?

A key question about the current financial aid system is how well it meets the needs of nontraditional students. Numerous studies point to the significant unmet financial need traditional students face after accounting for all sources of government and institutional financial aid (Advisory Committee on Student Financial Assistance 2001, 2002). Similar patterns are found for nontraditional, independent students. The total amount of unmet need was slightly lower on average for independent students, at $4,800, than it was for dependent students, at $5,900 (Berkner and Wei 2006). However, the incidence of unmet need was higher among nontraditional, older students. After all forms of financial aid were allocated, 54.4 percent of independent students still had financial need, in comparison to 45.6 percent of dependent students.

To summarize, nontraditional students appear to face financial hurdles to attending college that are just as high or higher than those of their younger counterparts. Such hurdles arise from several of the design elements of the aid system and programs. As noted above, the EFC calculation assumes that students will continue to make the same income while attending college as they did during the year before enrolling. Each dollar of student income greatly reduces eligibility for financial aid, with the assumption that most of the earnings can be applied to pay college costs. Additionally, by attending part time or less than half time and not enrolling in a particular educational program, independent students are often not eligible for financial aid. As noted by Berkner and Wei (2006), the type of institution attended can also influence the aid and need calculations because of differences in the average cost of attendance. The need for aid is highest at private for-profit and not-for-profit colleges and universities.

The differences between dependent and independent students are also reflected in how aid is distributed among students. Though a similar percentage of dependent and independent students received some kind of grant aid in 2003–2004 (50.4 and 51.0 percent, respectively), the average amount differed substantially. Dependent students averaged $5,200 in grants, while independent students received $2,900 on average. Once one controls for enrollment intensity by limiting the sample to full-time, full-year undergraduates, the differences are not as large but still evident—$6,100 for dependent as opposed to $4,600 for independent students (Berkner and Wei 2006).

It is important to note that these numbers reflect the best-case scenario in terms of unmet need. They are calculated based on those who actually make it into higher education and thus do not capture the unmet needs of adults who elected not to enroll in postsecondary study. Moreover, the unmet needs of older students are likely understated because of their less intense enrollment patterns, which reduce the costs they face. The implications of this unmet need are significant in terms of participation. According to research by Eduventures, nearly a quarter of prospective adult learners who choose not to enroll cite costs as an obstacle (Stokes 2006).

The Impact of Financial Aid on Older Students

While significant unmet need remains a major issue for independents, research suggests that nontraditional students do respond to financial aid policy. In fact, they appear to be more responsive than younger, dependent students. One study demonstrates this by focusing on the Pell Grant: Seftor and Turner (2002) examine how the introduction of the Pell Grant affected enrollment among students aged 22–35. They compare the trends for these students before and after the 1972 introduction of the program, using data from the October Current Population Survey. They conclude that the introduction of the Pell Grant increased the probability of attending college by 1.5 percentage points for men and 1.3 percentage points for women. Given mean enrollment rates at the time, this translates into 16 percent relative growth for men and 40 percent growth for women. In contrast, other work has found that Pell had little impact on attendance of traditional-age students, except for perhaps at community colleges (Hansen 1983; Kane 1995).

Given the family situations of nontraditional students, it may be the case that more than just grants applied to tuition could help them. Simmons and Turner (2004) instead focus on aid to help cover child care costs. They hypothesize that the need to pay for child care could impede participation in postsecondary training. To test this theory, they examine what happened when, in 1988–1989, up to $1,000 in child care costs were allowed in the calculations used to determine Pell Grant amounts. Using the 1979 National Longitudinal Survey of Youth (NLSY79), they find that the policy change resulted in increasing the college enrollment rate of women with children. However, they do not find gains in educational attainment corresponding to the higher enrollment rates.

There are several reasons that might explain the greater responsiveness of older, nontraditional students to financial aid policy. First, as noted above, this group likely faces greater credit constraints than younger students because their families are less likely to contribute to their education. Moreover, they may have dependents of their own and so cannot forgo earnings while in school. Therefore, any amount of aid might make a large difference in their decisions. Also, because older workers have more experience with processes such as tax and government support forms, they may be more adept at and less daunted by complex aid application processes (Seftor and Turner 2002). Older students are also more likely to choose a convenient, local college, such as a community college, and so they do not have to cover major transition costs such as moving expenditures; tuition support is the main thing they need to attend college. Finally, the types of colleges many nontraditional students attend are unlikely to give aid or to respond to government policy by raising their prices. Therefore, government support may be more likely to have a substantial impact on the participation of independent rather than dependent students.

SUPPORTING OLDER WORKERS: REFORMING COLLEGE FINANCIAL AID FOR THE FUTURE

There are many things that the government and other institutions could do to improve the financial support of older workers seeking postsecondary training. As noted above, many programs have been designed with the traditional-age, dependent student in mind, but in order to help older workers, aid programs need to take into account the enrollment patterns more common among older, nontraditional students. In terms of federal financial aid, Bosworth and Choitz (2002) suggest changing the eligibility criteria for aid programs to include students who attend less than half time and those in short-term programs that do not necessarily result in a formal degree or certificate.[3] New financing instruments could also be especially beneficial for older workers. In his issue paper for the Secretary of Education's Commission on the Future of Higher Education, Stokes (2006) supports programs such as Lifelong Learning Accounts and Career Advancement Accounts.

The interaction with other social programs is another thing to consider in aid reform. Bosworth and Choitz (2002) encourage policymakers to consider how social programs, such as food stamps and Medicare, interact with government financial aid programs, so that one benefit does not adversely affect another. Voorhees and Lingenfelter (2003) note that states could also expand their use of TANF dollars, which often support only short-term training. Instead, they could "direct their flexible maintenance of effort funds to finance training that is longer than the 12 months designated by the federal standard. This would require collaboration between state agencies involved in higher education and those involved in implementing federal regulations" (p. 10).

Colleges and universities could also play a greater role in facilitating the enrollment of older workers in postsecondary institutions. By providing more local, accessible options with flexible schedules and programs, they would enable more participation among nontraditional students. Online options may also be a way to expand access. There is as well a need for more career-oriented programs tied to particular industries. Voorhees and Lingenfelter (2003) highlight the idea that community colleges could create employment-related programs that could be supported by the WIA's One-Stop Career Centers. These might not extend for as long a time as traditional offerings but could be more comprehensive than the brief programs typically supported through the WIA.

Beyond academic programs, colleges and universities could do more to address the particular needs of older workers. This includes providing support for child care, in terms of both finances and capacity. As suggested by Simmons and Turner (2004), subsidies for child care could significantly affect the participation of nontraditional students. The government could help with these types of initiatives by providing grants to colleges that create such programs to support older workers. In the past, Congress has supported the federal program Child Care Access Means Parents in School (Yachnin 2001).

Colleges and employers could also increase their level of partnership to support the postsecondary education of older workers. Beyond merely increasing the general amount of support, changing the timing of tuition collection and employer support could also have important benefits for nontraditional students. Currently, institutions collect tuition payments prior to enrollment, but employers often will not reimburse employees until after the course is satisfactorily completed. Introducing more flexible reimbursement policies, along with more accommodating institutional collection policies regarding tuition, could increase participation in such programs (Voorhees and Lingenfelter 2003).

CONCLUSION

The increased demand for skilled workers has made it necessary for many nontraditional students to seek additional training, and their numbers are expected to rise in coming years. It is therefore imperative for the government, colleges and universities, and employers to consider how best to enable these investments by reevaluating the design of the aid system as well as the supports provided. The resulting benefits to individuals, their families, and society are potentially large as the labor market becomes increasingly less forgiving of the unskilled.

Notes

1. Total cost of attendance, which is prorated based on the student's enrollment intensity (whether the student attends full or part time), includes tuition, fees, room and board, and other costs at the institution the student attends.
2. The calculations assume the person is a resident of Illinois and is 30 years old. A single adult with one child who made an income at the poverty threshold ($13,896) also would not be expected to contribute anything to his or her postsecondary training. However, at 150 percent of the poverty level ($20,844), the EFC would be $931, and at 200 percent of the poverty level ($27,792), the amount would be $1,974.

3. On the other hand, the likelihood of successfully completing an educational program increases with enrollment intensity, and so it is important for the government to provide enough aid to enable students to take larger course loads and complete programs faster.

References

Acs, Gregory, Katherin Ross Phillips, and Daniel McKenzie. 2000. *On the Bottom Rung: A Profile of Americans in Low-Income Working Families.* New Federalism: Issues and Options for the States No. A-42. Washington, DC: Urban Institute.

Advisory Committee on Student Financial Assistance. 2001. *Access Denied: Restoring the Nation's Commitment to Equal Educational Opportunity.* Washington, DC: Advisory Committee on Student Financial Assistance.

————. 2002. *Empty Promises: The Myth of College Access in America.* Washington, DC: Advisory Committee on Student Financial Assistance.

Autor, David H. 2001. "Why Do Temporary Help Firms Provide Free General Skills Training?" *Quarterly Journal of Economics* 116(4): 1409–1448.

Autor, David H., Frank Levy, and Richard J. Murnane. 1999. "Skills Training in the Temporary Help Sector: Employer Motivations and Worker Impacts." A Report to the Department of Labor, Education and Training Administration. Cambridge, MA: Massachusetts Institute of Technology.

Becker, Gary. 1964. *Human Capital: A Theoretical and Empirical Analysis, with Special Reference to Education.* Chicago: University of Chicago Press.

Berkner, Lutz, and Christina Chang Wei. 2006. *Student Financing of Undergraduate Education: 2003–04, with a Special Analysis of the Net Price of Attendance and Federal Education Tax Benefits.* NCES 2006-186. Washington, DC: National Center for Education Statistics.

Bosworth, Brian, and Victoria Choitz. 2002. *Held Back: How Student Aid Programs Fail Working Adults.* Belmont, MA: FutureWorks.

————. 2004. *Title X: A New Federal-State Partnership in Higher Education for Working Adults in the 21st Century.* Belmont, MA: FutureWorks.

Carnevale, Anthony P., and Donna M. Desrochers. 1999. "Getting Down to Business: Matching Welfare Recipients' Skills to Jobs That Train." *Policy and Practice of Public Human Services* 57(1): 18–24.

Choitz, Victoria, and Rebecca Widom. 2003. *Money Matters: How Financial Aid Affects Nontraditional Students in Community Colleges.* New York: MDRC.

Choy, Susan. 2002. *Nontraditional Undergraduates: Findings from The Condition of Education, 2002.* Report No. NCES-2002-012. Washington, DC: National Center for Education Statistics.

College Board. 2007. *Trends in Student Aid, 2007*. Trends in Higher Education Series. Washington, DC: College Board.

DeBell, Matthew, and Gail Mulligan. 2005. *Reasons for Adults' Participation in Work-Related Courses, 2002–03*. NCES Issue Brief 2005-088. Washington, DC: National Center for Education Statistics.

FinAid. 2008. *Streamlined Expected Family Contribution (EFC) Calculator*. Cranberry Township, PA: FinAid. http://www.finaid.org/calculators/faaefc .phtml (accessed November 2, 2008).

Goldin, Claudia, Lawrence F. Katz, and Ilyana Kuziemko. 2006. "The Homecoming of American College Women: The Reversal of the College Gender Gap." *Journal of Economic Perspectives* 20(4): 133–156.

Golonka, Susan, and Lisa Matus-Grossman. 2001. *Opening Doors: Expanding Educational Opportunities for Low-Income Workers*. New York: Manpower Demonstration Research Corporation (MDRC); and Washington, DC: National Governors Association Center for Best Practices.

Hansen, W. Lee. 1983. "Impact of Student Financial Aid on Access." In *The Crisis in Higher Education*, Joseph Fromkin, ed. New York: Academy of Political Science, pp. 84–96.

Internal Revenue Service. 2006. *Tax Benefits for Education*. Publication 970. Washington, DC: Department of the Treasury, Internal Revenue Service.

Jacobson, Louis, Robert J. LaLonde, and Daniel Sullivan. 2005. "The Impact of Community College Retraining on Older Displaced Workers: Should We Teach Old Dogs New Tricks?" *Industrial and Labor Relations Review* 58(3): 398–415.

Kane, Thomas J. 1995. "Rising Public College Tuition and College Entry: How Well Do Public Subsidies Promote Access to College?" NBER Working Paper No. 5164. Cambridge, MA: National Bureau of Economic Research.

Leigh, Duane E., and Andrew M. Gill. 1997. "Labor Market Returns to Community Colleges: Evidence for Returning Adults." *Journal of Human Resources* 32(2): 334–353.

Lerman, Robert I., Signe-Mary McKernan, and Stephanie Riegg. 2001. *Employer-Provided Training and Public Policy*. Washington, DC: Urban Institute. Paper presented at America's Workforce Network Research Conference, held in Washington, DC, June 26–27.

Long, Bridget Terry. 2004. "The Impact of Federal Tax Credits for Higher Education Expenses." In *College Choices: The Economics of Where to Go, When to Go, and How to Pay for It*, Caroline M. Hoxby, ed. Chicago: University of Chicago Press, pp. 101–168.

National Center for Education Statistics. 2007. *Digest of Education Statistics, 2006*. Washington, DC: National Center for Education Statistics.

http://nces.ed.gov/pubsearch/pubsinfo.asp?pubid=2007017 (accessed November 11, 2008).

O'Donnell, Kevin. 2005. *National Household Education Surveys Program of 2003: Tabular Summary of Adult Education for Work-Related Reasons: 2002–2003*. NCES 2005-044. Washington, DC: National Center for Education Statistics.

Seftor, Neil S., and Sarah E. Turner. 2002. "Back to School: Federal Student Aid Policy and Adult College Enrollment." *Journal of Human Resources* 37(2): 336–352.

Simmons, Sarah M., and Sarah E. Turner. 2004. "Taking Classes and Taking Care of the Kids: Do Childcare Benefits Increase Collegiate Attainment?" Paper presented at Southern Economic Association Annual Meeting, held in New Orleans, LA, November 21–23.

Stokes, Peter J. 2006. "Hidden in Plain Sight: Adult Learners Forge a New Tradition in Higher Education." Issue paper for the Secretary of Education's Commission on the Future of Higher Education. Boston: Eduventures.

Stuart, Lisa, and Emily Dahm. 1999. *21st Century Skills for 21st Century Jobs*. Washington, DC: U.S. Government Printing Office. Ithaca, NY: Cornell University, ILR School.

Voorhees, Richard A., and Paul E. Lingenfelter. 2003. *Adult Learners and State Policy*. Denver: State Higher Education Executive Officers (SHEEO); and Chicago: Council for Adult and Experiential Learning (CAEL).

Yachnin, Jennifer. 2001. "Congress Puts More Money into Aid for Child-Care Centers on Campuses." *Chronicle of Higher Education*, February 2, A: 22.

8

Can Residential Mobility Programs Improve Human Capital?

Comparing Social Mechanisms in Two Different Programs

James E. Rosenbaum
Northwestern University

Underlying some arguments for residential mobility is an implicit assumption that low-income individuals' capabilities can be improved by residential moves. We can conceive of four kinds of social influences by which residential moves might improve individuals' human capital: 1) schools, 2) labor markets, 3) informal social interaction, and 4) safety. Each of these mechanisms might have a different kind of influence on the value of individuals' human capital.

First, and most simply, school quality varies across different locations in the United States. Affluent neighborhoods have schools with better-paid teachers, more resources, and higher achievement test scores. If residential mobility moves low-income families from areas with poor schools to areas with much better schools, children's human capital can increase because of better instruction and higher standards.

Second, residential mobility can move low-income families from labor markets with weak demand for their labor to labor markets with stronger demand for their labor—in other words, places offering semi-skilled jobs. Even adults with modest skills will see the value of their human capital increase. For instance, if suburban employers have more difficulty than urban employers in finding individuals to take semi-skilled jobs (e.g., as sales clerks, service workers, etc.), then individuals seeking such jobs will have much better employment prospects (and perhaps better wages) if they move from urban to suburban locations.

Third, residential mobility can move participants to areas where informal social interaction (social capital) supports employment and school effort. For children, moving away from schools and friends that discourage school effort and into areas that encourage school effort may improve their academic performance. For adults, moving to neighborhoods where they make new friends who strongly encourage employment may make them more motivated to work, which may increase their human capital.

Fourth, residential mobility can move families to safer areas, and adults' and children's human capital will be less impaired by anxiety and depression. Research has shown the debilitating effects of violent neighborhoods (Garbarino 1995), so moves away from such neighborhoods may reduce these influences.

Obviously, each mechanism is complex, and marshaling evidence on any one of these would be a large endeavor, beyond the scope and purpose of this chapter. Here, I merely propose these four mechanisms as a means of understanding the possible ways in which residential mobility programs might affect human capital. I use this concept to examine whether these social influences are altered by two different residential mobility programs.

This chapter seeks to identify dimensions on which these two residential mobility programs differ, to describe the neighborhood placements and social influences created by these programs, and to consider how these social influences might explain individual outcomes. In contrast with literature that focuses on mobility's effects on individual outcomes, this review focuses on program procedures, program placements, and the social influences that participants encounter. Although I also present empirical findings on individual outcomes, I am less concerned about inferring the average causal relationship between mobility and outcome behavior than in considering variations in the kinds of mobility procedures and their implications for creating a wide spectrum of different placements and social influences, which are the crucial forces that affect outcomes. In effect, I am proposing a model in which outcomes are a direct byproduct of social influences, which mediates "mobility effects." The key unanswered question is not what is the relationship between mobility and outcomes, but rather, what kinds of social influences do residential mobility program procedures create? Once we know what social influences are created, we will better understand what behavioral outcomes result.

The chapter begins by describing two residential mobility programs, Moving to Opportunity for Fair Housing (MTO) and the Gautreaux Assisted Housing Program (Gautreaux). I then describe procedures in the two programs that influence placements. The next two sections describe the kinds of neighborhood placements and the social influences created by each program. I find that the programs differ in the kinds of placements and in three aspects of social influences (whether participants attend good schools, change labor markets, or change social interactions), but are similar in improving perceived safety. I examine the specific procedures used by these two programs and consider how these procedures might influence the kinds of placements and social influences created by the two programs. I suggest that residential ability programs can alter human capital through these mechanisms, but that they must include program procedures that have a strong impact on improving social influences.

PLACES MATTER—SOMETIMES

Spatial mismatch has long been noted (Holzer 1991). Big differences have been shown in the resources and opportunities available in different locations (Briggs 2005). Some analyses contend that negative influences in neighborhoods with concentrated poverty may undermine the benefits of job and education programs (Wilson 1996).

Such observations have led to suggestions that residential mobility programs might provide more effective solutions. This is a profound contention—it suggests that mobility might increase human capital.

However, all moves don't have the same impact. Having observed enormous differences in the quality of public schools between affluent suburbs and inner-city neighborhoods, affluent families choose to buy homes based on the quality of the public schools. Can residential mobility programs serving low-income families have the same impact?

This chapter shows that two residential mobility programs with similar goals lead to placements in very different neighborhoods, which produce different social influences—which in turn may have implications for participants. The questions of which moves have an impact and how they do so are of great policy importance.

PROGRAM DESIGN OF TWO RESIDENTIAL
MOBILITY PROGRAMS

Gautreaux was a court-ordered demonstration program in Chicago, removed from the political process and conducted with low visibility. As a result of a consent decree, between 1976 and 1998, Gautreaux placed low-income black families who lived in housing projects (or were on the waiting list) into certain units in mostly white middle-income suburbs or in low-income mostly black urban neighborhoods. A few hundred families moved each year, and only a few families moved into any single neighborhood. Because of this, the program had low visibility, although 7,000 families ultimately moved through the program, about half of whom moved to white middle-income suburbs (Polikoff 2006).

Gautreaux was not designed as a research study; few premove measures were collected, and families were not randomly assigned to suburbs or city. However, assignments to the two conditions created a quasi-experimental design. According to reports in the 1980s by housing counselors implementing the program, families were assigned to one of the two conditions on a first-come, first-served basis. Although clients could refuse an offer, only 5 percent did so since they were unlikely to get another in the six months of their program eligibility (Rubinowitz and Rosenbaum 2000). As a result, placements approximated random assignment, but they were not perfectly random.

Suburb and city participants, on average, were highly similar before the move in personal attributes (age, number of children, education, marital status, public aid, years in program, etc.), but a few differences were noted in premove neighborhoods. While suburban movers came from slightly lower poverty tracts than city movers (a poverty rate of 40.6 percent versus 43.8 percent), they moved to census tracts with dramatically lower poverty rates (5.0 percent versus 27.3 percent [DeLuca and Rosenbaum 2003]). Although it is possible that preexisting differences may affect outcomes, there are reasons to think this impact is relatively small. First, it seems reasonable to infer that the large outcome differences are probably explained less by the 3-percentage-point difference in initial neighborhoods than by the 22-percentage-point difference in placements. Second, multivariate analyses that control for baseline attributes and locations found large, significant impacts of placement neighborhood attributes on outcomes an average of 14 years after program placement (DeLuca and Rosenbaum 2003; Keels et al. 2005).

The MTO program was modeled on the Gautreaux program, but MTO was a random assignment experiment. Eligible families were placed in treatments by random assignment, and analysis considered all families who received offers (regardless of whether they moved or not). This allowed researchers to assess the impact of being given the chance to move compared to what similar people did in the absence of this opportunity.

MTO departed from the Gautreaux program design in several respects besides random assignment. First, whereas Gautreaux placed families in specific units, MTO specified census tracts and let families choose any housing unit in any neighborhood, as long as it was located in a qualifying tract. MTO designers may have felt that further constraints beyond census tract were unnecessary or not politically desirable. Although some counselors found units for families (much like the Gautreaux housing staff), that was not common, so most families were on their own to find units. Counseling practices were not specified in the program design. It is not clear what MTO counselors told families about neighborhoods, but some reports suggest that some counselors encouraged addresses where participants would find neighbors similar to themselves.

Second, while Gautreaux moved experimental group families to distant suburbs, MTO focused on specifying census tract poverty concentration, and it permitted any kind of move, including moves within the city. The emphasis in MTO was on meeting the tract poverty-rate goal quickly and efficiently.

Third, while Gautreaux was a racial integration program that moved experimental-group families into mostly white suburbs, all of which were low-poverty, MTO gave no consideration to tract racial composition, and many MTO program movers chose residences that met the poverty requirements but were located in mostly black neighborhoods (Orr et al. 2003).

The two programs also had somewhat different entrance rules. All MTO participants and most Gautreaux participants were housing project residents, but some Gautreaux participants were on the housing project wait list. While wait-list families were not in housing project circumstances, their housing circumstances were no better than those of housing project residents, and perhaps they were worse—the families were either in crowded conditions, constantly moving, on the verge of eviction, or in homeless shelters (Rubinowitz and Rosenbaum 2000). The fact that they desired to enter Chicago public housing, despite its well-known dangers, suggests that they considered their living conditions worse than the housing projects.

In terms of education and welfare receipt, two important population characteristics, there are small differences between the programs. While similar portions of household heads had completed high school or gotten a GED in MTO and Gautreaux (60.3 to 63.9 percent), more MTO families were on public aid than in Gautreaux (61 versus 50 percent [Orr et al. 2003, Table C-2; Rubinowitz and Rosenbaum 2000, p. 79]). Participants in the two programs were probably not greatly different.

PLACEMENTS IN THE TWO PROGRAMS

In both programs, families in the experimental group were intended to be placed into a different type of neighborhood than the control group. I describe the kinds of neighborhoods into which the experimental groups of each program were actually placed. I look at three aspects of neighborhoods: census tract, microneighborhood, and distance from baseline neighborhood. I find that the programs differ on all three. Results are summarized in Table 8.1.

Census Tracts

Although both programs aimed to move families to less-poor neighborhoods, the programs led participants to neighborhoods with different compositions of poverty and race. Gautreaux's suburban placements were all in low-poverty census tracts. Indeed, based on an analysis of a 50 percent random sample of Gautreaux movers between 1976 and 1990 using administrative data, the 743 suburban movers were placed in census tracts where the average percentage of poverty was 5.3. Moreover, most neighbors were affluent; the mean family income in the suburban

Table 8.1 Program Design Elements for MTO and Gautreaux Movers (all numbers in %)

	MTO	Gautreaux[a]
Moving distance		
Moves less than 10 miles	84	10
Neighborhood placements		
(census tract attributes)		
Placements' average percent poverty	12.4	5.3
Placement in over 40% black areas	38	5
Microneighborhoods		
Procedures to prevent enclaves?	no	yes
Created enclaves?	yes?	no
Social contexts		
Schools		
School district change?	30	~100
Schools w/above-average test scores	10	88
Labor markets		
Change labor market?	no?	yes?
Labor market comparison	strong→strong	weak→strong
Social interactions		
Contact with former peers?	often?	rare?
Safety improved	yes	yes
Duration		
Retention rate in placement	44 after	66 after
neighborhoods[b]	4–7 years	15+ years

NOTE: A question mark indicates best estimate from qualitative or administrative data; the rest is based on systematic evidence.

[a] These figures include the families who relocated to suburban communities outside of the city of Chicago. See DeLuca and Rosenbaum (2003) for a more detailed analysis of all Gautreaux program moves.

[b] For MTO, this means that the neighborhood at the follow-up survey was less than 10 percent poor; for Gautreaux, it means that the neighborhoods at last follow-up were less than 30 percent African American. Note, however, that Gautreaux has a much longer follow-up period (see Orr et al., p. 33).

census tracts was $71,545 (DeLuca and Rosenbaum 2003, p. 323). The suburban locations were required to be less than 30 percent black, and almost all (90 percent) placement tracts were less than 16 percent black. Overall, the average placement tract had no more than 10 percent black households (p. 325).

In contrast, MTO placements did not consider racial composition. Although it was hoped that the program would increase racial integration, it was not required, and the results indicate that it often did not happen. In 1997, not long after the move, about 38 percent of experimental group movers were living in highly black areas (over 40 percent black [Goering and Feins 2003]), while less than 5 percent of Gautreaux's suburban movers' placements were in such areas (DeLuca and Rosenbaum 2003).

MTO appeared to accomplish its goals in terms of 1990 census figures, but some of these figures failed to capture the reality of changing census tract composition, and MTO ultimately fell short because of this. Nearly all movers (94 percent) went to areas with less than 11 percent poverty, based on the 1990 census data available at the time of placement (Orr et al. 2003, p. 29). However, because of changes in tract composition after 1990, the actual composition of census tracts at the time of the move averaged 12.4 percent. Based on the 2000 census data, the program estimated that "just half of the moves were to areas estimated to have poverty rates below 10 percent at the time of the move, and another third were to areas of 10 to 15 percent poverty at the time. All told, 97 percent moved to areas with less than 20 percent poverty" (p. 30). While moving participants from tracts with over 40 percent poverty to tracts with less than 20 percent poverty is a big improvement, these neighborhoods may have had different characteristics than the intended 10 percent goal. Both programs moved one group to low-poverty census tracts, but the programs led to different kinds of neighborhoods.

Microneighborhoods

Beyond that, the programs led to different microneighborhoods as well. Gautreaux placed families in specific apartments. Real-estate staff located units that avoided enclaves, and counselors made sure to avoid creating enclaves. No more than three families were placed in any neighborhood, and neighborhoods were avoided if many African American families already lived there. The program also avoided areas located near concentrations of black or low-income families (Rubinowitz and Rosenbaum 2000).

In contrast, MTO defined neighborhoods only in terms of census tracts, and did not consider microneighborhoods within census tracts. MTO had no rules or procedures to avoid enclaves within census tracts, and some counselors thought that enclaves were desirable because they provided social support. MTO families chose their own housing units, choices that were presumably based on their preferences, housing availability, and landlord willingness. Unlike Gautreaux, where real-estate staff convinced reluctant landlords to take participants, the MTO program did not provide such opportunities. Consequently, in MTO, participant choices influenced microneighborhoods.

Did MTO move families into enclaves? Casual observation of maps of MTO placements raises concerns. While experimental group placements in Gautreaux are widely scattered (as depicted on a map on a wall at the Leadership Council), some placements in MTO indicate more than three families placed close together. Some placements are located on census-tract boundaries adjoining higher-poverty census tracts (Goering et al. 1999), a finding similar to observations of another housing voucher program (Cronin and Rasmussen 1981). Although we do not have geo-coded data on MTO placements, it is possible to generate such geo-codes, and research could be done to compare the programs on whether microneighborhoods allowed concentration. If enclaves are created, one must wonder whether and how they may insulate families from the potential benefits of low-poverty census tracts.

Distance from Prior Neighborhoods

Part of the social impact of these programs may be in removing participants from the influence of old neighborhoods. If "prior neighborhoods seem to be magnets" (Briggs 1997), and if the power of magnets declines with distance, moving distance may influence whether old neighbors continue to influence families. The experimental group in the two programs experienced quite different moves in this respect.

For Gautreaux movers, the average suburban placement was 25 miles (Keels et al. 2005), and fewer than 10 percent of moves were less than 10 miles.[1] In contrast, 84 percent of MTO experimental group moves were less than 10 miles from the baseline address, and some participants moved less than 1 mile (Kling et al. 2004, Table A14). These differences raise concerns about whether families actually left their old neighborhood. While the difficulty of traveling 10 miles may differ according to public transit routes, we suspect that more participants will continue interactions with old friends from 1 to 10 miles away than will do so with ones 25 miles away, and they may continue to be influenced by peer pressures from their former high-poverty neighborhoods.

In summary, program design elements of Gautreaux and MTO appear to have created moves to very different types of neighborhoods (based on poverty and racial characteristics), different microneighborhood influences, and different distances from initial residences.

SOCIAL INFLUENCES IN THE TWO PROGRAMS

Having seen the actual placements, we might expect that the two programs would create different social influences. New neighborhoods present different institutions and conditions that offer the possibility of new influences. These "social influences" refer to broad conditions offered within neighborhoods, not individual outcomes. This section considers four kinds of influences relevant to neighborhoods: 1) schools, 2) local labor markets, 3) social interaction, and 4) safety.

1) Schools: Did Residential Mobility Change Schools and School Quality?

One of the most striking aspects of American public education is the way schools vary by geography. Within a large metropolitan area, schools often vary enormously in quality between affluent suburban areas and less affluent urban areas. In part, this is due to local funding differences and to differential ways that funding is spent (i.e., whether school funds are spent on curricula and instruction or on security and building maintenance [Jencks and Phillips 1998]). If low-income minority families moved to better neighborhoods, we might expect that they would attend better schools.

In Gautreaux, nearly all families moving to suburbs changed school districts and began attending different schools (Rubinowitz and Rosenbaum 2000). They generally attended much better schools than they had in the city. Indeed, 88 percent of Gautreaux suburban movers attended schools where the average test scores were in the top half of national standards (Orr et al. 2003; Rosenbaum et al. 1993).

In contrast, while the MTO experimental group changed neighborhoods, they rarely changed school districts. Seventy percent of the MTO treatment group movers stayed in the same school district. Overall, the average experimental-group child was in a school in the twenty-first percentile, and less than 10 percent attended schools that ranked above the fiftieth percentile (Orr et al. 2003, pp. 110–111).

In summary, the two residential mobility programs led children to very different sets of schools. Research is clearly needed to understand why there was so little school improvement for MTO movers. Perhaps the short moves explain part of this school difference. Research has begun to examine how parents make these choices (see Briggs et al. 2006).

2) Labor Market: Did Moving to a Different Labor Market Mean Moving to a Stronger Labor Market?

One of the most intriguing possibilities suggested by mobility programs is that residential mobility might directly increase the value of the movers' human capital. Individuals with low-level skills and limited education may have little market value in high poverty neighborhoods, where many people have the same qualifications and available jobs are quickly filled. If these individuals move to distant affluent suburbs, where the demand for low-skilled workers exceeds the supply, these individuals will be in greater demand and perhaps have greater value.

Gautreaux occurred during the 1980s, when employment opportunities in the suburbs were strong, while they were weak in inner-city areas. The spatial mismatch theory posits that the distance between available unskilled jobs (in the suburbs) and available semiskilled workers (in the city) contributes to unemployment of semiskilled workers (Holzer 1991). These distances often require long commutes, which are particularly onerous given poor public transportation, and the low pay of these jobs is not sufficient to justify the high costs of commutes in time and money.

Given the well-documented spatial mismatch between suburban labor markets and city residents, the Gautreaux program made exactly the kinds of moves that were likely to put semiskilled adults into labor markets with strong demand and few competitors. In contrast, as noted, the MTO treatment group made short-distance moves, so it isn't clear whether those workers actually moved to a "different labor market."

In addition, there are indications that the MTO program treatment group was already in strong labor markets prior to moving. MTO occurred in the late 1990s, during a strong economy, when labor market demand for semiskilled workers was very high. In addition, at the same time, the TANF program of welfare reform had pushed large numbers of families off public assistance and into jobs. As a result, the labor markets in low-income neighborhoods improved for everyone. The treatment group moved out of strong labor markets that would likely have improved their prospects if they had stayed.

3) Social Interaction: How Much Did Families Really Leave Prior Neighborhoods Behind?

Third, residential mobility can move participants to areas where informal social interaction (social capital) supports employment and school effort. For children, moving away from schools and friends that don't encourage school effort and into areas where social norms support school effort may improve those students' own school efforts. If adults move to neighborhoods where they make new friends who strongly encourage employment, they may be more motivated to work, which may increase the value of their human capital. Obviously, these social influences on mothers and children are complex and require detailed analyses (see Rosenbaum, DeLuca, and Tuck 2005).[2] However, all of them are premised on the assumption that mothers and children stop interacting with their former friends, which may not be true.

Residential mobility studies implicitly assume that residential changes influence social interaction. Mothers and children whose homes are in new neighborhoods will have new neighbors and institutions with which to interact. Thus it is important to consider whether families maintain their ties with individuals and institutions in the old neighborhood.

In interviews, Gautreaux suburban movers reported that weekday visits to their former neighborhoods were very rare. With average suburban moves of 25 miles, mothers and children could not easily travel back to the old neighborhood on a daily basis. Some suburban movers returned to the old neighborhood for occasional weekend visits with relatives or to go to church; these Sunday visits were often to family dinners and churches, and they occurred in the daytime, not at night. While it was theoretically possible for some children to continue attending their old schools (if they pretended to live with a relative), this almost never happened, and the few times it did was for summer school. Thus, children's contacts with old neighbors were limited to occasional visits and mostly in the presence of adults (Rubinowitz and Rosenbaum 2000).

While these rare visits had the downside of causing initial feelings of isolation, this may have increased the impact of the move. At the time of the second interview, over seven years after moving, very few mothers or children were socially isolated. Most of the children interacted with white classmates after school, often in each other's homes (Rosenbaum et al. 1993, p. 1538).

In contrast, the MTO short moves probably made it easier to maintain old support networks. Research suggests that many children continued to interact with friends from the old neighborhood. The interim report finds that the experimental-group movers were less likely to visit with friends from old neighborhoods (or to still be living there) compared to the control group. However, 43 percent of experimental-group children still visited their friends from the old neighborhood, and the rate was somewhat higher for boys.

These children moved to residences out of their old neighborhoods, but they may not have left the old neighborhood *socially*. It is important to note here that we do not know what children are doing when they visit friends in the old neighborhood, how often these visits happen, or how much these visits reduce exposure to the new neighborhood.

Despite changing residence, many MTO experimental-group families spent part of their social lives in their old neighborhoods and presumably were influenced by their former neighbors. It is important to

further explore both the reasons for and the implications of social interaction with the old neighborhood. While this may have been comfort-
ing, it altered the social influences of "moving."

4) Safety: Did Moving to a New Neighborhood Make Families Feel Safer?

Given the higher incidence of crime and assaults in low-income
neighborhoods, it is generally expected that moves to low-poverty
neighborhoods would lead to less exposure to crime and greater feelings of safety. In the Gautreaux program, suburban movers reported
feeling much safer than city movers, and also much safer than they had
themselves felt when they lived in the city. For instance, only 31 percent of suburban movers said the suburban area was dangerous at night,
while 71 percent of city movers said their neighborhood was dangerous
at night (Rubinowitz and Rosenbaum 2000, p. 94).

Similarly, MTO families reported large increases in feelings of
safety. In 2001, compared to the control group, the MTO experimental
group was much more likely to feel safe at night (85 percent versus 55
percent), much less likely to have been victimized in the last six months
(12 percent versus 21 percent), and much less likely to be dissatisfied
with the police (77 percent versus 48 percent) [Orr et al. 2003, Table
3.5]. These moves did have an effect on perceptions of safety. These
changes are likely linked to the big improvements in mental health noted below.

In summary, these findings indicate that moves in both programs
led to improved neighborhood influences. However, some evidence
suggests that moves in Gautreaux were accompanied by greater exposure to low-poverty neighborhoods and more social separation from the
old neighborhood than the MTO moves. Future research would benefit
from understanding the issues of social exposure to new and old neighborhoods and the positive and negative aspects of each.

INFLUENCES ON INDIVIDUAL OUTCOMES: EDUCATION, EMPLOYMENT, SUBSEQUENT MOVES, AND MENTAL HEALTH

Do residential moves affect individuals' outcomes? The following sections examine the effects of the two programs on four different outcomes theorized to be related to neighborhoods: 1) education, 2) employment, 3) subsequent moves, and 4) mental health.

1) Education—Can Moves Improve School Outcomes without Improved Schools?

The Gautreaux studies found dramatic differences between the suburban and city groups in educational outcomes. Compared to children who moved within the city, suburban movers were more likely to complete a high school diploma, to be on a college track in high school, to attend college, and to attend a four-year college. These were statistically significant and large differences (Rosenbaum 1995). In contrast, MTO has not had enough time to see such long-term effects; however, four to seven years after random assignment, children in the MTO experimental group did not perform better than control-group children on reading and math achievement tests, or in terms of suspensions, expulsions, and school engagement (Kling et al. 2004).

Although MTO's superior research design may explain the different findings, alternative explanations are possible. As noted, MTO moves rarely resulted in students changing school districts or attending above-average schools, and sometimes resulted in no change of schools. In contrast, nearly all suburban movers in Gautreaux moved to new school districts, many of which were dramatically better than those for the control group (whose members moved within the city). Given the radical disparities in school quality in different locations, many hoped residential mobility would provide access to good schools. As noted, less than 10 percent of the MTO experimental group attended schools with above-average achievement test scores, while 88 percent of Gautreaux experimental-group students did so. MTO's findings may indicate that residential mobility without better schools has little impact on educational outcomes (particularly if children keep interacting with old friends). Merely improving the composition of neighbors (in a census tract) does not by itself improve children's educational achievement.

This raises an important policy implication: policymakers need to think carefully about how school choices are incorporated into neighborhood choices. Middle-class families often choose neighborhoods based on school quality, but many MTO families ignored school quality, and the program provided no information or advice about school quality. It is likely that without moving children to areas with above-average schools, there will be no discernible education effects.

2) Employment—Moves to Different or Stronger Labor Markets

Do moves put people in different labor markets?

A second focus of research was on adult employment. The early Gautreaux survey research showed that mothers' employment was significantly higher in the suburbs, but that mothers' earnings and hours worked were no different. Later analyses, using administrative data from a much larger random sample, suggest that the primary influence was neighborhood composition, not the city/suburb distinction (DeLuca and Rosenbaum 2003; Mendenhall, DeLuca, and Duncan 2006; Rosenbaum, DeLuca, and Miller 1999). Research found that while the city/suburb distinction did not have a significant effect on public-aid receipt, "public-aid rates went from 26 percent to 39 percent for families placed in the highest and lowest quintile neighborhoods, with respect to education level of the tract . . . The difference remains very strong and significant even after controlling for years in the program, age, and premove public aid" (DeLuca and Rosenbaum 2003, p. 312). Similar findings with more extensive controls (and a different distinction, one based on race and poverty, not education) were found for employment outcomes and public aid (Mendenhall, DeLuca, and Duncan 2006).

Employment was also a major focus of the MTO research. The main finding was summarized in a subheading of the executive summary of the interim impacts evaluation: compared to the control group there were "no effects on employment or earnings" (Orr 2003, p. xiii). However, there are two questions that arise.

The first is whether MTO actually moves families to different labor markets. Unlike Gautreaux, where 25-mile moves from declining inner-city neighborhoods to high-growth suburbs clearly put families in different labor markets, MTO's less-than-10-mile moves (often within city limits) may not have put them in a different labor market, and it may not have even reduced commuting time.

Did MTO move people *from* strong labor markets?

The second question is whether MTO moved families from strong labor markets to (other) strong labor markets. While the Gautreaux program moved families from weak to strong labor markets (Rosenbaum et al. 1993), MTO moved families who were already in strong labor markets. MTO occurred during a strong economy, when labor market demand for semiskilled workers was very high. MTO results were measured between 1994 and 2000, when an unusually strong economy, strong welfare reform policy (TANF), and expanded earned income tax credit encouraged many poor people to work (Blank 2002). As a result, the labor markets in low-income neighborhoods improved, leading to less difference in labor market influences between MTO experimental and control group families.

The strength of premove labor markets is seen in the control group. The control group's employment gains were extraordinary—100 percent gains. The MTO control group employment increased from 23.6 to 50.9 percent (Blank 2002, p. 127). One hundred percent gains are rare in experimental groups of powerful programs (Barnow 1987; Bassi and Ashenfelter 1986; Bloom et al. 1993; Cave and Doolittle 1991). Obviously, the premove labor market that the control group represented was a very strong labor market. Although the treatment group's gains were no larger than the control group's gains, both groups resided in very strong labor markets.

Indeed, in the context of such a strong labor market, one must wonder whether those still unemployed might have serious physical or psychological barriers to working—in other words, are there ceiling effects against further gains? Or are residential mobility effects effective for the same people who already benefited? One must also doubt that these findings would generalize to more ordinary historical periods.

In summary, while Gautreaux families moved from weak to strong labor markets, it is not clear whether MTO families moved to different labor markets and, even if they did, it appears the experimental group moved out of labor markets that were getting very strong—markets that led to 100 percent gains in employment for the control group.

3) Duration—Did Families Stay?

One indication of whether families see benefits to their move is whether they choose to stay. In turn, duration may influence the impact of moves. To the extent that they return to low-income neighborhoods, we might infer that they got few benefits in their new locations. Conversely, short-duration moves are likely to have little impact.

Using administrative data, research located Gautreaux participants an average of 15 years after they had made their initial move in the program. Selecting a 50 percent random sample of all families who had moved between 1976 and 1990 (1,507 families), researchers located recent addresses of 1,504 of these 1,507 families (DeLuca and Rosenbaum 2003). The research found that about two-thirds of families placed in the suburbs still remained in mostly white suburbs an average of 15 years later. Further analyses of these data indicate that families "continued to reside in neighborhoods with income levels that matched those of their placement neighborhoods . . . Families who were placed in low-crime and suburban locations were more likely to reside in low-crime neighborhoods years later" (Keels et al. 2005, p. 51).

In contrast, over a much shorter time interval (five years), MTO studies found that only 44.4 percent of the experimental-group movers still lived in low-poverty census tracts (15 percent poverty or less [Orr et al. 2003, pp. 30, 34]). In addition, a majority (59 percent) of the experimental-group movers were living in 80-percent-plus minority tracts (pp. 34, 37). As the interim report notes, many of these subsequent moves were "to areas more like the ones where the Section 8 families and control group movers lived . . . [and] to high-minority neighborhoods" (pp. 33, 37).

Ironically, although the Gautreaux moves imposed more disruption on participants' lives than did the MTO moves, the 15-year retention rate in Gautreaux was substantially higher than the shorter, five-year retention rate in MTO (66 percent versus 44 percent). Despite Gautreaux participants' initial fears about these moves, their preferences changed. Families reported that, over time, they formed friendships with neighbors and their children also made friends and became part of their schools and communities (Rubinowitz and Rosenbaum 2000). While children had initial difficulties in school, they gradually did better. Ironically, after the program induced families to move to areas they might not have chosen otherwise, families came to appreciate the new neighborhoods.

In contrast, since MTO families didn't move far, families may have continued interacting with their old friends, so they may not have made friends in their new neighborhoods. Although retaining old friends preserved social support and made the transition smoother, it also meant that the old neighborhood remained a social magnet (Briggs 1997), which often created a strong pull.

4) Mental Health—Do Moves Improve Families' Outlooks?

Gautreaux did not study health outcomes, but I include this topic because it is one of the most important discoveries of the MTO research, which found significant improvements in mental health.

Despite the many countervailing influences I have identified that might have reduced the impact of MTO moves, the MTO experimental group showed strong significant differences from the control group in terms of mothers' and daughters' perceptions of neighborhood safety, as well as psychological distress, depression, and obesity (Orr et al. 2003, p. 77). These findings are extremely impressive. The magnitude of difference is as great as one might see from programs devoted specifically to improving mental health (Kling et al. 2004). These are consistent differences, repeatedly found over time and in separate measures—not just statistical flukes.

CONCLUSION

MTO is a truly impressive study. It offers a carefully designed program and a well-administered research design that provides the strongest study in this area. Although MTO offers a stronger research design than Gautreaux, it offers a weaker program, leading to much weaker changes in social influences. MTO is useful for examining the impact of modest moves and modest changes in social influences.

However, MTO is not a good test of whether residential mobility can have a strong impact. If we are interested in discovering the potential impact of residential mobility on individual outcomes, we must examine a program that creates bigger changes in social influences. I have identified specific procedures that may contribute to those kinds of placements and social influences.

While the MTO studies provide stronger research evidence, the Gautreaux program creates larger changes in the environment. The two programs create different placements and different social influences, which are likely to explain some of the discrepancies in program outcomes (see Table 8.1).

Some observers have argued that the low-income families selected for the Gautreaux program would have moved to these kinds of neighborhoods even without the program. MTO shows that this is a wrong assumption—most MTO families were comparable, but virtually no MTO families moved 25 miles to mostly white affluent neighborhoods on their own. Obviously, Gautreaux-type moves would not have happened without the strong program requirement and assistance provided by Gautreaux. Program design has a crucial impact on what kinds of moves happen.

This chapter has shown that similar programs can lead to dramatically different placements and social influences, which are the key intervening mechanisms influencing human capital. These might have been altered if programs had been run slightly differently. In other words, the devil is in the details. It would have been easy to move many families into low-income enclaves if the Gautreaux program had not been more committed to avoiding enclaves (at the block level). If Gautreaux had been less committed to expanding housing options into new areas, it would have easily focused on a few nearby suburbs. Reducing the distance of moves would have been more convenient for housing counselors who took families to see available units. These minor changes in procedures would have met the conditions demanded by the consent decree, and they would have looked pretty good in terms of census tract poverty rates. Recognizing the possibility that slight modifications of Gautreaux might have led to much weaker social influences can help us think about ways to design residential programs that have stronger benefits.

POLICY IMPLICATIONS

In examining whether a residential mobility program is designed in a way that could improve human capital, we have asked what kinds of moves and social influences it creates. If a program moves families but leaves 90 percent of students in below-average schools, do we really expect improved educational achievement? If the program moves families only a few miles, do we expect that they have entered a different labor market, which will improve the value of their human capital? If children don't move far enough to change friendships and interactions, will they retain old friends, former gang memberships, and prior activities and interests?

I have identified specific procedures that may contribute to big changes in placements and social influences. One can easily conceive of MTO including one or more of these procedures, and, as a result, offering participants quite different placements and social influences. As we try to imagine what kinds of programs might create such social influences, we might consider minor modifications of MTO as realistic possibilities that might have such impact. Below, I suggest some minor modifications and some hypotheses (HYP) about potential consequences.

HYP 1: MTO + identify and require units not in low-income enclaves → higher human capital.

HYP 2: MTO + moves 20 miles from old address → less interaction with old friends. Higher human capital.

In Gautreaux, real estate staff located appropriate housing units that were not in enclaves, were in better neighborhoods, and many were quite distant. On their own, participants were unlikely to even know about these neighborhoods, and so it isn't surprising that MTO participants did not find such units. Real-estate staff could potentially have had a strong beneficial impact on MTO.

Counseling advice can also make a difference. Although both programs had housing counselors, MTO counselors did not provide information about school quality or labor market demand, nor did they provide advice about why participants should base their choices on such information. Gautreaux counselors mentioned both factors to help participants see the advantages of the distant moves they were offering. Residential mobility programs should give some thought to using housing counseling about these issues. Housing counseling may have a strong influence on participants' choices and could lead to better outcomes, as posited below.

HYP 3: MTO + identify locations with above-average schools + advice on how to choose them → better schools. Higher human capital.

HYP 4: MTO + identify locations with better job opportunities (for participants' level of skills) + advice on how to choose them → better employment outcomes. Higher human capital.

On the latter point, it is noteworthy that in some two-year colleges that provide occupational training, job placement counselors often advise their graduates to consider residential moves to improve their employment prospects (Rosenbaum, Deil-Amen, and Person 2006). These college advisers realize the practical barriers imposed by spatial mismatch—their graduates who live in low-income neighborhoods often live very far from the areas of employment growth, and many job vacancies require one-to-two-hour commutes. Besides providing skills and training to their graduates, these colleges advise their graduates to consider residential moves. Since they advise residential moves of 20–40 miles, we might expect that residential mobility programs may need to advise participants to go similar distances to get employment benefits.

As noted, children who make short moves may keep interacting with old friends and experience little change in social norms, social skills, or motivation. MTO studies have found that girls benefit from the move but boys often do not. Although such gender differences might arise from biology or early socialization—factors that programs can't change—gender differences might also arise from present influences, i.e., parents' different rules for boys and girls, which may mean that boys actually don't experience changes of "social influences."

We suspect that boys and girls may differ in their "traveling radius"—the distance they are allowed to travel to see friends after school.

If boys can travel greater distances than girls, then boys who moved only a few miles in MTO can frequently return to old neighborhoods. New residential neighborhoods may not change their social networks or social norms—boys may retain old friends, former gang memberships, and prior activities and interests. If so, we can hypothesize the following modifications that would reduce gender differences and increase the benefits to boys.

HYP 5: MTO + moms prevent boys from returning to old neighborhood → change social interactions and outcomes. Higher human capital.

HYP 6: MTO + move 25 miles → boys can't return easily, change social interactions and outcomes. Higher human capital.

We now have evidence about the kinds of placements and social influences created by two different programs. This comparison suggests that small procedural details can make a big difference. Besides the two programs described here, many other programs have arisen over the past decade. Many have entailed minor changes (despite its name, Gautreaux II strongly resembles MTO), but some have required dramatic changes in placements and social influences. For instance, another program created by a court decision, the Thompson decision in Baltimore, is being studied by Professor DeLuca at Johns Hopkins University, and it may provide new evidence about the issues raised here.

As we have seen, residential mobility is not a single entity. The two cases described here show how similar programs lead to very different placements and social influences. I have suggested that it is these intervening mechanisms that are likely to explain whether a residential mobility program improves the value of individuals' human capital, and I have suggested some detailed procedures that might contribute to such improvement. I hope that future policy discussions consider these issues.

Notes

1. This latter number was a special calculation that Micere Keels computed and reported to me in a conversation on February 23, 2006.
2. We studied only mothers, not fathers, because there were very few fathers in the program.

References

Barnow, Burt S. 1987. "The Impact of CETA Programs on Earnings: A Review of the Literature." *Journal of Human Resources* 22(2): 157–193.

Bassi, Laurie J., and Orley Ashenfelter. 1986. "The Effect of Direct Job Creation and Training Programs on Low-Skilled Workers." In *Fighting Poverty: What Works and What Doesn't*, Sheldon H. Danziger and Daniel H. Weinberg, eds. Cambridge, MA: Harvard University Press, pp. 133–151.

Blank, Rebecca M. 2002. "Evaluating Welfare Reform in the United States." *Journal of Economic Literature* 40(4): 1105–1166.

Bloom, Howard S., Larry L. Orr, George Cave, Stephen H. Bell, and Fred Doolittle. 1993. *The National JTPA Study: Title II-A Impacts on Earnings and Employment at 18 Months*. Research and Evaluation Report Series 93-C. Washington, DC: U.S. Department of Labor.

Briggs, Xavier de Souza. 1997. "Moving Up versus Moving Out: Neighborhood Effects in Housing Mobility Programs." *Housing Policy Debate* 8(1): 195–234.

———, ed. 2005. *The Geography of Opportunity: Race and Housing Choice in Metropolitan America*. Washington, DC.: Brookings Institution.

Briggs, Xavier de Souza, Kadija S. Ferryman, Susan J. Popkin, and María Rendón. 2006. "Can Expanded Housing and Neighborhood Choice Improve School Outcomes for Low-Income Children? Evidence from the Moving to Opportunity Experiment." Unpublished manuscript. Massachusetts Institute of Technology, Cambridge, MA.

Cave, George, and Fred Doolittle. 1991. *Assessing JOBSTART: Interim Impacts of a Program for School Dropouts*. New York: Manpower Demonstration Research Corporation.

Cronin, Francis J., and David W. Rasmussen. 1981. "Mobility." In *Housing Vouchers for the Poor: Lessons from a National Experiment*, Raymond J. Struyk and Marc Bendick Jr, eds. Washington, DC: Urban Institute Press, pp. 107–128.

DeLuca, Stefanie, and James E. Rosenbaum. 2003. "If Low-Income Blacks Are Given a Chance to Live in White Neighborhoods, Will They Stay? Examining Mobility Patterns in a Quasi-Experimental Program with Administrative Data." *Housing Policy Debate* 14(3): 305–345.

Garbarino, James. 1995. *Raising Children in a Socially Toxic Environment*. San Francisco: Jossey-Bass.

Goering, John, and Judith D. Feins, eds. 2003. *Choosing a Better Life? Evaluating the Moving to Opportunity Social Experiment*. Washington, DC: Urban Institute Press.

Goering, John, Joan Kraft, Judith D. Feins, Debra McInnis, Mary Joel Holin, and Huda Elhassan. 1999. *Moving to Opportunity for Fair Housing Demonstration Program: Current Status and Initial Findings*. Washington, DC: U.S. Department of Housing and Urban Development, Office of Policy Development and Research. http://www.huduser.org/Publications/pdf/mto.pdf (accessed February 10, 2009).

Holzer. Harry J. 1991. "The Spatial Mismatch Hypothesis: What Has the Evidence Shown?" *Urban Studies* 28(1): 105–122.

Jencks, Christopher, and Meredith Phillips, eds. 1998. *The Black-White Test Score Gap*. Washington, DC: Brookings Institution Press.

Keels, Micere, Greg J. Duncan, Stefanie DeLuca, Ruby Mendenhall, and James E. Rosenbaum. 2005. "Fifteen Years Later: Can Residential Mobility Programs Provide a Long-Term Escape from Neighborhood Segregation, Crime, and Poverty?" *Demography* 42(1): 51–73.

Kling, Jeffrey R., Jeffrey B. Liebman, Lawrence F. Katz, and Lisa Sanbonmatsu. 2004. "Moving to Opportunity and Tranquility: Neighborhood Effects on Adult Economic Self-Sufficiency and Health from a Randomized Housing Voucher Experiment." Princeton IRS Working Paper 481. Princeton, NJ: Princeton University. http://www.nber.org/~kling/mto/481.pdf; appendix tables available at http://www.nber.org/~kling/mto/481a.pdf (accessed February 10, 2009).

Orr, Larry, Judith D. Feins, Robin Jacob, Erik Beecroft, Lisa Sanbonmatsu, Lawrence F. Katz, Jeffrey B. Liebman, and Jeffrey R. Kling. 2003. *Moving to Opportunity Interim Impacts Evaluation*. Washington, DC: U.S. Department of Housing and Urban Development, Office of Policy Development and Research.

Mendenhall, Ruby, Stefanie DeLuca, and Greg J. Duncan. 2006. "Neighborhood Resources, Racial Segregation, and Economic Mobility." *Social Science Research* 35(4): 892–923.

Polikoff, Alexander. 2006. *Waiting for Gautreaux: A Story of Segregation, Housing, and the Black Ghetto*. Chicago: Northwestern University Press.

Rosenbaum, James E. 1995. "Changing the Geography of Opportunity by Expanding Residential Choice: Lessons from the Gautreaux Program." *Housing Policy Debate* 6(1): 231–270.

Rosenbaum, James E., Stefanie DeLuca, and Shazia R. Miller. 1999. "The Long-Term Effects of Residential Mobility on AFDC Receipt: Studying the Gautreaux Program with Administrative Data." Paper presented at the Joint Center for Poverty Research's conference "Neighborhood Effects on Low-Income Families," held in Chicago, IL, September 9–10.

Rosenbaum, James E., Stefanie DeLuca, and Tammy Tuck. 2005. "New Capabilities in New Places: Low-Income Black Families in Suburbia." In *The

Geography of Opportunity: Race and Housing Choice in Metropolitan America, Xavier de Souza Briggs, ed. Washington, DC: Brookings Institution Press, pp. 150–175.

Rosenbaum, James E., Regina Deil-Amen, and Ann E. Person. 2006. *After Admission: From College Access to College Success.* New York: Russell Sage Foundation.

Rosenbaum, James E., Nancy Fishman, Alison Brett, and Patricia Meaden. 1993. "Can the Kerner Commission's Housing Strategy Improve Employment, Education, and Social Integration for Low-Income Blacks?" *North Carolina Law Review* 71(5): 1519–1556.

Rubinowitz, Leonard S., and James E. Rosenbaum. 2000. *Crossing the Class and Color Lines: From Public Housing to White Suburbia.* Chicago: University of Chicago Press.

Wilson, William Julius. 1996. *When Work Disappears: The World of the New Urban Poor.* New York: Vintage.

9
What Might Improve the Employment and Advancement Prospects of the Poor?

Harry J. Holzer
Georgetown University and
The Urban Institute

During the past few decades, millions of less-educated workers have poured into the labor market in the United States, many as a result of welfare reform and immigration. But, while many of these workers have become successfully attached to the labor market, their wages often languish. Indeed, the wages of low earners (i.e., those at the tenth or twentieth percentile of all workers) have stagnated over time, relative to those at the middle or top of the labor market (Blank, Danziger, and Schoeni 2006). Advancement prospects for these workers also appear quite limited (Andersson, Holzer, and Lane 2005; French, Mazumder, and Taber 2006).

In addition, millions of other potential workers—especially black men from low-income families and neighborhoods—fail to attach regularly to the labor market at all. If anything, while the employment rates of single poor mothers improved quite dramatically in the 1990s, the labor force activity of less-educated black men continued to decline, as it has for each of the past several decades.

In this chapter, I review some research evidence on the causes of low earnings among the working poor and on the causes of weak labor-market activity among low-income men. I then consider some potential policy responses to these problems.

THE WORKING POOR AND THE NONATTACHED: WHAT ARE THEIR PROBLEMS?

In an economy that continues to reward skills at ever-higher levels, the skill deficits of the poor (relative to the nonpoor) are their greatest handicaps. These deficits include the following:

- poor levels of education, including high rates of dropping out of high school;
- weak cognitive skills and problem-solving abilities;
- weak "soft" skills, including written and verbal communication; and
- lack of occupational training and specific experience that would grant access to particular high-demand sectors of the economy, such as health care and construction.

For the nonattached, a lack of general work experience often signals to employers that applicants may have difficulties with even basic levels of job-readiness.

However, earnings in the labor market depend not only on worker skills but also on employer policies and practices. Of course, some sectors—such as construction, durable goods manufacturing, and transportation—clearly pay higher wages than others for workers of a given skill level. But even within very detailed industries and localities, employers often choose to pay more or less than their competitors to workers of comparable skills. Employers paying higher wages choose to compete on the basis of higher productivity and lower turnover, while those paying lower wages compete on the basis of lower compensation costs (Appelbaum, Bernhardt, and Murnane 2003). Furthermore, these employer wage premiums can account for large fractions of the observable differences in earnings across workers (Abowd and Kramarz 1999). In sum, "good jobs" contribute to higher earnings as well as "good skills."

But poor workers have very limited access to good jobs. This lack of access can be attributed to lack of information, lack of informal contacts, weak transportation, and employer discrimination—especially for minority workers (Holzer 2004). Poor access might inhibit workers from receiving the kind of on-the-job training and work experience that help build skills as well as pay. And if high-wage employers are becoming scarcer in the labor market as employment in some sectors shrinks (e.g., durable goods manufacturing) and newer competitive forces (e.g., from employers like Wal-Mart in retail trade) drive out higher-wage employers, then it will become even more difficult for the poor to gain the higher-paying jobs that still exist. On the other hand, as baby boomers retire from key sectors of the economy, replacement demand might generate new job availability in these sectors for many less-skilled workers.

The working poor suffer from other problems besides poor skills and limited access to good jobs. Many suffer from repeated job turnover and have difficulty retaining employment. Of course, not all job turnover is bad—indeed, voluntary turnover is often associated with strong job growth, especially for young workers (Andersson, Holzer, and Lane 2005; Topel and Ward 1992). But involuntary job instability might be caused by poor work performance, or by frequent absenteeism and tardiness, which are associated with difficulties in child care, transportation, or health (Holzer and LaLonde 2000; Holzer and Stoll 2001). Low wages can also limit workers' incentives to retain jobs.

Finally, millions of low-income (especially African American) men fail to develop consistent labor-market attachments for a variety of additional reasons. Growing up in poor and fatherless families and in highly segregated schools and neighborhoods, many boys and young men fall behind quickly and then disconnect from school at very early ages (Edelman, Holzer, and Offner 2006; Fryer and Levitt 2004). Once this disconnection occurs, these young men often fail to further develop their skills or complete school, and many obtain very little formal work experience of any kind. Furthermore, they also become more likely to engage in other nonmainstream behaviors, such as illegal activity and fathering children out of wedlock (Hill, Holzer, and Chen 2009).

The combination of criminal activity and unwed fatherhood almost guarantees that these young men will become incarcerated and also that they will receive child support orders (Holzer and Offner 2006). Upon release from prison, their ex-offender status will further inhibit their labor market prospects, as employers become even more reluctant to hire them and as their own skills and labor market contacts further depreciate (Holzer, Raphael, and Stoll 2004, 2006). Indeed, employer reluctance to hire those with criminal records might even cause these employers to engage broadly in "statistical discrimination" against less-educated black males (Holzer, Raphael, and Stoll 2004; Pager 2003).

Added to this, those who are noncustodial fathers almost certainly will be in arrears, or debt, on their child support orders, since the orders remain in effect while they are incarcerated. Those in arrears face very high tax rates on their limited earnings—up to 65 percent. And, since the child support collections are not always passed through by states to low-income families if they have been on public assistance, the incentives for the fathers to work in the formal economy and make these payments are very low, if they can escape detection by the child-support enforcement system.

Finally, it is important to note other problems and barriers that limit the labor force activity of various groups, including current or former welfare recipients. These individuals, often referred to as the "hard to employ," frequently have physical or mental health disabilities, substance abuse problems, and very poor skills and work experience (Bloom and Butler 2007; Danziger et al. 2000).

POLICIES TO IMPROVE ADVANCEMENT AND LABOR MARKET PARTICIPATION

Given the somewhat different situations and problems experienced by the working poor as opposed to those who are largely not attached to the labor market, somewhat different policy prescriptions apply to each group.

For the working poor, their advancement prospects would be best served by a combination of further job training, job placement assistance, and other supports and services, which would enable them to get access to better jobs in the labor market. Community or vocational colleges provide credentials that private sector employers will respect. However, work experience in the relevant sector might also be necessary. And, since there are clearly well-paying jobs available in certain high-demand sectors of the economy, strategies in which labor market intermediaries help link workers to existing jobs with engaged employers might offer the best chance of success (Giloth 2004).

These strategies now come in many forms (Holzer and Martinson 2005). They include the following:

- *sectoral training*, in which training is targeted towards key high-demand sectors in the economy and intermediaries work with local employers in these sectors to place trained workers into jobs;

- *incumbent-worker training*, in which training is provided by employers to workers whom they have already hired, to improve their chances of upward mobility in the firm;

- *career-pathway development*, in which intermediaries work with employers on devising new combinations of career education and work experience, to create more pathways for workers (incumbent or prospective) to attain good jobs and promotions in their industries; and

- *apprenticeships and internships.*

The intermediaries—which can include community-based organizations or various not-for-profit or for-profit companies—might direct workers to the relevant sources of training and then to employers who will hire them. They thus help less-skilled workers to overcome the informational problems (and perhaps discrimination) that can limit access to better jobs. Assistance with child care or transportation is sometimes provided as well. Financial assistance to pay for training—in the form of Pell Grants or other supports—can also be arranged. And other forms of enhanced financial incentives to encourage work can be used as well, such as enhanced Earned Income Tax Credit (EITC) benefits at the state level or rental subsidies for those maintaining employment who live in public housing.

Are these approaches cost-effective? Rigorous evaluation results have often been lacking to date. Some rigorous evidence does show positive impacts that are large enough to make programs cost-effective (this evidence comes from the Job Training Partnership Act [JTPA] evaluation, the Portland site in the National Evaluation of Welfare-to-Work Strategies [NEWWS], the evaluation of the Center for Employment Training [CET] in San Jose, and a few other studies), though the overall evidence is somewhat mixed.[1] A great many promising but nonrigorous evaluations of other strategies are available. Somewhat stronger evidence of positive impacts exists for incumbent worker training (though not necessarily for the poor) and for work supports such as the EITC and the public housing rental subsidies in Jobs Plus (Holzer 2007a).[2] Evidence from the more recent Employment Retention and Advancement project (ERA), which has sites around the country, has generated mixed results, though the interventions at most sites have been very modest.[3] Clearly, much more evaluation work needs to be done in this area.

What about efforts to improve labor market participation among youth? A sensible strategy here would center on three broad goals (Edelman, Holzer, and Offner 2006): 1) improving education and employment outcomes while preventing early disconnection, 2) extending the EITC to childless young adults to improve their incentives to accept low-wage jobs, and 3) reducing the various barriers and disincentives that ex-offenders and noncustodial fathers face in the labor market.

Strategies to improve early outcomes and prevent disconnection would involve the following four approaches: 1) utilizing youth development efforts aimed at adolescents (like Big Brothers/Big Sisters or the Harlem Children's Zone); 2) creating multiple pathways to success in high schools, including high-quality Career and Technical Education (CTE) options (such as apprenticeships and the Career Academies—see Kemple and Scott-Clayton [2004] and Lerman [2007]) as well as options stressing direct access to higher education; 3) "second chance" programs (such as YouthBuild and the Youth Service and Conservation Corps) and dropout prevention or recovery efforts; and 4) the resurrection of community-based models like the Youth Opportunity Program, which has created employment centers in low-income neighborhoods that track at-risk youth and refer the youth to available services. The available evidence suggests that at least some of these approaches are cost-effective, but in other cases more evidence is needed.[4]

Options for extending the EITC to childless adults appear in Berlin (2007); Edelman, Holzer, and Offner (2006); and Raphael (2008). The notion that this category of young men might potentially be quite responsive to these incentive programs receives support in evaluations of New Hope (Duncan, Huston, and Weisner 2007) and in statistical estimates of "labor supply elasticity" (or the responsiveness of work effort to net wages) by Grogger (1998) and others.

Efforts for ex-offenders include prisoner reentry programs, like the Center for Employment Opportunity, which provides a paid but temporary "transitional job" for each participant (Bloom et al. 2007); early evaluation evidence shows little impact by this program on earnings over time but a sharp reduction in recidivism for those who move quickly from prison into the program. Legislative or executive efforts among states to reduce the many legal barriers at the state level that limit employment options and other rights for ex-offenders (Holzer, Raphael, and Stoll 2004) are also important.[5] For noncustodial fathers, arrears management efforts and full "pass through" of collections to families would offer the best chance of success. Suspending the accumulation of arrears during incarceration should also be considered.

Finally, efforts to improve the skills and work experience of the poor and their access to good jobs would likely be more successful if more such jobs existed. Higher minimum wages (in real terms) and greater ability of workers to organize would be helpful—so long as wages are not raised to levels that generate substantial disemployment.[6] Perhaps some local economic development efforts (such as Community Benefit Agreements) that reward firms that are providing good jobs and training might also be helpful in this regard, though more careful study of their impacts is needed at this time.

While the cost-effectiveness of all of these approaches has not yet been established, the enormous costs of doing nothing for these young men (as measured in terms of the costs of crime and incarceration, poor health, and intergenerational effects) must be considered as well. Greater financial support at the federal level should be available for these efforts through higher funding of Pell Grants, the Workforce Investment Act, and other legislative vehicles such as the Second Chance Act for prisoner reentry programs. At the same time, the federal government should incentivize and assist states and localities as they devise their own programs and policies along these lines, while also requiring rigorous evaluation.[7]

Notes

1. For instance, the positive impacts of JTPA tend to fade over time, though they remain large enough to make the program cost-effective. All other sites besides Portland in NEWWS showed a lack of cost-effectiveness over time. The CET replication across the country did not generate positive impacts over time, though the "high fidelity" sites in California (in other words, those that adhered most closely to the original CET model) showed strong earnings growth among both treatment groups and controls where the latter attended community college in large numbers.

2. For example, a quasi-experimental study showed that incumbent-worker training grants in Michigan in the late 1980s led to productivity improvements among workers that presumably improved their earnings over time, while somewhat more descriptive evidence in California also suggests positive impacts on worker earnings. The EITC has clearly raised the employment rates of low-income single mothers, while Jobs Plus has also improved employment rates among public housing residents.

3. Hamilton (2008) shows that sites in Texas that supplemented the EITC with additional earnings subsidies generated higher earnings among workers over time, while a site in Illinois that helped workers find and apply for better jobs generated positive impacts as well. Community-based groups in Riverside, California, that provided a range of employment services also had positive impacts on the earnings of low-wage workers there.

4. The Big Brothers/Big Sisters program and Career Academies have proven to be clearly cost-effective in experimental evaluations. Econometric evidence suggests similar positive impacts of Tech Prep and other CTE models. Early evidence for the Youth Service and Conservation Corps (in a short-term, random-assignment evaluation) was also very positive, while more descriptive evidence on the Youth Opportunity program was quite positive relative to other high-poverty neighborhoods during the same time period.

5. The Legal Action Center in New York and the Sentencing Project in Washington, D.C., have led efforts to induce states to reconsider the restrictions on employment and voting rights that exist for ex-offenders. Florida, among others, has recently undertaken a review of these barriers and has made some efforts to reduce both kinds.

6. A legislative proposal known as the Employee Free Choice Act would make it easier for workers to organize into unions without representation elections, though more competitive labor markets might still restrict their ability to raise wages without generating employment losses. See Hirsch (2008) for a good discussion of these issues.

7. In Holzer (2007b), I propose a new competitive grant by the federal government to states that build "advancement systems," in which the federal government would match new state and local expenditures while providing substantial technical assistance and requiring formal evaluation.

References

Abowd, John M., and Francis Kramarz. 1999. "The Analysis of Labor Markets Using Matched Employer-Employee Data." In *The Handbook of Labor Economics*, Orley C. Ashenfelter and David Card, eds. Vol. 3B. Handbooks in Economics 5. Amsterdam: North Holland, pp. 2629–2710.

Andersson, Fredrik, Harry J. Holzer, and Julia I. Lane. 2005. *Moving Up or Moving On: Who Advances in the Low-Wage Labor Market?* New York: Russell Sage Foundation.

Appelbaum, Eileen, Annette Bernhardt, and Richard J. Murnane, eds. 2003. *Low-Wage America: How Employers Are Reshaping Opportunity in the Workplace*. New York: Russell Sage Foundation.

Berlin, Gordon L. 2007. "Rewarding the Work of Individuals: A Counterintuitive Approach to Reducing Poverty and Strengthening Families." *Future of Children* 17(2): 17–42.

Blank, Rebecca M., Sheldon H. Danziger, and Robert F. Schoeni. 2006. "Work and Poverty during the Past Quarter-Century." In *Working and Poor: How Economic and Policy Changes Are Affecting Low-Wage Workers*, Rebecca M. Blank, Sheldon H. Danziger, and Robert F. Schoeni, eds. The National Poverty Center Series on Poverty and Public Policy. New York: Russell Sage Foundation, pp. 1–20.

Bloom, Dan, and David Butler. 2007. "Overcoming Employment Barriers: Strategies to Help the 'Hard to Employ.'" In *Reshaping the American Workforce in a Changing Economy*, Harry J. Holzer and Demetra Smith Nightingale, eds. Washington, DC: Urban Institute Press, pp. 155–180.

Bloom, Dan, Cindy Redcross, Janine Zweig, and Gilda Azurdia. 2007. *Transitional Jobs for Ex-Prisoners: Early Impacts from a Random Assignment Evaluation of the Center for Employment Opportunities (CEO) Prisoner Reentry Program*. New York: MDRC.

Danziger, Sandra, Mary Corcoran, Sheldon H. Danziger, Colleen Heflin, Ariel Kalil, Judith Levine, Daniel Rosen, Kristin Seefeldt, Kristine Siefert, and Richard Tolman. 2000. "Barriers to the Employment of Welfare Recipients." In *Prosperity for All? The Economic Boom and African Americans*, Robert Cherry and William M. Rodgers III, eds. New York: Russell Sage Foundation, pp. 245–278.

Duncan, Greg J., Aletha C. Huston, and Thomas S. Weisner. 2007. *Higher Ground: New Hope for the Working Poor and Their Children*. New York: Russell Sage Foundation.

Edelman, Peter, Harry J. Holzer, and Paul Offner. 2006. *Reconnecting Disadvantaged Young Men*. Washington, DC: Urban Institute Press.

French, Eric, Bhashkar Mazumder, and Christopher Taber. 2006. "The Changing Pattern of Wage Growth for Low-Skilled Workers." In *Working and Poor, How Economic and Policy Changes Are Affecting Low-Wage Earners*, Rebecca M. Blank, Sheldon H. Danziger, and Robert F. Schoeni, eds. The National Poverty Series on Poverty and Public Policy. New York: Russell Sage Foundation, pp. 141–172.

Fryer, Roland G. Jr., and Steven D. Levitt. 2004. "Understanding the Black-White Test Score Gap in the First Two Years of School." *Review of Economics and Statistics* 86(2): 447–464.

Giloth, Robert P., ed. 2004. *Workforce Intermediaries for the Twenty-First Century*. Philadelphia: Temple University Press.

Grogger, Jeff. 1998. "Market Wages and Youth Crime." *Journal of Labor Economics* 16(4): 756–791.

Hamilton, Gayle. 2008. "Promoting Stable Employment and Wage Progression: Findings from the Employment Retention and Advancement (ERA) Project." Paper presented at the Administration for Children and Families' Eleventh Annual Welfare Research and Evaluation Conference, held in Washington, DC, May 28–30.

Hill, Carolyn J., Harry J. Holzer, and Henry Chen. 2009. *Against the Tide: Household Structure, Opportunities, and Outcomes among White and Minority Youth*. Kalamazoo, MI: W.E. Upjohn Institute for Employment Research.

Hirsch, Barry. 2008. "Sluggish Institutions in a Dynamic World: Can Unions and Industrial Competition Coexist?" *Journal of Economic Perspectives* 22(1): 153–176.

Holzer, Harry J. 2004. "Encouraging Job Advancement among Low-Wage Workers: A New Approach." Brookings Institution Policy Brief: Welfare Reform and Beyond No. 30. Washington, DC: Brookings Institution.

———. 2007a. "Collateral Costs: The Effects of Incarceration on the Employment and Earnings of Young Workers." IZA Discussion Paper No. 3118. Bonn, Germany: Institute for the Study of Labor.

———. 2007b. "Better Workers for Better Jobs: Improving Worker Advancement in the Low-Wage Labor Market." Hamilton Project Discussion Paper 2007–15. Washington, DC: Brookings Institution.

Holzer, Harry J., and Robert J. LaLonde. 2000. "Job Change and Job Stability among Less Skilled Young Workers." In *Finding Jobs: Work and Welfare Reform*, David Card and Rebecca M. Blank, eds. New York: Russell Sage Foundation, pp. 125–159.

Holzer, Harry J., and Karin Martinson. 2005. "How Can We Improve Job Retention and Advancement among Low-Income Parents?" Low-Income Working Families Paper. Washington, DC: Urban Institute.

Holzer, Harry J., and Paul Offner. 2006. "Trends in Employment among Less-Educated Young Men, 1979–2000." In *Black Males Left Behind*, Ronald B. Mincy, ed. Washington, DC: Urban Institute Press, pp. 11–38.

Holzer, Harry J., Steven Raphael, and Michael A. Stoll. 2004. "Will Employers Hire Former Offenders? Employer Preferences, Background Checks, and Their Determinants." In *Imprisoning America: The Social Effects of Mass Incarceration*, Mary Pattillo, David Weiman, and Bruce Western, eds. New York: Russell Sage Foundation.

———. 2006. "Perceived Criminality, Background Checks, and the Racial Hiring Practices of Employers." *Journal of Law and Economics* 49(2): 451–480.

Holzer, Harry J., and Michael A. Stoll. 2001. *Employers and Welfare Recipients: The Effects of Welfare Reform in the Workplace.* San Francisco: Public Policy Institute of California.

Kemple, James J., and Judith Scott-Clayton. 2004. *Career Academies: Impacts on Labor Market Outcomes and Educational Attainment.* New York: MDRC.

Lerman, Robert. 2007. "Career-Focused Education and Training for Youth." In *Reshaping the American Workforce in a Changing Economy*, Harry J. Holzer and Demetra Smith Nightingale, eds. Washington, DC: Urban Institute Press, pp. 41–90.

Pager, Devah. 2003. "The Mark of a Criminal Record." *American Journal of Sociology* 108(5): 937–975.

Raphael, Steven. 2008. "Boosting the Earnings and Employment of Low-Skilled Workers in the United States: Making Work Pay and Removing Barriers to Employment and Social Mobility." In *A Future of Good Jobs? America's Challenge in the Global Economy*, Timothy J. Bartik and Susan N. Houseman, eds. Kalamazoo, MI: W.E. Upjohn Institute for Employment Research, pp. 245–304.

Topel, Robert H., and Michael P. Ward. 1992. "Job Mobility and the Careers of Young Men." *Quarterly Journal of Economics* 107(2): 439–479.

10
What We Know about the Impacts of Workforce Investment Programs

Burt S. Barnow
Johns Hopkins University

Jeffrey A. Smith
University of Michigan

This chapter briefly reviews the recent literature that seeks to evaluate employment and training programs, as well as important older papers. We focus on the question of whether the programs have measurable and economically relevant impacts on labor market outcomes.

We do not focus on the economics of such programs but do lean on the "dismal science" when interpreting the findings in the literature. We also do not focus on the econometrics of program evaluation, though our views about the credibility of various combinations of econometric strategies and data affect our choice of which evaluations to highlight and how we interpret the overall literature.

Readers interested in more in-depth surveys of the substantive literature should consult Heckman, LaLonde, and Smith (1999). Smith (2000, 2004) provides a relatively nontechnical guide to the evaluation literature, while Abbring and Heckman (2007); Angrist and Krueger (1999); Friedlander, Greenberg, and Robins (1997); Heckman, LaLonde, and Smith (1999); Heckman and Vytlacil (2007a,b); and Imbens and Wooldridge (forthcoming) provide technical overviews.

EVALUATIONS OF THE MAJOR U.S. FEDERAL PROGRAMS

Employment and training programs in the United States have a relatively brief history. In addition to the public employment programs of the Great Depression, the Manpower Development and Training Act (MDTA, 1962–1972), the Comprehensive Employment and Training Act (CETA, 1973–1982), the Job Training Partnership Act (JTPA, 1982–1998), and the Workforce Investment Act (WIA, 1998–present) have provided vocational training, along with remedial education, subsidized on-the-job training, and job search assistance to disadvantaged youth and adults as well as displaced workers. CETA also provided public service employment.

Perry et al. (1975) review the literature on the MDTA. Except for Ashenfelter (1978), this literature largely reflects the nascent stage of evaluation methodology at the time. The U.S. Department of Labor (USDOL) funded a number of evaluations of the CETA program, all of which relied on the same data source, the Continuous Longitudinal Manpower Survey (CLMS), which combined random samples of participants with nonexperimental comparison group data from the Current Population Survey (CPS) and included matched calendar year Social Security earnings data for both groups. Barnow (1987) summarizes these nonexperimental evaluations, which relied largely on crude matching estimators or difference-in-differences strategies, and obtained widely varying estimates. The sensitivity of the difference-in-differences estimates in the CETA studies to the choice of the "before" period foreshadows a similar finding in Heckman and Smith (1999). Despite the high-quality (but only annual) administrative outcome data, the CLMS lacked the detailed information on local labor markets found to be important in Heckman et al. (1998), as well as the information on recent labor market and program participation choices (at a fine level of temporal detail) found to be important in Card and Sullivan (1988); Dolton, Azevedo, and Smith (2006); and Heckman et al. (1998).

The wide variety of CETA estimates led to a decision by the USDOL to evaluate the JTPA using a social experiment, called the National JTPA Study (NJS), which operated at a nonrandom sample of 16 (of about 600) local JTPA sites from approximately November 1987 to September 1989. Doolittle and Traeger (1990) describe the details of the experiment, and Bloom et al. (1997) and Orr et al. (1996) present the results. The NJS included disadvantaged adults and out-of-school youth but not in-school youth and dislocated workers.

The U.S. General Accounting Office (USGAO 1996) provides impact estimates for five years after random assignment based on Social

Security earnings data. The USGAO finds stable impacts of around $800 a year for adult (22 and older) men and women, but these impacts lose statistical significance over time. In contrast, the estimates for male and female youth remain near zero throughout the follow-up period. The NJS found substantial treatment-group nonparticipation (around 40 percent) and control group substitution (also around 40 percent) into alternative providers of similar services. As a result, these estimates approximate (because of differences in service intensity between the treatment and control groups) what Imbens and Angrist (1994) call local average treatment effects: average impacts on those who receive services if assigned to the treatment group but who would not have received JTPA services if assigned to the control group. Heckman, LaLonde, and Smith (1999, Table 20) show that JTPA produced a net social benefit for adults but not for youth, generally irrespective of (reasonable) assumptions about benefit duration beyond five years, the discount rate, or the welfare cost of taxation.

Mueser, Troske, and Gorislavsky (2007) employ modern matching methods, as described in, for example, Smith and Todd (2005), combined with relatively rich administrative data, to estimate the earnings impact of JTPA in Missouri for program years 1994 and 1995, using a comparison group of individuals registering with the Employment Service. In real terms, their preferred estimates resemble those from the NJS.

Finally, although the WIA program has been operating nationwide since July 2000, there exist no published econometric evaluations. In 2008, the USDOL funded a random assignment evaluation of WIA.

EVALUATIONS OF SELECTED OTHER U.S. PROGRAMS

Job Corps

Job Corps, established in 1964, provides intensive and comprehensive services, including vocational and academic activities as well as support services, to about 60,000 disadvantaged youth, ages 16–24, in 119 residential centers. The program has had two major evaluations: a thoughtful, nonexperimental evaluation in the 1970s, summarized in Long, Mallar, and Thornton (1981), and an experimental evaluation in the 1990s, summarized in Schochet, Burghardt, and McConnell (2006). The two have remarkably parallel findings; we focus on the experiment.

The first key finding is that removing disadvantaged young men from their local neighborhoods dramatically reduces their criminal behavior in the short run. Second, there is a notable effect on educational attainment in the short run, measured in terms of hours, literacy and numeracy, and GED and vocational certificate receipt. Third, the Job Corps program generates substantial sustained earnings impacts for 20- to 24-year-old participants, but not for younger participants. As a result, because of its high cost, the program does not come close to passing a cost-benefit test (which includes the impacts on crime) for younger participants but does come close for the 20- to 24-year-olds. Despite the lack of an efficiency justification for the program, at least for the 20- to 24-year-olds it actually has a substantial impact on labor market outcomes, which puts it well ahead of many other youth programs, such as JTPA, where the impacts equaled approximately zero.

Worker Profiling and Reemployment Services

The Worker Profiling and Reemployment Services (WPRS) system assigns mandatory reemployment services to new Unemployment Insurance (UI) claimants predicted to have long spells of UI receipt or high probabilities of UI benefit exhaustion. A desire to proactively serve UI claimants likely to exhaust their benefits early in their benefit spells, rather than waiting to serve them until after they have experienced a long spell, motivates the program. The WPRS poses two separate evaluation problems. First, what effect do the mandatory services have on those who receive them and, second, how well does the existing system, which is based on predicted labor market outcomes in the absence of the mandatory services, do at allocating such services?

We know of two evaluations that address the first question. Dickinson, Decker, and Kreutzer (2002) summarize the results of a larger project that includes linear selection-on-observables estimates of the impact of WPRS referral on weeks and amount of UI received as well as earnings and employment for six states. They find substantively important and statistically significant impacts on the UI variables but no systematic effects on labor market outcomes; this suggests that the WPRS system reduces UI usage without imposing a large cost on referred claimants via lower-quality job matches, although neither does the program provide any benefits to the recipients.

More recently, using data from Kentucky and exploiting the particular institutional features of the profiling system in that state, Black et al. (2003) provide experimental evidence of the impact of the re-employment services requirement on claimants who are on the margin for the service requirement, given their employment histories and local area characteristics. They find that the program has a substantial effect relative to its (very small) cost, with that effect consisting largely of a deterrent effect, whereby some claimants immediately find employment upon receiving notice of the requirement that they receive services.

Black et al. (2003) also address the second question, and they find little difference in the impacts by profiling score. Keeping in mind the relative imprecision of their estimates, this suggests that the existing allocation mechanism does not advance economic efficiency. Pope and Sydnor (2007) argue that the existing mechanism fails on normative grounds as well, though their argument hinges critically on the view that the WPRS treatment represents a burden rather than a benefit.

EMPLOYER-FOCUSED PROGRAMS

Although it might sound obvious that workforce programs should focus on the labor demand side as well as the labor supply side, until recently there has been a disproportionate emphasis on the latter. In this section we briefly review the literature on three approaches to employer-focused programs: on-the job training (OJT), customized training, and sectoral training.

On-the-Job Training

Subsidized on-the-job training (OJT) at private firms dates back at least to MDTA. This service provides a (typically 50 percent) wage subsidy for a limited period (typically six months) to firms hiring and informally training certain specified types of workers. Program staff members recruit firms to provide OJT positions (a time-consuming task), and firms always retain the right to reject candidates prior to hiring and to dismiss workers during or after the subsidy period. Though the training provided is supposed to exceed that provided to other new workers, anecdotal evidence strongly suggests that OJT recipients often receive the same training as unsubsidized workers (and, in some cases, little or no training at all).

Subsidized OJT has several rationales. The wage subsidy component seeks the purely redistributional goal of getting employers to try out workers who may appear more risky because of weak labor market histories or other problems. As the OJT participants are not considered regular employees, employers are more willing to risk hiring them because if the OJT participants are let go at the end of the OJT period, it is not the same as terminating a regular worker. Tying training by the firm to the wage subsidy aims to increase the skills of workers lacking the resources or credit to obtain training either directly from providers or indirectly from firms via lower wages (where the minimum wage may also limit the ability of workers to trade lower wages for training).

Most evaluations suggest positive impacts of OJT on participant employment and earnings. For example, Barnow's (1987) review of the CETA evaluations finds OJT to have greater impacts than all other service types. The NJS provides suggestive evidence on this point as well. However, OJT impacts likely embody more displacement than impacts for classroom training and other services that focus exclusively on increasing human capital and not also on redistributing jobs. As a result, partial equilibrium estimates like those noted here do less well at capturing the impacts relevant for a social cost-benefit calculation.

Customized and Sectoral Training

Customized training is defined as training characterized by employer input and approval authority for the curriculum, employer authority to establish eligibility criteria for participants and to select participants if the employer desires, and a commitment by the employer to hire successful program completers. Sectoral training projects consist of customized employment and training services provided to a group of employers in the same industry or sector of the economy; see, e.g., Dresser and Rogers (1998) and Elliott and King (1999) for discussions. Though program advocates enthuse about these programs, they do so without good evidence regarding their impacts.

Sectoral programs, like OJT, have the potential to provide opportunities for human capital enhancement to disadvantaged workers who might be overlooked by employers. To warrant government support, more evidence is needed on their effectiveness in increasing earnings, and care should be taken to ensure that the training is provided to workers who ordinarily would not be trained at employer expense. Thus, we recommend that rigorous evaluations be conducted to determine whether these programs produce earnings gains that exceed their (full social) costs. We further recommend that programs be structured so that workers who receive the training have labor market disadvantages, and so that the training is general in nature and useful at other firms in addition to the one hiring the workers.

ANALYTIC ISSUES

This section highlights the four most important analytic issues in the literature.

The first concerns heterogeneity in the effects of active labor market policies. This heterogeneity arises in part from the fact that programs themselves often provide quite heterogeneous services under headings such as "classroom training." The substantial differences across groups defined by sex and age in average treatment effects, noted earlier in the chapter, strongly suggest that even relatively homogeneous services will have varying effects across individuals as well. In such an environment, evaluation researchers must pay close attention to exactly what treatment effect their analysis estimates, and policy analysts must take care to link the estimates they consider to the policy questions of interest. For example, an experiment with no control-group substitution estimates the mean impact of "treatment on the treated." This mean impact represents the correct impact estimate for a cost-benefit analysis that seeks to address the question of either keeping or scrapping the existing program. It does not provide the correct impact estimate for an analysis of whether the program should receive a larger budget so as to allow it to expand the set of persons served; a simple economic model of program participation in which those with the largest impacts choose to participate suggests that average impacts for individuals on the margin of service receipt will lie below the mean impact of treatment on the treated.

Second, many studies do not even attempt a cost-benefit analysis, and those that do often provide relatively low-quality analyses, either because of lack of required inputs or failure to follow the best practices outlined in the literature. Without a serious cost-benefit analysis, even a relatively strong positive impact estimate has little to say about policy. Without data on all relevant outcomes (as when relying solely on administrative earnings data for outcomes when programs may also affect, say, criminal behavior and health), policymakers end up making decisions based on incomplete information about impacts. Many government programs lack even rudimentary information on either average or marginal program costs, let alone detailed information on the marginal and average costs for particular services and client types. Finally, as noted in Heckman, LaLonde, and Smith (1999), many cost-benefit analyses fail to take full account of the costs of tax funding by omitting consideration of the marginal excess burden of taxation, and proceeding instead as if a dollar of tax funding costs society only a dollar.

Third, most evaluations estimate impacts over relatively short periods from the time of service initiation or random assignment. Recent evidence indicates the dangers this poses to correct inferences about program value. In the negative direction, the early positive impacts found in the National Job Corps Study turned out to largely fade away when longer-term follow-up data became available. In the positive direction, classroom training sometimes takes several years to yield its full impact, as in the long-term follow-up of the California GAIN program by Hotz, Imbens, and Klerman (2006) and the long-term evaluation of German classroom training by Lechner, Miquel, and Wunsch (2004). At the same time, the long-term follow-ups of the Supported Work experiment by Couch (1992) and of the JTPA experiment in USGAO (1996) show that sometimes program impact estimates remain rock solid at the level observed shortly after program participation. With only a handful of studies that provide credible impact estimates more than two or three years out (this paragraph lists nearly all of them), we cannot draw any conclusions about program types or client characteristics associated with particular patterns of long-term impacts.

Fourth, and finally, only a handful of papers look seriously at general equilibrium effects. Put differently, most evaluations ignore the effects that programs may have on the behavior of those who do not participate in them. In addition to indirect effects working through the tax system, these include displacement effects, whereby individuals induced to search harder (or smarter) by a program, or whose skills increase as the result of a program, take jobs that would otherwise have gone to individuals not participating in the program. Programs can also have price effects; for example, a program that produces large numbers of trained auto mechanics or nurses' aides should drive down wages in those labor markets. In many cases, failing to take account of general equilibrium effects leads to overly positive conclusions about program performance.

Calmfors (1994) and Johnson (1980) provide early conceptual discussions of these issues. The small but growing empirical literature includes Davidson and Woodbury (1987), who find modest but not trivial displacement effects of UI bonuses in a search context. Heckman, Lochner, and Taber (1999) find large price effects of a subsidy to university tuition, effects that imply that a partial equilibrium analysis wildly overstates the enrollment effects of the subsidy. Lise, Seitz, and Smith (2006) consider the Canadian Self-Sufficiency Project, which provided a generous earnings subsidy to some welfare recipients, and find that taking account of displacement and changes in the amount of effort applied to searching by those without the subsidy changes the sign of the cost-benefit calculation for the program. Finally, Kabbani (2001) finds evidence using data from the NJS that training programs may increase the earnings of nonparticipants by moving the participants into a different labor market.

CONCLUSION

First, most employment and training programs have either no impact or modest positive impacts. Many do not pass careful social cost-benefit tests, though some that fail may be worth doing on equity grounds. Existing evaluations have important analytic limitations that bias them in favor of programs with short-term impacts and large spillover effects on nonparticipants from displacement or price changes. In general, employment and training programs work best for adult women and least well for youth. The literature provides no good explanation for this demographic pattern.

For reasons of space we have omitted a variety of topics, such as recent studies that examine program design by looking at performance management systems (Barnow and Smith 2004; Heckman, Heinrich, and Smith 2002), at the efficacy of caseworkers (Bell and Orr 2002; McConnell, Decker, and Perez-Johnson 2006), and at statistical treatment rules as an alternative to caseworkers (Eberts, O'Leary, and Wandner 2002; Lechner and Smith 2007). We have also omitted some program categories, such as welfare-to-work programs (Ashworth et al. 2004; Bloom, Hill, and Riccio 2003) and the Trade Adjustment Act, as well as all evidence from outside the United States (Betcherman, Olivas, and Dar 2004; Kluve 2006). The general lessons from the omitted literature parallel those from what we have covered.

References

Abbring, Jaap H., and James J. Heckman. 2007. "Econometric Evaluation of Social Programs, Part III: Distributional Treatment Effects, Dynamic Treatment Effects, Dynamic Discrete Choice, and General Equilibrium Policy Evaluation." In *Handbook of Econometrics,* James J. Heckman and Edward E. Leamer, eds. Vol. 6B. Amsterdam: North-Holland, pp. 5145–5306.

Angrist, Joshua D., and Alan B. Krueger. 1999. "Empirical Strategies in Labor Economics." In *Handbook of Labor Economics,* Orley Ashenfelter and David Card, eds. Vol. 3A. Amsterdam: North-Holland, pp. 1277–1366.

Ashenfelter, Orley. 1978. "Estimating the Effect of Training Programs on Earnings." *Review of Economics and Statistics* 60(1): 47–57.

Ashworth, Karl, Andreas Cebulla, David Greenberg, and Robert Walker. 2004. "Meta-Evaluation: Discovering What Works Best in Welfare Provision." *Evaluation* 10(2): 193–216.

Barnow, Burt S. 1987. "The Impact of CETA Programs on Earnings: A Review of the Literature." *Journal of Human Resources* 22(2): 157–193.

Barnow, Burt S., and Jeffrey A. Smith. 2004. "Performance Management of U.S. Job Training Programs: Lessons from the Job Training Partnership Act." *Public Finance and Management* 4(3): 247–287.

Bell, Stephen H., and Larry L. Orr. 2002. "Screening (and Creaming?) Applicants to Job Training Programs: The AFDC Homemaker–Home Health Aide Demonstrations." *Labour Economics* 9(2): 279–301.

Betcherman, Gordon, Karina Olivas, and Amit Dar. 2004. "Impacts of Active Labor Market Programs: New Evidence from Evaluations with Particular Attention to Developing and Transition Countries." World Bank Social Protection Discussion Paper No. 0402. Washington, DC: World Bank.

Black, Dan A., Jeffrey A. Smith, Mark C. Berger, and Brett J. Noel. 2003. "Is the Threat of Reemployment Services More Effective than the Services Themselves? Evidence from Random Assignment in the UI System." *American Economic Review* 93(4): 1313–1327.

Bloom, Howard S., Carolyn J. Hill, and James A. Riccio. 2003. "Linking Program Implementation and Effectiveness: Lessons from a Pooled Sample of Welfare-to-Work Experiments." *Journal of Policy Analysis and Management* 22(4): 551–575.

Bloom, Howard S., Larry L. Orr, Stephen H. Bell, George Cave, Fred Doolittle, Winston Lin, and Johannes M. Bos. 1997. "The Benefits and Costs of JTPA Title II-A Programs: Key Findings from the National Job Training Partnership Act Study." *Journal of Human Resources* 32(3): 549–576.

Calmfors, Lars. 1994. "Active Labour Market Policy and Unemployment: A Framework for the Analysis of Crucial Design Features." *OECD Economic Studies* 22(Spring): 7–47.

Card, David, and Daniel Sullivan. 1988. "Measuring the Effect of Subsidized Training Programs on Movements In and Out of Employment." *Econometrica* 56(3): 497–530.

Couch, Kenneth A. 1992. "New Evidence on the Long-Term Effects of Employment Training Programs." *Journal of Labor Economics* 10(4): 380–388.

Davidson, Carl, and Stephen A. Woodbury. 1987. "The Displacement Effect of Reemployment Bonus Programs." *Journal of Labor Economics* 11(4): 575–605.

Dickinson, Katherine P., Paul T. Decker, and Suzanne D. Kreutzer. 2002. "Evaluation of WPRS Systems." In *Targeting Employment Services*, Randall W. Eberts, Christopher J. O'Leary, and Stephen A. Wandner, eds. Kalamazoo, MI: W.E. Upjohn Institute for Employment Research, pp. 61–90.

Dolton, Peter, João Pedro Azevedo, and Jeffrey A. Smith. 2006. "The Econometric Evaluation of the New Deal for Lone Parents." Department for Work and Pensions Research Report No. 356. London: Department for Work and Pensions.

Doolittle, Fred C., and Linda Traeger. 1990. *Implementing the National JTPA Study*. New York: Manpower Demonstration Research Corporation.

Dresser, Laura, and Joel Rogers. 1998. "Networks, Sectors, and Workforce

Learning." In *Jobs and Economic Development: Strategies and Practice,* Robert P. Giloth, ed. Thousand Oaks, CA: Sage Publications, pp. 64–82.

Eberts, Randall W., Christopher J. O'Leary, and Stephen A. Wandner. 2002. *Targeting Employment Services.* Kalamazoo, MI: W.E. Upjohn Institute for Employment Research.

Elliott, Mark, and Elisabeth King.1999. *Labor Market Leverage: Sectoral Employment Field Report.* Philadelphia, PA: Public/Private Ventures.

Friedlander, Daniel, David H. Greenberg, and Philip K. Robins. 1997. "Evaluating Government Training Programs for the Economically Disadvantaged." *Journal of Economic Literature* 35(4): 1809–1855.

Heckman, James J., Carolyn Heinrich, and Jeffrey A. Smith. 2002. "The Performance of Performance Standards." *Journal of Human Resources* 37(4): 778–811.

Heckman, James J., Hidehiko Ichimura, Jeffrey A. Smith, and Petra E. Todd. 1998. "Characterizing Selection Bias Using Experimental Data." *Econometrica* 66(5): 1017–1098.

Heckman, James J., Robert J. LaLonde, and Jeffrey A. Smith. 1999. "The Economics and Econometrics of Active Labor Market Programs." In *Handbook of Labor Economics,* Orley Ashenfelter and David Card, eds. Vol. 3A. Handbooks in Economics 5. Amsterdam: North-Holland, pp. 1865–2097.

Heckman, James J., Lance Lochner, and Christopher Taber. 1999. "General-Equilibrium Cost-Benefit Analysis of Education and Tax Policies." In *Trade, Growth, and Development: Essays in Honor of Professor T.N. Srinivasan.* Gustav Ranis and Lakshmi K. Raut, eds. Amsterdam: Elsevier Science, pp. 291–349.

Heckman, James J., and Jeffrey A. Smith. 1999. "The Pre-Programme Earnings Dip and the Determinants of Participation in a Social Programme: Implications for Simple Programme Evaluation Strategies." *Economic Journal* 109(457): 313–348.

Heckman, James J., and Edward J. Vytlacil. 2007a. "Econometric Evaluation of Social Programs, Part I: Causal Models, Structural Models, and Econometric Policy Evaluation." In *Handbook of Econometrics,* James J. Heckman and Edward E. Leamer, eds. Vol. 6B. Handbooks in Economics 2. Amsterdam: North-Holland, pp. 4779–4874.

————. 2007b. "Econometric Evaluation of Social Programs, Part II: Using the Marginal Treatment Effect to Organize Alternative Econometric Estimators to Evaluate Social Programs, and to Forecast Their Effects in New Environments." In *Handbook of Econometrics,* James J. Heckman and Edward E. Leamer, eds. Vol. 6B. Handbooks in Economics 2. Amsterdam: North-Holland, pp. 4875–5144.

Hotz, V. Joseph, Guido W. Imbens, and Jacob A. Klerman. 2006. "Evaluating

the Differential Effects of Alternative Welfare-to-Work Training Compo-
nents: A Reanalysis of the California GAIN Program." *Journal of Labor Economics* 24(3): 521–566.

Imbens, Guido W., and Joshua D. Angrist. 1994. "Identification and Estimation of Local Average Treatment Effects." *Econometrica* 62(2): 467–475.

Imbens, Guido W., and Jeffrey M. Wooldridge. Forthcoming. "Recent Developments in the Econometrics of Program Evaluation." *Journal of Economic Literature.*

Johnson, George E. 1980. "The Theory of Labor Market Intervention." *Economica* 47(187): 309–329.

Kabbani, Nader S. 2001. "The Effect of Public Sector Training Programs on the Employment and Earnings of Non-Participant Workers." Unpublished doctoral dissertation. Baltimore: Johns Hopkins University.

Kluve, Jochen. 2006. "The Effectiveness of European Active Labor Market Policy." IZA Discussion Paper No. 2018. Bonn, Germany: Institute for the Study of Labor.

Lechner, Michael, Ruth Miquel, and Conny Wunsch. 2004. "Long-Run Effects of Public Sector Sponsored Training in West Germany." IZA Discussion Paper No. 1443. Bonn, Germany: Institute for the Study of Labor.

Lechner, Michael, and Jeffrey A. Smith. 2007. "What Is the Value Added by Caseworkers?" *Labour Economics* 14(2): 135–151.

Lise, Jeremy, Shannon Seitz, and Jeffrey Smith. 2006. "Equilibrium Policy Experiments and the Evaluation of Social Programs." NBER Working Paper 10283. Cambridge, MA: National Bureau of Economic Research.

Long, David A., Charles D. Mallar, and Craig V.D. Thornton. 1981. "Evaluating the Benefits and Costs of the Job Corps." *Journal of Policy Analysis and Management* 1(1): 55–76.

McConnell, Sheena, Paul Decker, and Irma Perez-Johnson. 2006. "The Role of Counseling in Voucher Programs: Finding from the Individual Training Account Experiment." Canadian Labour Market and Skills Researcher Network Working Paper No. 21. Princeton, NJ: Mathematica Policy Research.

Mueser, Peter R., Kenneth R. Troske, and Alexey Gorislavsky. 2007. "Using State Administrative Data to Measure Program Performance." *Review of Economics and Statistics* 89(4): 761–783.

Orr, Larry L., Howard S. Bloom, Stephen H. Bell, Fred Doolittle, and Winston Lin. 1996. *Does Training for the Disadvantaged Work? Evidence from the National JTPA Study*. Washington, DC: Urban Institute Press.

Perry, Charles R., Bernard E. Anderson, Richard L. Rowan, and Herbert R. Northrup. 1975. *The Impact of Government Manpower Programs: In General, and on Minorities and Women*. Philadelphia: Industrial Research Unit, Wharton School, University of Pennsylvania.

Pope, Devon G., and Justin R. Sydnor. 2007. "Implicit Statistical Discrimination in Predictive Models." Working Paper No. 2007-09-11. Philadelphia: Wharton School, University of Pennsylvania.

Schochet, Peter Z., John Burghardt, and Sheena McConnell. 2006. *National Job Corps Study and Longer-Term Follow-Up Study: Impact and Benefit-Cost Findings Using Survey and Summary Earnings Records Data*. Final Report. Princeton, NJ: Mathematica Policy Research.

Smith, Jeffrey A. 2000. "A Critical Survey of Empirical Methods for Evaluating Employment and Training Programs." *Swiss Journal for Economics and Statistics* 136(3): 247–268.

————. 2004. "Evaluating Local Economic Development Policies: Theory and Practice." In *Evaluating Local Economic and Employment Development: How to Assess What Works among Programmes and Policies*, Alistair Nolan and Ging Wong, eds. Paris: Organisation for Economic Co-operation and Development, pp. 287–332.

Smith, Jeffrey A., and Petra E. Todd. 2005. "Does Matching Overcome LaLonde's Critique of Nonexperimental Estimators?" *Journal of Econometrics* 125(1–2): 305–353.

U.S. General Accounting Office (USGAO). 1996. *Job Training Partnership Act: Long-Term Earnings and Employment Outcomes*. Report to Congressional Requesters. GAO/HEHS-96-40. Washington, DC: U.S. General Accounting Office (USGAO).

11

Correctional Programs in the Age of Mass Incarceration

What Do We Know about "What Works"?

John H. Tyler
Jillian Berk
Brown University

THE AGE OF MASS INCARCERATION

Beginning in the mid-1970s the convergence of several social and economic forces changed the size, face, and nature of the U.S. penal system. In terms of the size of the penal system, changes in criminal justice policies associated with the government's fight against drugs and crime mean that more convictions now lead to a prison sentence than in the past, and the prison sentences they lead to tend to be of longer duration than in the past. The overall result of these policy shifts is a rising penal population. As of June 2006 there were 1.5 million prisoners held in our federal and state prisons, compared to 329,000 in 1980—more than a fourfold increase (Bureau of Justice Statistics [BJS] 2008a).[1] In terms of imprisonment rates, the United States is the world's leader. In 2005, out of every 100,000 U.S. citizens, 705 were in jail or prison, a 500 percent increase over the last 30 years. That rate is higher than in all other developed countries, including Russia, and almost twice as high as in South Africa (Mauer 2003). Currently the corrections "industry" in our nation is a $65 billion enterprise, a sum that represents an increase of almost 600 percent since 1982 (BJS 2008b).

At the same time that we have been imprisoning and releasing increasing numbers of individuals, changes in our economy have led to declining economic opportunities for low-skilled individuals. These changes, coupled with the exodus of inner-city job opportunities for the low- and medium-skilled, have resulted in declining labor market opportunities for young, poorly educated minority men. As a result, these individuals have become especially vulnerable to the new, more punitive criminal justice regime. The statistics are stark: by 1999, almost 60 percent of black male dropouts between the ages of 30 and 34 had been imprisoned at some point, compared to about 10 percent of white male dropouts (Pettit and Western 2004).[2] As our economy has become more highly skilled, our prison populations have become disproportionately low-educated (two-thirds of prisoners now lack a regular high school diploma [Harlow 2003]) and African American (40 percent as of 2005 [Harrison and Beck 2006]).

The importance of these criminal justice and economic trends lies in this undeniable reality: almost all of these individuals will leave prison one day and return to free society.[3] Over 600,000 people will leave prison this year, three and a half times more than the 170,000 who were released in 1980. Furthermore, a disproportionate number will be returning to a relatively small number of distressed communities and neighborhoods. Not only will a large proportion of these individuals have low levels of education, but many will also have low levels of skills, work experience, and preprison earnings, while at the same time criminal justice reforms during this "age of mass incarceration" will ensure that they will have substantially less postrelease supervision and assistance than in the past. In addition, the experience with the criminal justice system itself can present barriers to postrelease employment. A felony conviction can leave ex-offenders with a social stigma that Nagin (1998) likens to a "scarlet letter." Pager (2003) has shown through audit studies that this stigma is mediated and compounded through the lens of race. In addition to the potential stigma attached to a felony record, state laws often prohibit the employment of convicted felons in a variety of jobs from child care providers to barbers, and many jobs now require mandatory criminal background checks. Given these realities, many argue that the roles for prison-based education and vocational and work-experience programs are potentially more important than ever. Of course, the extent to which these programs can help ex-offenders reintegrate into mainstream society and stay out of prison depends on how effective they are.

THE EVIDENCE ON CORRECTIONAL EDUCATION, VOCATIONAL, AND EMPLOYMENT PROGRAMS

Prisoners, Prisons, and Prison-Based Programs

As a first step, it is worth stepping back to characterize the "typical" prisoner in our nation's state and federal prisons, along with the common prison experience faced by the typical offender. In addition to the low education levels cited earlier, 90 percent of prison inmates are male, a third are less than 30 years of age, and half are serving sentences for nonviolent crimes (Harrison and Beck 2006). The dominant track in prison for an offender sentenced to a nonviolent crime is characterized by a relatively short stay in prison (less than 15 months on average, with many in state prisons serving less than a year), spent mostly in medium- or minimum-security prisons before his release (Austin 2001). Even though the skill and education levels of the average prisoner are low, and even though time in prison could be seen as an opportunity to positively affect human capital levels, relatively small numbers of inmates are participating in prison-based education or vocational programs at any given time. A report issued by the BJS indicates that about one-half of the inmates in state and federal prisons were participating in some kind of education or vocational program in 1997, with the great bulk of these participating in General Educational Development (GED) testing programs or vocational education programs. This means that at the time of the 1997 survey, fully one-half of the nation's inmates were not engaged in any kind of education or training program while in prison. Also, it is likely that these participation rates are even worse now—prisons have had to deal with increased crowding and strained resources as inmate populations have swelled since 1997.

The low rates of prison-program participation reflect several realities associated with prison life, beginning with a shortage of staff and instructional space, as these resources have often failed to keep up with the explosive growth in the prison population. Adding to these institutional constraints are three considerations: 1) security issues trump the programmatic needs of offenders; 2) prison time is often given to work assignments within the prison associated with facility maintenance, services, and upkeep; and 3) prisoners often move from one facility to another as their custody level changes and in response to the balance between available bed space and differences in security levels across facilities. As one experienced correctional education officer stated, "Inmates face lots of idle time, but it is punctuated with lots of interruptions, from security checks and lockdowns to medical issues that require attention, to mundane jobs they are often required to do" (LoBuglio 2007). The overall picture is one where individuals with substantial educational and skill deficits arrive at prison's door for a relatively short stay, and because of institutional arrangements and resource allocation decisions, they receive relatively little sustained education and vocational programming while they are in prison.

Previous Evidence on Program Impact

Situated in the prison setting just described are three basic kinds of programs that focus chiefly on increasing the postrelease employability of ex-offenders: 1) classroom education programs (chiefly Adult Basic Education and preparation to pass the GED exam), 2) vocational training programs, and 3) employment programs designed to provide general work experience and training on specific jobs.[4] What do we currently know about the effectiveness of these kinds of corrections-based programs in reducing recidivism and assisting ex-offenders in reintegrating into the labor market? Most observers would say that until recently the answer is that we know very little about the causal impact of corrections-based skill and employment programs. It is not for lack of study that we know so little about the effectiveness of correctional programs. Indeed there have been hundreds of studies over the years of the many different prison and community-based programs designed to rehabilitate offenders and ex-offenders.[5] The problem lies in the quality and rigor of program evaluation in the correctional field. For example, in a 1999 meta-analysis of 33 corrections-based education, vocational, and work programs, Wilson et al. (1999) note, "Few studies [that were included in the meta-analysis] made any serious attempt . . . to control for biases produced by . . . self-selection into programs." Wilson et al. go on to state the following:

> Future research that merely compares participants with nonparticipants of these programs is not needed to resolve the questions of the effectiveness of these programs, for it is well established

that participants do reoffend at a lower rate than nonparticipants. Rather, the field needs high-quality evaluation studies that can provide a strong basis for establishing a causal connection between the activities of the programs and future positive changes in inmate behavior. (p. 17)

In a paper published the next year, Wilson, Gallagher, and MacKenzie (2000) had this to say about the models that were used to evaluate the impact of correctional education programs on outcomes: "Although close to half of the [33] studies included in this synthesis performed some form of post hoc matching or statistical control, these controls were generally restricted to adjustments for the age and race distributions between groups" (p. 361).

A survey of the correctional program evaluation literature suggests that the conclusions drawn by Wilson and his coauthors extend beyond the studies they examine to include much of the research in this field. While there are some notable examples where serious attempts were made to balance program participants and nonparticipants on observable variables (e.g., Saylor and Gaes [1996]), and while there have been some random assignment experiments of corrections-based programs, the results from these stronger studies give, at best, a mixed picture, and the great bulk of the field is made up of the far less rigorous studies characterized by Wilson et al. In another study, Farrington and Welsh (2005) conclude their meta-analysis of the 84 random assignment evaluations conducted in criminology between 1982 and 2004 with the observation that "rigorous evaluations of contemporary employment interventions for former prisoners are sorely needed" (p. 311).

This same conclusion is reached by Bloom in the most up-to-date review of employment-focused programs for ex-prisoners (Bloom 2006). The following points effectively summarize Bloom's findings:

- While there are no clear-cut patterns of successful programs, "there are hints of success for older offenders, for programs that provide integrated services both before and after release, and perhaps for models using financial incentives."

- The evidence to date does not support a conclusion that we already know what works and simply need to fund it, and this is primarily because some of the most promising findings that one sees in the literature come from some of the more weakly designed evaluations.

- The shifting economic and criminal justice contexts of the last decade and a half mean that a clear need for more definitive evidence as to "what works" still remains.

This survey of the literature leaves one both dissatisfied and discouraged. After many evaluation efforts over dozens of years, it appears that we still do not have a good sense of the programs or even the kinds of programs that can help offenders reintegrate into society. This pessimistic outlook should, however, be tempered by the convergence of three trends that may well influence corrections-based evaluations in the coming years. We argue that a similar convergence had an impact on education-related research in the 1990s, with the two related results that 1) program evaluation in that field has gotten much stronger and more rigorous over the last decade and a half and 2) we therefore know more about key features of this field, such as the importance of class size or teacher quality on student achievement, than we otherwise would have.

The first trend has to do with awareness. Much like what has happened in the world of education research and education policy, a consensus is emerging among researchers and practitioners in the correctional field that in order to solicit support from policymakers, funders, and legislative bodies, programs will be required to provide strong evidence that they are effective. And, in order for evidence to be considered "strong," it will have to come from evaluations that are much more rigorous than in the past. The message seems clear: public money and foundation funds are tight, and the people controlling these sources of support have become a more careful, knowledgeable, and skeptical bunch. This happened in the world of education, and, just as in education, this recognition is an important first step toward better evaluation research.

Second, just as more rigorous research is required, research designs and methods have become increasingly more powerful, appropriate, and sophisticated. It is likely that random assignment evaluations will play an increasingly important role in the corrections world—again, this is comparable to what has happened in the last decade in education. However, as is the case in education and other public policy spheres, there will be many times when experimental evaluation is not possible. Advances in econometrics and statistics, combined with a new generation of researchers who bring training and experience to issues associated with causal inference, give one substantial hope that future non-experimental evaluations of corrections-based programs will be much more rigorous than the nonexperimental evaluations of the past.

Third, as more rigorous evaluations are demanded and as our techniques for using data in more appropriate ways grow, corrections-based data collection and management are beginning to catch up with the twenty-first century. Again, this is similar to what has happened in education. Just as in that enterprise, federal and state agencies, and even some individual facilities and programs, have begun to collect, store, use, and share their data with researchers. These rich administrative data sources can be extremely useful and often essential when it comes to evaluating programs and interventions. Also, with the increasing knowledge that definitive answers to the "what works" question require and rely on good data, governmental agencies and private foundations are more aware that the funding of large-scale surveys can have net social benefits.

If our analogy to what has happened in education research is correct, we should see stronger evaluations of correctional programs in the future. In the next section we present results from three recent studies that are suggestive of the potential direction of correctional program evaluation.

WHAT HAVE WE LEARNED RECENTLY? THREE DIFFERENT APPROACHES

A Random Assignment Study: The Center for Employment Opportunities (CEO) Evaluation

The Center for Employment Opportunities (CEO) is one of the nation's largest and most well-regarded employment programs for ex-offenders. The goal of CEO is to improve the postrelease outcomes of ex-offenders by providing immediate employment upon release via a highly structured and tightly supervised transitional employment program, as well as by continuing to monitor and offer services to program participants after they move out of transitional employment into "independent" employment. The CEO experience begins with place-ment on a work crew within one week of enrollment in CEO. This work experience is highly structured and monitored and pays the New York state minimum wage. CEO staff work with program participants to help them develop good work habits while they are in the transitional jobs, and then they help participants move off of the work crews into regular jobs. After the initial, transitional job phase, CEO remains as involved as possible with program participants as they enter and compete in the labor market. One way CEO does this is by providing cash rewards of up to $600 a year for individuals in jobs who bring in their pay stubs to CEO on a regular basis. The purpose of this reward system is to keep CEO staff connected to former program participants so that they can monitor how participants are doing in their regular jobs and inter-vene with assistance when necessary. As part of the Hard-to-Employ Demonstration and Evaluation Project funded by the U.S. Department of Health and Human Services, MDRC, in partnership with the Urban Institute, is evaluating the CEO program with a random assignment design.

Random assignment of CEO applicants between January of 2004 and October of 2005 resulted in 568 program participants who received the full CEO "treatment" and 409 control subjects who received some job search assistance. The first-year results (i.e., one year after random assignment) from the CEO evaluation are interesting and tantalizing. These patterns emerge:[6]

- The employment effects of CEO participation are not impres-sive. Employment differences between the treatment and control groups heavily favor the treatment group in the first quarter after random assignment when the treatment group members work in CEO transitional jobs. This CEO advantage falls steadily over the next three months, so that by the fourth quarter after random assignment there are no statistical differences between the two groups in the probability of being employed.

- On the other hand, the effects of CEO on recidivism appear to be rather substantial, at least for the subgroup who came to CEO within three months of their release from prison and were randomly assigned at that point.[7] Within this reentry subgroup, those randomized into the CEO program had statistically significantly lower arrest rates (1.7 percent versus 6.2), lower parole revocations (18.8 percent versus 27.0), lower reincarceration rates in the state prison system for any reason (9.6 versus 19.7), and lower reincarceration rates in the state prison system for a new conviction (0.5 versus 5.1) than did those in the reentry subgroup who were randomized out of the CEO treatment. These differences in recidivism largely disappeared when the whole experimental sample—those who applied within three months of release *and* those who applied at some later time—was used.

Taken together, these initial results from the CEO evaluation suggest some interesting conclusions to consider. First, since the recidivism results largely disappear when the whole sample is used, it appears that the CEO program model is most effective for offenders who come to the program and get employment assistance relatively soon after release (as do three-quarters of all CEO participants). Second, the fact that by the fourth quarter the CEO employment effects had largely disappeared among the reentry subgroup, even as this group had lower rates of recidivism than did the control group, suggests that the mechanisms through which employment reduces recidivism may need more careful thought. That is, typical economic models of crime suggest that if higher wages and a greater probability of employment can replace the economic component of crime, the result should be a lower probability of engaging in criminal behavior. The CEO results suggest there may be other mechanisms through which gainful employment reduces criminal activity. For example, it may be that even though early gainful employment may not lead to greater employment by the end of the fourth quarter, employment in the months close to prison release helps ex-offenders get through what criminologist Shawn Bushway calls "the toxic first year" after release.[8] Subsequent follow-ups in the CEO evaluation may help us better understand some of these interesting first-year findings and shed light on the linkages between employment, wages, and recidivism.

Lessons from a Large-Scale Longitudinal Survey Study: Evaluation of the Serious and Violent Offender Reentry Initiative (SVORI)

In 2003, the U.S. Departments of Justice, Labor, Housing and Urban Development, and Health and Human Services established the Serious and Violent Offender Reentry Initiative (SVORI), a large-scale program providing over $100 million to 69 grantees to develop programming, training, and state-of-the-art reentry strategies at the community level. The SVORI programs are intended to reduce recidivism as well as to improve employment, housing, and health outcomes of participating released prisoners. RTI International, a nonprofit research firm, and the Urban Institute are involved in a five-year evaluation of SVORI-funded programs. The 15-month postrelease results from that evaluation are now available, and the results, while less than encouraging, are nonetheless instructive.

In the SVORI evaluation, all ex-offenders who participated in SVORI-supported programs across 16 programs over 14 states and in more than 300 jails and prisons form the treatment group. A comparison group was constructed from ex-offenders in the same facilities who were released at approximately the same time, and the groups are balanced as effectively as possible using propensity score-matching techniques. In a baseline survey prior to release, 74 percent of the treatment group and 73 percent of the comparison group indicated that they felt that they needed employment, education, or skill-building services. Follow-up surveys indicated that only 39 percent of the treatment group and 24 percent of the comparison group had received any employment, education, or skill-building services. Postrelease, only 15 percent of the treatment group and 8 percent of the comparison group had received any services, and nine months after release the figures were 12 percent and 8 percent, respectively.

The central lesson from these results is that the overall level of service provision, including services from the SVORI programs that were receiving federal funding, was substantially below what offenders indicated they needed prior to their release. So, even though SVORI program participants received a somewhat greater level of services both before and after release, there was still much unmet need, according to the reports of the sample members. Given the relatively low level of service provision, even among the treatment group members, it is hardly surprising that 15-month postrelease results showed very few statistically significant differences in outcomes between treatment and comparison group members. The evaluation considers roughly 100 different outcomes across the broad categories of "self-sufficiency and quality of life," "health," and "reduced criminality." In only 19 of 107 instances did SVORI participants have statistically significantly better outcomes than the comparison group in the propensity score results.[9] Thus, it is not clear what the ultimate message is at the early stage of this evaluation: that SVORI programs are mostly ineffective, or that there is a substantial amount of unmet need when it comes to programming designed to help offenders reintegrate.

The lessons about unmet need as documented by the SVORI evaluation should be placed beside what we already know about how the realities of prison life can disrupt or prevent program provision, program enrollment (as offenders move between facilities that do and do not offer programs they desire), and program attendance. Taken together, these facts of prison life and what the SVORI evaluation tells us about program provision suggest that it may be the case that few programs are delivered with integrity relative to their design. If it is indeed the case that few enrollees are getting the full treatment in any given program, it could be hard for even effective programs to show an impact.

Learning about Education, Vocational, and Work Programs Using Administrative Data: The Florida Case

Between 2000 and 2002, John H. Tyler and Jeffrey Kling worked with three state agencies in Florida to assemble a series of data sets that could be used to study criminal justice questions and issues. For this project the Florida Department of Corrections, the Florida Department of Law Enforcement, and the Florida Education and Training Placement Information Program worked in concert to provide the necessary criminal justice and labor market administrative records. The linkable data sets delivered to Tyler and Kling were stripped of all personally identifiable information and contain information on more than one million records on all individuals arrested in Florida since 1990, with a complete panel on arrests, convictions, incarceration spells, rehabilitative program participation, and Florida unemployment insurance (UI) earnings since 1994. The quality and richness of these data provide an opportunity to conduct rigorous evaluations of the effectiveness of corrections-based programs in Florida, a state with one of the largest prison populations in the nation.

Using the Florida data, Tyler and Kling (2007) found that white male offenders who entered prison as dropouts and obtained a GED had no better earnings after three years than did white dropouts who did not obtain a GED while in prison. On the other hand, this study found that minority-group male offenders (everyone coded as nonwhite in the data) who entered as dropouts but obtained a GED in prison had earnings that were about 15 percent higher in the first year after release than minority group offenders who entered prison as dropouts but did not obtain a GED.[10] Both findings are based on a specification that includes a rich set of personal demographic and criminal justice history variables as well as preprison earnings. The model also controls for all unobservable differences between program participants and nonparticipants that are time invariant, a so-called fixed effects model.[11]

While the results for minority group offenders are encouraging, the first-year earnings gains for the GED holders fall in both the second and third years after release, so that by the end of the third year there are no statistical differences between those minority offenders who did and those who did not obtain a GED while in prison. It is worth noting that Tyler and Kling (2007) were able to show that for all groups, any simple comparisons (without controls) between those with and those without a GED obtained while in prison would show a large, positive, and statistically significant effect of the GED on earnings.

For this paper, we returned to the Tyler and Kling data from Florida to estimate the effects of six different prison-based education, vocational, or employment programs. An interesting feature of conducting this analysis is that we can compare program effects on the same population of inmates using the same techniques and the same data. Specifically, we examine three classroom programs (Adult Basic Education or ABE, GED preparation, and vocational training) and three work experience programs (prison industries, work camps, and work release).[12] We look at the effects of these programs on earnings for three years following prison release, limiting our sample to male inmates who enter prison without a high school diploma to ensure that everyone is in need of educational programming.

As did Tyler and Kling, we first showed that, for all of the programs except ABE, simple comparisons between program participants and nonparticipants would show that program participation was associated with higher earnings and lower recidivism rates three years after release. However, when we applied the same fixed-effects model used in Tyler and Kling, controlling for the available set of covariates, only two of the programs showed any positive effects. Based on the fully specified model, offenders who participated in a prison industry had earnings that were about 15 percent higher than nonparticipants', and those who participated in work release had quarterly earnings that were about 24 percent higher than the earnings of nonparticipants. We found no recidivism effects for prison industry participation, but work release participants had recidivism rates that were 4, 5, and 6 percentage points lower than the comparison group in the first, second, and third years after release, respectively. These recidivism gains occur against baseline recidivism rates that show 30 percent return to prison within one year, 45 percent within two years, and 53 percent within three years of release. Again, most of the programs show recidivism effects across the three postrelease years in models with no control variables.

Although our detailed data allow us to move beyond much of the nonexperimental research on prison programming, it is still important to wrestle further with questions of program selection based on unobservables. In other research, Berk (2008) investigates the work release program more carefully. Using propensity score matching, this work tests whether the effect of work release participation on earnings varies with the propensity to be treated. We do find evidence that the earnings effect is largest in the tails of the propensity score distribution. We interpret this as evidence of a heterogeneous treatment effect or the increased importance of selection on unobservables in this portion of the distribution.

An insight from this research is that it is important to consider that interventions targeting employment might not be right for all inmates. If we take an economic model of crime seriously, one might not expect corrections-based employment programs, even effective ones, to have the same impact for all offenders. The reason is that one of the primary goals of corrections-based employment programs is to increase the employability and earnings of released offenders and, hence, reduce their proclivity to engage in criminal activity. Financial gain, however, does not motivate all crime, and so it is not clear how effective employment programs might be expected to be when it comes to "non-income-generating" offenses. To explore this possibility, Berk separates offenders into two groups—those who committed income-generating offenses (robbery, burglary, property theft, and drug sales) and those who committed nonincome-generating offenses (violent crime, drug use, weapons possession, and other offenses). While both groups of offenders have improved employment outcomes after participating in work release, only the income-generating crime group has a drop in recidivism. In many respects, this result is intuitive, but it is crucial to consider its implications. There is not one type of prison inmate, and there will never be one type of prison program that meets the needs of all inmates. We do need to think carefully about what types of employment programs improve labor market outcomes, but we also need to realize that better labor market opportunities will not eliminate the recidivism problem.

CONCLUSION

The explosion in the prison population in this nation has translated into an explosion in the number of released ex-offenders who return to our nation's communities every day of every year. Given this reality, understanding the extent to which various correctional programs help or do not help ex-offenders reintegrate into mainstream society has never been more important. We argue that the relatively low quality of correctional program evaluation that has been the norm until recently has left us uncertain as to which, and even which types of, programs work. We further argue that research into what works in corrections may be at a critical juncture, similar to that faced by education research in the 1990s when three trends converged: 1) a growing recognition of the importance of more rigorous program evaluation centered on the idea that random assignment evaluations constitute the gold standard in program evaluation, 2) the development and increased use of more powerful and appropriate statistical and econometric research methods that could be brought to bear when random assignment was not possible, coupled with the emergence of a new generation of researchers who were much more accustomed to thinking hard and deeply about causal inference in the social sciences and were better equipped to do so, and 3) the emergence and availability of rich administrative data sets that could be used in program evaluation when random-assignment field experiments were not in place.

Against this backdrop, this paper asks, "What do we learn from the latest research regarding what works in rehabilitative programming?" We believe that the most important lessons from recent research are the following:

- First, it is very hard to have a substantial impact on the lives of adult criminal justice offenders. That is, research that seriously tries to account for positive selection into rehabilitative programs is often unable to reject the null hypothesis of no program effect on outcomes, be they labor market outcomes or recidivism.

- Second, this result should not be completely surprising given what we know about how hard it is to change life trajectories,[13] what we have learned thus far from the SVORI evaluation about the apparent underprovision of programs, and what we know about how the institutional realities of prisons and prison life make it difficult to deliver rehabilitative programs in ways that comport with how the programs were designed to be delivered.

- Third, the early results of the CEO evaluation that show no effects of the program on employment, even as program participation reduces recidivism, suggest that we need to think hard about the mechanisms through which an employment program might affect recidivism and employment.

- Fourth, the results from Berk's recent work-release research suggest that the targeting of scarce program resources at particular types of offenders and ex-offenders could potentially have big payoffs. In particular, her findings tell us that perhaps we should target employment programs at offenders who commit income-generating crimes, with the potential corollary being that we might target cognitive-behavior or substance-abuse programs at offenders who are in prison for nonincome-generating crimes, such as violent crime, drug use, and weapons possession.

Notes

1. An additional 750,000 individuals were in local jails in 2006, for a total penal population of 2.25 million.
2. According to Pettit and Western (2004), the comparable figures in 1979 were 17.1 percent for black male dropouts and 4.0 percent for white male dropouts.
3. Approximately 95 percent of the individuals who are incarcerated are eventually released. The 5 percent who are not are composed of those who die while in prison, who are executed, or who are serving life-without-parole sentences.
4. Prison programs also focus on drug treatment and recovery, life skills, and cognitive behavioral skills designed to change the decision-making processes of criminal justice offenders. While any of these programs could, if effective, improve the labor market outcomes of individuals, since their primary goal is not to improve employment outcomes, they are not considered in this study.
5. It is worth noting at this point that almost all of the program evaluation research has been focused on the effects of program participation on recidivism, with very few studies looking at labor market outcomes such as wages, earnings, or employment as the outcome of interest. This is partly because most criminologists are primarily interested in program effects on recidivism and partly because, until recently, labor market information on ex-offenders has been difficult to obtain. The increased use of state unemployment-insurance wage records by researchers is changing the latter constraint.
6. The following results and figures come from the presentation of MDRC's Dan Bloom at the June 2007 Welfare Research and Evaluation Conference, hosted by the Administration for Children and Families and held in Washington, D.C. These publicly available slides can be found at http://www.acf.hhs.gov/programs/opre/wrconference/agenda.html.
7. This "reentry subgroup," as it is called in the evaluation, is a valid subgroup from the experimental evaluation standpoint, since those who came to CEO within three months of their release and were randomized into treatment were compared with those who came to CEO within three months of release and were randomized into the control group. That is, the reentry subgroup is not an endogenously defined subgroup, and so any treatment-control differences in outcomes can be attributed to CEO participation. See Orr (1998) for a discussion of endogenously defined subgroups.
8. After three years, approximately 60 percent of released prisoners will have returned to prison. Half of these individuals return within the first year after release (BJS 2008c).
9. Also, the comparison group had better outcomes that were statistically significant in two instances.
10. Whites (treatment and comparison groups) had higher preprison earnings than did nonwhite offenders (treatment and comparison groups).
11. The earnings fixed-effects model is
$$Yit = AFT_{it}\beta_{40} + GED_{it}\delta_4 + AGE_{it}\beta41 + YRQTR_{it}\beta42 + AFT_{it} \times X_i\beta43 + \alpha_i + \varepsilon_{4it},$$

where i indexes person, t indexes time in quarters before or after prison, α is the individual fixed effect, AFT is an "after prison" indicator, GED is a dummy variable indicating the possession of a GED in quarter t, AGE is age at time t, $YRQTR$ is a vector of year-quarter dummy variables, and X is a vector of variables that includes education level upon prison entry, predicted sentence length, marital status and number of children upon prison entry, years in Florida prior to prison entry, whether a Florida resident, state or region of birth, whether employed prior to arrest, industry and occupation prior to arrest, whether or not an English speaker and whether a confirmed U.S. citizen or an alien, cumulative years in prison prior to the current prison spell, number of disciplinary reports ever accumulated in prison, type of offense for this imprisonment spell, and a measure of cognitive skills at prison entry. This fixed-effects specification allows for the variables in X to affect postrelease earnings. For another example of this type of flexible specification in a fixed-effects model, see Jacobson, LaLonde, and Sullivan (1993).

12. Florida's prison industries engage in a variety of tasks—inmates grow sugar cane, digitize government documents, and make cardboard boxes. Inmates working in prison industries receive a nominal wage (20¢–55¢ an hour). Inmates in work camps clean roadways, perform grounds and building maintenance, and work on public construction projects. These inmates receive no remuneration. Inmates nearing the end of their sentences are eligibile for work-release assignments. Inmates at a work-release facility hold jobs in the community during the day and return to the secure facility at night. Inmates are paid the prevailing wage but these wages are garnished for room and board, victim restitution, and family support.

13. For a discussion and evidence on this topic, see Heckman (2000).

References

Austin, James. 2001. "Prisoner Reentry: Current Trends, Practices, and Issues." *Crime and Delinquency* 47(3): 314–334.

Berk, Jillian. 2008. "Does Work Release Work?" Unpublished manuscript. Providence, RI: Brown University.

Bloom, Dan. 2006. "Employment-Focused Programs for Ex-Prisoners: What Have We Learned, What Are We Learning, and Where Should We Go from Here?" Paper presented at the Nation Poverty Center conference "Research on Prisoner Reentry: What Do We Know and What Do We Want to Know?" held in Ann Arbor, MI, May 24.

Bureau of Justice Statistics (BJS). 2008a. *Prison Statistics*. Washington, DC: U.S. Department of Justice, Bureau of Justice Statistics. http://www.ojp.usdoj.gov/bjs/prisons.htm (accessed May 20, 2009).

———. 2008b. *Direct Expenditure for Each of the Major Criminal Justice Functions (Police, Corrections, Judicial) Has Been Increasing*. Washington, DC: U.S. Department of Justice, Bureau of Justice Statistics.

————. 2008c. *Federal Bureau of Justice Statistics Recidivism Study.* Washington, DC: U.S. Department of Justice, Bureau of Justice Statistics. http://www.cor.state.pa.us/stats/lib/stats/BJS%20Recidivism%20Study.pdf (accessed December 5, 2008).

Farrington, David P., and Brandon C. Welsh. 2005. "Randomized Experiments in Criminology: What Have We Learned in the Last Two Decades?" *Journal of Experimental Criminology* 1(1): 9–38.

Harlow, Carolline Wolf. 2003. *Education and Correctional Populations.* Bureau of Justice Statistics Special Report. Washington, DC: U.S. Department of Justice, Bureau of Justice Statistics.

Harrison, Paige M., and Allen J. Beck. 2006. *Prisoners in 2005.* Bureau of Justice Statistics Bulletin. Washington, DC: U.S. Department of Justice, Bureau of Justice Statistics.

Heckman, James J. 2000. "Policies to Foster Human Capital." *Research in Economics* 54(1): 3–56.

Jacobson, Louis S., Robert J. LaLonde, and Daniel G. Sullivan. 1993. "Earnings Losses of Displaced Workers." *American Economic Review* 83(4): 685–709.

LoBuglio, Stefan (Chief of Pre-Release Services, Montgomery County [Maryland] Department of Corrections and Rehabilitation). 2007. Interview by John H. Tyler. Tape recording. October 19. Montgomery County Department of Corrections and Rehabilitation, Rockville, MD.

Mauer, Marc. 2003. *Comparative International Rates of Incarceration: An Examination of Causes and Trends.* Presented to the U.S. Commission on Civil Rights. Washington, DC: The Sentencing Project.

Nagin, Daniel S. 1998. "Criminal Deterrence Research at the Outset of the Twenty-First Century." *Crime and Justice* 23: 1–42.

Orr, Larry L. 1998. *Social Experiments: Evaluating Public Programs with Experimental Methods.* Thousand Oaks, CA: Sage Publications.

Pager, Devah. 2003. "The Mark of a Criminal Record." *American Journal of Sociology* 108(5): 937–975.

Pettit, Becky, and Bruce Western. 2004. "Mass Imprisonment and the Life Course: Race and Class Inequality in U.S. Incarceration." *American Sociological Review* 69(2): 151–169.

Saylor, William G., and Gerald G. Gaes. 1996. *PREP: Training Inmates through Industrial Work Participation and Vocational and Apprenticeship Instruction.* Washington, DC: U.S. Department of Justice, Federal Bureau of Prisons.

Tyler, John H., and Jeffrey R. Kling. 2007. "Prison-Based Education and Reentry into the Mainstream Labor Market." In *Barriers to Reentry? The Labor Market for Released Prisoners in Post-Industrial America,* Shawn Bushway,

Michael A. Stoll, and David F. Weiman, eds. New York: Russell Sage Foundation, pp. 227–256.

Wilson, David B., Catherine A. Gallagher, Mark B. Coggeshall, and Doris L. MacKenzie. 1999. "A Quantitative Review and Description of Corrections-Based Education, Vocation, and Work Programs." *Corrections Management Quarterly* 3(4): 8–18.

Wilson, David B., Catherine A. Gallagher, and Doris L. MacKenzie. 2000. "A Meta-Analysis of Corrections-Based Education, Vocation, and Work Programs for Adult Offenders." *Journal of Research in Crime and Delinquency* 37(4): 347–368.

12

Comparing Apples to Oranges When Evaluating Community-Based Programs and Services

Robert J. LaLonde
University of Chicago

Community organizations have proliferated over time. These non-profit entities may provide a range of services, or they may provide a very specific set of services targeted to residents of a geographically defined area, such as a neighborhood, a school community, a parish, or even a city or town. Their services include, but are not limited to, the following:

- prisoner reentry
- community policing
- job placement
- school tutoring
- job training for new immigrants
- home visitation for new mothers
- drug treatment and drug treatment referrals
- domestic violence counseling and centers
- early childhood education initiatives
- programs to encourage minority arts participation
- small business assistance for low-income persons
- food banks and services for the homeless

These services have been provided by both nonsectarian and faith-based organizations. They are designed to improve outcomes for recipients of the services, for their families, and for the communities in which they live.

Financing for these services usually comes from charitable contributions, from members of the community organization providing the service, and from outsiders, but it can also come from grants from foundations. Each year these foundations provide community organizations with billions of dollars of support through grants.[1]

In recent years foundations have increasingly asked community organizations to evaluate the programs and services that have been at least partially financed by their giving. Although it is not always clear what these foundations have in mind when they ask their grantees for these evaluations, and sometimes what they ask for is inappropriate or infeasible, they are correct to ask their grantees to be quantitatively more accountable than they have been in the past for the dollars that they have spent.

In this chapter, I explain why evaluations often do not constitute a cost-effective use of foundation resources, nor do they constitute a productive use of the time and resources for the community organizations that receive the grants. This point holds especially true for "impact" or "cost-effectiveness" evaluations. In addition to the list of services given above, empowerment or enterprise zones, tax increment financing methods (TIFs), recycling programs, and "NIMBY" ("not in my backyard") disputes over such issues as the siting of a transfer station or a power generating plant also can fall under this rubric of community-level services. One of my conclusions here is that despite this varied list of services and policies, the challenges associated with evaluating them are virtually identical.

These challenges include not enough baseline information to complete a timely and rigorous evaluation, too little quantitative information on the services provided, who receives them, and how the services delivered differ from those intended. At other times the size of the intervention is relatively small and its impacts could only be detected with an extremely large sample of participants.

However, even when impact evaluations or cost-effectiveness evaluations are inappropriate, there is usually other valuable information about the community organizations' practices and performances that the organizations can collect and quantify. This information is valuable, not only to the foundations and other nonprofit and public-sector organizations that fund these community organizations' services, but also to their stakeholders and the organizations themselves as a tool to improve their program operations.

WHAT TO EVALUATE?

Should evaluators assess for community organizations the impact of grants that they receive on the services that they provide to their clients or the impact of their services on participants' outcomes? In the former case, suppose a foundation asks its grantee to assess the impact of the foundation's funding on the quantity or quality of services it provides to members of its community. In the second case, suppose a foundation asks its grantee to evaluate the impact of the community organization's primary services on the residents it serves and on who receives services.

The Impact of Grants on a Single Organization's Performance Cannot Be Evaluated

The first of these objectives—to evaluate the effects of the foundation's funding on the services that a single community organization provides—is not feasible. Although foundations would like to know what difference their giving has made to the organizations that have received the grants, and the organizations that received them would like to tell all the foundations that support their programs how important their funding was to them, yet without including often implausible assumptions into the analysis it is not possible to evaluate this question for a single community organization. In practice, there are many factors affecting the quality and quantity of services provided by a community organization. Besides the foundation's grant, the community organization's services also are affected by grants from other foundations and from the public sector, hiring and departures of personnel, and changing social and economic factors in the community.

To see the difficulty associated with the task of evaluating how a foundation's funding affects a community organization's services and performance, I manipulate the terms in a simple framework. First I define some notation:

A = a measure of services provided by the community organization *after* it received funding from the foundation.

A' = a hypothetical measure of services that would have been provided by the community organization if its proposal for funding from the foundation had been rejected.

A_{-1} = a measure of services provided by the community organization *before* it received funding from the foundation.

B = a measure of services provided by another community organization whose proposal for funding from the foundation had been rejected.

D = a measure of services provided by another community organization that never even applied for funding from the foundation.

In order to assess whether its grants have made a difference, a foundation may ask community organizations to provide it with a measure of the following impact:

IMPACT = A − A' .

This impact measures the difference between the quantity (or quality) of services provided after the community organization received the foundation's grant (A) and the quantity (or quality) of services that would have been provided if the community organization had not received the foundation's grant (A'). Notice that measure A' is not the same as the measure of services provided by the community organization before it received funding from the foundation (i.e., A_{-1}).

Put this way, the problem is readily apparent. Although the term A can be measured, the term A' cannot. To measure A' requires literally turning back the clock to the point at which the foundation was making its funding decisions (Holland 1986). Once events have been theoretically returned to that time, the foundation then rejects the community organization's proposal and term A' measures the services provided under this alternative scenario.

Program evaluators refer to this problem of not being able to turn back the clock as "the evaluation problem" (Heckman, LaLonde and Smith 1999). Since turning back time is impossible, evaluators must fill in these missing data with an estimate of measure A'. In one approach, to estimate A', evaluators use a measure from a similar community organization that did not receive funding from the foundation. One possibility in this approach is to use information from another community organization whose proposal for funding was rejected by the foundation (denoted by B), as follows:

(1) $IMPACT = A - B$.

Another possibility is to use information from another community organization that never applied for funding (denoted by D), as follows:

(2) $IMPACT = A - D$.

Finally, a third possibility is to use information from the community organization before it received funding from the foundation (denoted by A_{-1}), as follows:

(3) $IMPACT = A - A_{-1}$.

Immediately, it is apparent that we have at least three different estimators of the impact of the foundation's grant-making, and none of them are necessarily equal to the true impact of the foundation's grant-making, which is $A - A'$.

All three of the foregoing impact measures have the same shortcoming: namely, that measures B, D, and A_{-1} are not the same as measure A'. They are oranges, and measure A' is the apple. Consider the following rearrangement of terms in the three impact measures:[2]

(1') $IMPACT = A - B = (A - A') + (A' - B)$;

(2') $IMPACT = A - D = (A - A') + (A' - D)$;

(3') $IMPACT = A - A_{-1} = (A - A') + (A' - A_{-1})$.

The implication of these three estimators of the impact of a foundation's giving on a (single) community organization's services or performance is that evaluators can reliably and precisely estimate the counterfactual value A' using measures based on data from other community organizations or from the same community organization at some point before it was funded by the foundation. Experience indicates that neither of these possibilities works well in practice.

To understand why not, consider the first of these measures: A − B. Information drawn for measure B is from another community organization that applied for funding but whose proposal was rejected by the foundation. As a result, this rejected community organization is one that the foundation has looked at carefully and decided that its proposal and its likely performance were inferior to those of the community organization it decided to fund. It would be remarkable if the counterfactual measure A' for the funded community organization would be well approximated by measure B from another community organization whose application for funding was rejected.

Foundations' funding decisions are carefully made. Foundations fund proposals that best serve their objectives and mission. So it is unlikely that the set of funded community organizations would be like their unfunded counterparts. However, suppose for the sake of argument that foundations' funding decisions were not carefully made. Even in the extreme and unlikely case where the foundation did not deliberate over the proposals it received and instead flipped a coin to determine funding, it would be likely that the impact measure of A − B is in error. To be sure, the coin flip ensures that *on average* the impact measured by A − B approximates the true impact measured by A − A'. However, this point only holds on average, not for any single comparison between a funded community organization and one of its rejected counterparts.

The problem with using even a randomly rejected community organization's measure of services or performance, B, so as to use A − B to estimate the true impact of the foundation's funding, A − A', is matching error. Even in the absence of the foundation's funding, these community organizations are not the same, and as a consequence their measures of performance also should not be the same. The difference A' − B contains both the performance differences between the community organizations and the errors associated with comparing or matching organizations that are not the same. These expressions tell us that in order to measure the impact of a foundation's giving on a community organization's services and performance, it is necessary that we compare measures for organizations that are the same or essentially the same.

This point raises another question: since other community organizations are not the same, could evaluators use the information on the same community organization before it was funded by the foundation? The problem here, as I explained above, is that many factors affect an organization's performance—including different personnel, funding from other nonprofit organizations, changing economic and social factors within the targeted communities, even the entry or emergence of another community organization in the area. Even here there is "matching error." An organization in the past is not the same organization as it is constituted in the present.

Evaluate the Average Impact of Funding on a Group of Organizations' Performances

The discussion in the preceding section explains why evaluators contend that we cannot evaluate the impact of an intervention—such as a foundation's giving—on the performance of a single organization. This principle also extends to individuals, and for the same reasons. There are many influences on an individual's outcomes besides those associated with the services that they receive from a community organization. A comparison between an individual who receives services from a community organization and another individual who does not receive such services usually tells us more about preexisting differences between these two people than it does about the differences in effectiveness of the services themselves.

The standout solution to what I described above as the matching-error problem is to evaluate the average impact of a foundation's giving on many different, but similar, community organizations by comparing their measures of performance to those of many other community organizations that have not received funding from the foundation. In this case, the expectation is that if the evaluators have done a good job of matching these other, unfunded community organizations to the funded community organizations, then the matching errors will average out.

The implication of this proposed solution to the evaluation problem is that it is not feasible to evaluate the performance of a set of, say, four or five community organizations that have been supported by a foundation. However, it may be feasible to evaluate the impact of a foundation's grant-giving by evaluating the average impact on a set of, say, 100 similar community organizations. In this latter case, it is possible that the matching errors average out, leaving a credible and possibly precise estimate of the average impact across the 100 organizations that the foundation chooses to fund. The underlying assumption is that the matching errors average out in large samples of community organizations or of service recipients.

In more colloquial terms, under some circumstances it may be an effective evaluation strategy to compare large numbers of apples to large numbers of oranges. To be sure, when evaluating the impact of foundation giving on a few community organizations' performances, we are faced with the familiar intractable problem of comparing apples to oranges. But when evaluating the impact of foundation giving on a large number of organizations, it is possible that the matching errors associated with comparing apples to oranges will average out. One setting in which they are likely to average out occurs under the hypothetical but unrealistic scenario that foundations' funding decisions are made randomly from their pools of applicants.

In practice, this proposed statistical solution does not help most foundations and nonprofits evaluate their giving, because of their practice of targeting their resources to a few community organizations with well-conceived proposals for providing innovative services. These foundations' giving policies are likely good ones. Yet despite this, in the vast majority of cases, it makes little sense for the foundations to insist that community organizations evaluate the impact of their funding.

Evaluate Services Regardless of the Source of Funding

The preceding discussion does not imply that foundations should forgo evaluation of important services targeted toward communities and individuals. Foundations can improve their own funding decisions and provide valuable information that will help community organizations operate their programs and deliver their services if they evaluate the services offered or the services received and not the organizations themselves.

Therefore, instead of asking, "What difference did our funding make to a particular organization and by extension to the organization's 'clients'?" foundations should ask instead, "What impact do these particular services have on individuals who receive them?" Such evaluations should focus on services and the individuals who received them and not on the improved performance of organizations that resulted from the funding provided by the foundation.

Even when taking this approach, it is not always an efficacious use of resources to insist on an impact evaluation. Prior to the impact evaluation, there are at least three other steps that foundation program officers and community organizations should take:

1) collect baseline and programmatic information on participants,

2) implement a study to see if the services are delivered as intended, and

3) assess the size of the intervention and its theoretical impacts.

In most cases community organizations' data collection efforts have lagged behind other important work that the organizations do. Since evaluation is a quantitative endeavor, outcomes of interest as well as services provided must be measured before any formal evaluation occurs.[3] The key point is that if the outcome cannot be measured, it cannot be evaluated.[4]

There is no point in evaluating a program or service before we learn how it operates in practice. An implementation study must precede an impact evaluation. Otherwise, even if the impact evaluation demonstrated that the service was effective, the potential for the service to be replicated would remain uncertain, because it would not be clear how the program actually operated in practice in the field. An implementation study should, among other things, document whether the services offered and received differ sufficiently from what is intended. Such differences arise because of the organization's or service provider's performance, because of a mismatch between the services and the recipients, or because resources are insufficient to implement the intended design. Before initiating an impact evaluation, such implementation questions need to be resolved.

Finally, the size of an intervention may be too small for its impact to be detected with a modest sample of recipients. For example, a 20-minute counseling session on how to find a job could be cost-effective, because the intervention is so inexpensive on a per-person basis. In this situation, the impacts would not need to be large for these services to be cost-effective.[5] However, an outcome such as employment rates or unemployment durations could be sufficiently variable among members of the community that a large sample of service recipients would be required in order to detect small impacts but cost-effective services.

These challenges associated with evaluating community organizations and their services are not unique and arise in other similar circumstances. For example, in evaluating enterprise zones, studies have addressed the evaluation problem by comparing economic activity in areas after they have been designated as enterprise zones to the economic activity prior to their receiving this designation.

A second approach compares these zones to areas with similar characteristics (Greenbaum and Engberg 2000; Holland 1986). Using both approaches, these areas have been defined as communities, census tracts, neighborhoods, or cities. In this alternative approach, evaluations attempt to construct a quasi-experimental setting in which areas that are designated as enterprise zones are compared to observationally similar areas that are not designated as enterprise zones.

No matter what approach is used, these evaluations cannot produce reliable estimates of the impact of a single or even a few enterprise zones on community and individual outcomes. In order for such evaluation studies to reliably measure impacts of enterprise zones, they must carefully measure outcomes and area characteristics for a sufficiently large number of these zones and their corresponding comparison areas. In this way, they measure the average impact of the enterprise zone strategy for a sample or particular "population" of communities.

CONCLUSION

High-quality evaluations are costly, and they are cost-effective only if they lead to some significant outcome. Saving an effective program or set of services that would otherwise be eliminated is a worthy purpose of evaluation. So is documenting socially significant net impacts for a new, innovative program.

However, in many instances involving community organizations, the goals of evaluation should be more modest. Often they should not focus on impact evaluation or cost-effectiveness, but on simply measuring and collecting data on program services. Providing operators and foundations with this information alone can provide valuable insight into how the program operates or how services are delivered and the challenges that must be overcome in order to affect recipients' outcomes. At the very least this information can improve program management. As I have explained above, this information also is essential for considering whether it is a good use of resources to initiate an impact evaluation of these programs and services.

Notes

1. See http://foundationcenter.org/findfunders/statistics/grantsampling.html for statistics on foundations believed to account for about half of all grant-making in the United States. Total grant giving from foundations for all purposes is thought to have amounted to about $40 billion in 2006.
2. In each case in Equations (1') through (3'), I simply subtract A' and add A' to Equations (1) through (3).
3. An example in Chicago is the study titled *Mapping Cultural Participation in Chicago* (LaLonde et al. 2006), funded by the Joyce Foundation. Originally, the foundation asked researchers at the National Opinion Research Center (NORC) and the Irving B. Harris Graduate School of Public Policy Studies to evaluate the effectiveness of various initiatives designed to promote minority participation in the large Chicago-area arts organizations. The researchers countered that without baseline information in hand such an evaluation would not succeed. So instead the foundation and the researchers agreed to collect baseline information on participation in the arts by individuals living in the Chicago metropolitan area. See LaLonde et al. (2006).
4. To address the costs of data collection and data management, smaller community organizations should consider hiring as interns the very talented students from the select high schools in their areas for data collection purposes. Many of these students have quantitative and computer skills that can be very useful to a standard community organization. They could be hired at very low cost.
5. An example of a small-sized intervention—a letter that unemployed job seekers were instructed to show potential employers—is discussed in Burtless (1985).

References

Burtless, Gary. 1985. "Are Targeted Wage Subsidies Harmful? Evidence from a Wage-Voucher Experiment." *Industrial and Labor Relations Review* 39(1): 105–114.

Greenbaum, Robert, and John Engberg. 2000. "An Evaluation of State Enterprise Zone Policies." *Policy Studies Review* 17(2/3): 29–46.

Heckman, James J., Robert J. LaLonde, and Jeffrey A. Smith. 1999. "The Economics and Econometrics of Active Labor Market Programs." In *Handbook of Labor Economics*, Orley C. Ashenfelter and David Card, eds. Vol. 3A. Handbooks in Economics 5. Amsterdam: North-Holland, pp. 1865–2084.

Holland, Paul W. 1986. "Statistics and Causal Inference." *Journal of the American Statistical Association* 81(396): 945–960.

LaLonde, Robert J., Colm O'Muircheartaigh, Julia Perkins, Ned English, Diane Grams, and Carroll Joynes. 2006. *Mapping Cultural Participation in Chicago*. Chicago: Cultural Policy Center, University of Chicago.

The Authors

David Autor (PhD Harvard) is professor of economics at the Massachusetts Institute of Technology, faculty research associate of the National Bureau of Economic Research, and editor in chief of the *Journal of Economic Perspectives*, published by the American Economic Association. Autor is currently engaged in two research programs, one on the growth of labor market intermediation, and one on job skill demands, technological change, and earnings inequality.

Burt S. Barnow (PhD Wisconsin) is associate director for research and principal research scientist at the Institute for Policy Studies at Johns Hopkins University. He has over 30 years of experience conducting research in the fields of workforce investment, program evaluation, performance analysis, labor economics, welfare, poverty, child support, and fatherhood.

Jillian Berk (PhD Brown) is a researcher at Mathematica Policy Research Inc. She studies the impact of education and employment programs on the labor market outcomes of disadvantaged populations, including ex-offenders and dislocated workers.

Harry J. Holzer (PhD Harvard) is a professor of public policy at Georgetown University, a senior fellow at the Urban Institute, and a former Chief Economist of the U.S. Department of Labor. His research focuses on the low-wage labor market and on policies to improve the earnings of disadvantaged workers.

Hilary Williamson Hoynes (PhD Stanford) is professor of economics at the University of California, Davis, and the coeditor of the *American Economic Journal: Economic Policy*. Hoynes specializes in the study of tax and transfer programs for poor families.

Robert J. LaLonde (PhD Princeton) is a professor at the Irving B. Harris Graduate School of Public Policy Studies at the University of Chicago. His research interests include program evaluation, education and training, immigration policy, worker displacement, unions and collective bargaining, and the consequences of incarceration.

Bridget Terry Long (PhD Harvard) is professor of education at the Harvard Graduate School of Education. Her research focuses on access and choice in higher education, the outcomes of college students, and the behavior of postsecondary institutions. Long is a faculty research associate of the National Bureau of Economic Research (NBER).

Bruce D. Meyer (PhD MIT) is McCormick Foundation Professor at the Harris School of Public Policy at the University of Chicago. His research has focused on social insurance, taxation, labor supply, and poverty.

As deputy director of MDRC's Young Adults and Postsecondary Education Policy Area, Lashawn Richburg-Hayes (PhD Princeton) is the principal researcher and project director of a national demonstration that will test the effectiveness of performance-based scholarship programs to increase retention and persistence in higher education. Her current research focuses on measuring various effects of new forms of financial aid, enhanced student services, and curricular and instructional innovations on community college retention and credit accumulation and nonexperimental methods of data analysis.

James E. Rosenbaum (PhD Harvard) is professor of sociology, education, and social policy at Northwestern University. His research has been published in sociology and policy journals and has been reported in the *New York Times*, the *Washington Post*, the *Wall Street Journal*, *Fortune Magazine*, the *Chronicle of Higher Education*, and on *60 Minutes*.

Jeffrey A. Smith (PhD Chicago) is professor of economics at the University of Michigan, and has also taught at the University of Western Ontario and the University of Maryland. His research centers on experimental and nonexperimental methods for the evaluation of interventions, with particular application to social and educational programs.

Maude Toussaint-Comeau (PhD University of Illinois at Chicago) is an economist in the microeconomics team of the economic research department of the Federal Reserve Bank of Chicago. Toussaint-Comeau's research has been on the use of formal and informal financial markets by minority groups and the use of alternative financial services, such as check-cashing outlets and payday loan companies. Her current research focuses on consumer sentiment and consumption expenditure and on diversity and firms' productivity.

John H. Tyler (EdD Harvard) is associate professor of education, economics, and public policy at Brown University. In addition to studying correctional education and the linkages between schooling and labor market outcomes, Tyler examines teacher quality issues, including how teachers use student performance data to inform their classroom instruction.

Index

The italic letters *f, n,* and *t* following a page number indicate that the subject information of the heading is within a figure, note, or table, respectively, on that page. Double italics indicate multiple but consecutive elements.

529 Plans, 112

ABE. *See* Adult Basic Education
Academic success
    lack of, as barrier to higher education,
        92, 104
    support structures for, 94–96, 95*t,*
        100, 104, 123*n*3
ACCESS project, New York, 93
Adult women workers
    effectiveness of employment training
        programs for, 28, 31–32, 91
    employment rates, 71, 72*f,* 73*ff,* 76*n*6
    married, 71, 72*f,* 73*f,* 76*n*4
    occupations and wages of, 56*t,* 59*t*
    See also Single women with children
AFDC. *See* Aid to Families with
        Dependent Children
Affordability barriers, 26, 92, 119
    overcoming (*see* Financial aid;
        Housing assistance programs)
African American families. *See* Black
        men; Black workers
Aid to Families with Dependent Children
        (AFDC), 16, 65
    caseloads, 66, 67*f*
    EITC and, 68, 70*f,* 76*n*4
American Community Survey,
        occupational data from, 61*n*7
Apprenticeships, 28, 157
Autor, David, conference participant, 39

Baltimore, Maryland, court decision in,
        149
Barnow, Burt S., conference participant,
        40
Barrow, Lisa, conference participant, 40
Basic Educational Opportunity Grants, 19

Beal, Frank, conference participant, 25,
        39
Bernanke, Ben S., quoted, 7
Berube, Alan, conference participant, 39
Big Brothers/Big Sisters (organization),
        27, 158, 160*n*4
Black men
    incarcerated, as school dropouts, 180,
        194*n*2
    labor force activity of, 9–10, 153, 155
Black workers, 11, 156
    earnings of, *vs.* white, 194*n*10, 194–
        195*n*11
    residential mobility programs with,
        130, 131, 134–135, 139, 144
Blinder, Alan S., conference participant,
        40
Block grants, 16, 26, 160*n*7
Bloom, Dan, corroborating data from,
        186–187, 194*n*6
BLS (Bureau of Labor Statistics). *See*
        U.S. Dept. of Labor
Boskin Commission, government bias
        and, 82
Boston, Massachusetts, TANF-eligible
        students in, 93
Brown, Gov. Edmund, commission
        appointed by, 23
Bush, Pres. George W., education policy
        of, 19
Butcher, Kristin F., conference
        participant, 40

California, 23, 160*n*3, 172
    CET in, 157, 160*nn*1–2
    community colleges with employment
        services in, 91, 93, 95*t*
    work-study funds for TANF students
        in, 116–117

Canadian Self-Sufficiency Project, 173
Career Academies, 27–28, 158, 160*n*4
Career Advancement Accounts, support
   for, 121
Career and Technical Education (CTE),
   27–28, 158, 160*n*4
Career pathway development, labor
   market intermediaries and, 157
Census of Populations, 61*n*2, 61*nn*7–8, 82
Census tracts, Chicago residential
   mobility and, 130–131, 132–134,
   133*t*
Center for Employment Opportunity
   (CEO) program, 27
   evaluation of, 29–30, 159, 185–187,
      193, 194*n*7
Center for Employment Training (CET),
   91–92
   cost-effectiveness of, 157, 160*n*1
CEO program. *See* Center for
   Employment Opportunity
CES. *See* Current Employment Statistics
CET. *See* Center for Employment
   Training
CETA. *See* Comprehensive Employment
   and Training Act
Chaffey College, California, Opening
   Doors project at, 95*t*
Chicago, Illinois, 9
   Metropolitan Planning Council,
      25–26, 43*n*15
   residential mobility programs in,
      23–25
      census tracts used for, 130–131,
         132–134, 133*t*
      Gautreaux compared to MTO,
         130–149
      neighborhoods studied, 129*t,*
         134–136
Child Care Access Means Parents in
   School program, 122
Children, 80
   adolescents, 27, 158
   care of, 120, 121–122, 155, 156
      (*see also* Day-care facilities)
   early childhood, 19, 36

effects of low-income assistance on,
      17–18
   neighborhood social interaction of,
      138–140, 144–145
   social interactions of, differ by gender,
      148–149
   See also Aid to Families with
      Dependent Children (AFDC); No
      Child Left Behind (NCLB); Single
      women with children
Civil disorders, violence in, 23
Civil rights, ex-offenders and, 159,
   160*n*5
Classroom training, 172, 190–191
Clinton, Pres. William J., commission
   appointed by, 23
CLMS. *See* Continuous Longitudinal
   Manpower Survey
College education, 11, 114, 116
   cost of, 20, 92, 119, 122*n*1
   EFC towards, 112–114, 115, 118,
      122*n*2
   nontraditional students and, 109–112,
      117–118, 120
   wage differential of, 62*n*11, 90
College retention. *See* Education
   retention programs
Commission on the Future of Higher
   Education, 121
Community-based organizations,
   199–209
   impact of
      group average, 205–206
      single organization, not evaluable,
         28, 201–205
   services provided by, 157, 160*n*3,
      199–200
      evaluation of, 4, 6, 31–34, 37–38,
         206–209
   See also Nonprofit community
      organizations
Community Benefit Agreements,
   rewarding employers with, 159
Community colleges
   employment services at, 27, 91, 121,
      148, 156

Community colleges, *cont.*
  Opening Doors demonstration at,
    93–104, 95*t*, 98*t*–99*t*, 102*t*–103*t*
  redressing mismatch of skills with
    jobs in, 21, 35
  role in American higher education,
    92–93, 117–118, 120
Community health, supportive factors, 9
Compensation, 154
  benefits in, 14, 18–19, 41*n*9
  inequality in, 79–80
  parental subsidies in, 42*n*14
Competition among employers, 154
Comprehensive Employment and
    Training Act (CETA), 26, 28,
    165–166, 170
Computer technology, 20, 80
  impacts of, 53–55, 61*nn*5–6
Connecticut Jobs First program, 18
Conservation Corps program, 28, 160*n*4
Construction sector, 154
Consumption poverty, 14, 81–82
Continuous Longitudinal Manpower
    Survey (CLMS), CETA
    evaluations and, 166
Corrections sector, 179, 184
Cost-benefit analysis, evaluation and, 172
Counseling services, 174
  residential mobility programs and,
    130–31, 147–148
  support structures for student, 94–96,
    95*t*, 148
Court-ordered decrees
  child support, 155–156
  equitable housing and, 130, 146, 149
Coverdell Savings Accounts, 116
CPS. *See* Current Population Survey
Criminal behaviors, 159, 168
  costs of, 159
  dropouts and, 155, 180
  prison programs to change, 193,
    194*n*4
  See also Violent behaviors
CTE. *See* Career and Technical
    Education

Current Employment Statistics (CES),
    calculation discrepancies and,
    61–62*n*9
Current Population Survey (CPS), 61*n*2,
    166
  women's employment rates, 72*f*, 73*ff*,
    76*n*6

Dahl, Molly, conference participant, 39
Data collection *vs.* evaluation, program
    services and, 32–33, 37–38
Day-care facilities, 22, 42*n*14, 120
DeLeire, Thomas, conference participant,
    39
Delgado Community College, Louisiana,
    Opening Doors project at, 95*t*,
    98*t*–99*t*, 102*t*–103*t*, 104*n*2
Detroit WorkFirst program, 17
Diaz, Evelyn, conference participant, 40,
    41*n*3
Disadvantaged populations, 166
  policies affecting, 3–7
  poverty and, 9*f*, 26
  workforce development of, 26–31, 36
  See also Ex-offenders; Nontraditional
    students; Single women with
    children; Youth
Displaced workers, 15, 111
  assistance to, 21, 26–27, 35, 42*n*12,
    166
District of Columbia, civil rights review
    in, 160*n*5
Dropouts
  criminal behaviors and, 155, 180,
    194*n*2
  preventing, 28, 92–93, 158
Duncan, Greg, conference participant, 40
Durable goods sector, 154, 155

Early childhood education, 19
  See also Day-care facilities
Earned Income Tax Credit (EITC)
  combating spatial mismatch with,
    42*n*14
  effectiveness of, 15, 17, 66

Earned Income Tax Credit (EITC), *cont.*
  employment rates and, 68, 71–75,
    72*f*, 73*ff*, 160*nn*2–3
  income assistance policy and, 16–17,
    35–36, 70*ff*, 75*n*2
  negative income effect of, 66–67,
    76*n*5
  proposed expansion of, 84–85, 158–
    159
  single women with children and, 4, 5,
    65–75, 69*ff*, 76*n*4
  state and federal programs for, 75–
    76*nn*2–3, 157
  welfare reform and, 66–68, 70*f*, 71,
    74–75
Earnings, 154, 160*n*2
  black compared to white workers and,
    194*n*10, 194–195*n*11
  data from Social Security program,
    166–67
  education and, 89–92, 101
  growth of, 60, 61*nn*2–3
  inequality of, 51–52, 52*f*, 53*f*
  subsidies for, 160*n*3, 173
Eberts, Randall W., conference
    participant, 39
Economic assumptions, quotes on, 7
Economic mobility, 36, 60, 62*n*12
  conference on improving, 7–40, 41*n*3
  improving, by combating spatial
    mismatch, 42–43*n*14, 60
  reflections on, and policy, 79–86
  workers and, 5, 12–14, 109
Education
  access to, 19–20, 28, 92, 116, 188
  alternative pathways to, 27–28, 158
  dropout prevention, 28, 92–93, 158
Education Amendments of 1972, 19
Education levels, 13, 20, 42*n*10, 168
  college, 11, 21, 62*n*11, 109–110
  early childhood, 19
  GED, 26, 114, 132
  high school, 11–12, 114, 132
  low, 9–10, 11, 16, 55, 56*t*, 61*n*8, 72,
    73*f*, 89–90, 154
  remedial, 166

  vocational, 28
Education policy, 19, 83, 119–120
  financial aid in, 120–122
Education retention programs, low-
    income adults and, 3, 4, 5, 21,
    90–105, 120
EFC. *See* Expected Family Contribution
EITC. *See* Earned Income Tax Credit
Employee Free Choice Act, union
    organization and, 160*n*6
Employers, 26, 157
  discrimination by, 154, 156
  investment in nontraditional students
    by, 116–117, 117–118
  rewards to, for training, 159, 170
Employment Retention and
    Advancement (ERA) projects, 91,
    158, 160*n*3
Employment sectors, 17, 61*n*8, 154, 157,
    170–171, 184
  natural resources occupations in, 56*t*,
    59*t*
Employment training programs, 9
  analytic issues of, 171–173, 182–185
  cost-effectiveness of, 157–158, 159
  demonstrated changes after, 28, 31,
    160*n*2
  evaluations of, 165–171, 173–174
    employer-focused programs and,
      169–171
    major U.S. federal programs and,
      165–167
    selected other programs and,
      167–169
  policies to provide, 5–6, 21, 26, 157
  redressing mismatch of skills and jobs
    with, 21, 34–35
  targeted
    customized training, 170
    former welfare recipients and, 3,
      90–91
    informal and indirect, 112, 116,
      117
    sectoral training, 157, 170–171
  See also On-the-job training (OJT)

ERA. *See* Employment Retention and
     Advancement projects
Evans, Charles L., conference
     participant, 39
Ex-offenders
     civil rights and, 159, 160*n*5
     employment and advancement of, 6,
          179–195
          (*see also* Center for Employment
          Opportunities [CEO])
     employment restrictions for, 160*n*5,
          180
     labor market reentry programs for, 3,
          4, 27, 29–31, 158, 159, 188–189,
          193
     recidivism and, 159, 182–183, 187,
          191–192, 194*n*5, 194*n*8
Expected Family Contribution (EFC)
     college costs and, 112–114, 115, 118,
          122*n*2
     independent students forgo, 113–
          114, 118–119, 120

FAFSA. *See* Free Application for Federal
     Student Aid
Family income, 114, 117
     EFC and, 112–113, 122*n*2
     growth of, over time, 86, 93
     median measurements of, 82, 83*f*
     volatility in, 80–81
Federal Reserve Bank, Chicago,
     conference sponsorship by, 3–6,
     39–40
Financial aid
     block grants to states, 16, 160*n*7
     FAFSA as first step in, 112–113, 115
     loan programs, 114
     nontraditional students and, 20,
          21–22, 110–122, 122*n*2
     Pell Grants to students, 19, 20, 104–
          105*n*3, 113, 114–115, 157, 159
     scholarships as, 94–97, 95*t*, 100, 101,
          104
     subsidies as, 42*n*14, 120, 121–122,
          157, 158, 160*n*3, 173
     support structures for, 94–97, 95*t*,

          100, 117–118, 120–122, 123*n*3
          See also Earned Income Tax Credit
          (EITC); Grants-in-aid; Low-
          income assistance policy
Financial aid reform, 120–121
Florida
     ex-offenders and, 30, 160*n*5
     prison program evaluation in, 189–192
For-profit companies, as labor market
     intermediaries, 157
Foreign-born workers, 111
     low wages and, 101, 153
     occupations and wages of, 56*t*, 59*t*
Foundations, grants-in-aid funded by,
     200, 209*n*1
Free Application for Federal Student Aid
     (FAFSA), 112–113, 115

GAIN program, long-term follow-up of,
     172
Gautreaux Assisted Housing Program,
     Chicago, 23–24
     design, 130–136, 133*t*
     individual outcomes from, 141–145
     policy implications of, 147–149
     social influences on, 133*t*, 136–140,
          146
     study conclusion, 145–146
GED. *See* General Educational
     Development
Gender differences
     children and social interaction, 148–
          149
     effectiveness of employment training
          programs, 28, 31–32
     EITC benefits and, 35–36
     See also Adult women workers;
          specific cohorts, e.g., Black men;
          Noncustodial fathers; Single
          women with children; White men
General Educational Development
     (GED), 28, 114
     effect on earnings, 90–91
     prison-based programs for, 181, 182,
          190
Georgia, tuition program in, 116

Giloth, Bob, conference participant, 33, 40, 41*n*3
Globalization, wage inequality and, 42*n*9, 101
Gosselin, Peter, conference participant, 39
Grants-in-aid, 19, 116
   average impact on group of organizations, 205–206
   block grants, 16, 26, 160*n*7
   evaluation of services funded by, 206–209
   foundation funding of, 200, 209*n*1
   impact not evaluable on single organization of, 201–205
   Pell Grants to students, 19, 20, 104–105*n*3, 113, 114–115, 157, 159
Great Depression, public employment in, 165–166
Greenspan, Alan, quoted, 7

Harlem Children's Zone (organization), 27, 158
Head Start program, 19
Health, 188
   poor, 155, 159
Health care sector, access to, 154
Hibbs, Maria, conference participant, 40, 41*n*3
Hispanic workers, 11
Holzer, Harry J., conference participant, 40
Hope Tax Credit, 114–115
Houseman, Susan, conference participant, 39
Housing affordability, 24–26, 157, 158
Housing assistance programs
   employment rates and, 158, 160*n*2
   human capital improvement through, 127–149
   school quality and, 127, 129
   spatial mismatch and, 3, 5, 23–24, 36–37, 43*n*14
   See also Residential mobility programs

Hoynes, Hilary Williamson, conference participant, 39
Human capital
   employer investment in nontraditional students, 117–118
   improvement of, and residential mobility, 127–128, 129, 137–140, 144–145, 146–149
   investments to enhance, 19, 20–21, 60, 80, 83, 86, 171

Illinois
   job support services in, 30–31, 160*n*3
   residential mobility in (*see under* Chicago, Illinois)
   state EITC supplement to federal program, 76*n*3
   state housing legislation in, 25, 26
   student aid in, 113, 116, 122*n*2
Immigrant workers. *See* Foreign-born workers
Incarceration
   employability upon release from, 10, 155–156, 182, 190
   (*see also* Ex-offenders)
   penal population characteristics, 179–181, 192, 194*nn*1–3
   prison programs during, 181–182, 189–192, 194*n*4
   impact of, 182–185, 193
   recidivism and, 159, 182–183, 187, 191–192, 194*n*5, 194*n*8
Income volatility, 15, 79, 80–81
Inner cities. *See* Urban areas
Integrated Public Use Microdata Series (IPUMS), occupational data from, 61*nn*7–8
Internships, 157
IPUMS. *See* Integrated Public Use Microdata Series

Job Corps, 6, 28, 167–168, 172
Job information centers, 42*n*14, 121
Job Opportunities and Basic Skills (JOBS) training program, 16

Job readiness, work experience as, 154
Job retention, 91, 155
Job Search Assistance program, 31, 166
Job skills, 16, 20
    deficit, of working poor, 9, 154
    employment training programs and,
        34–35, 101, 112, 122, 170
    polarization of, and wages, 52–55,
        58–60, 61n4
    semiskilled jobs and spatial
        mismatches, 127, 137–138
Job Training Partnership Act (JTPA), 26,
    172
    effectiveness of, 28, 91, 157, 160n1,
        168
    NJS evaluation of, 166–167
    public employment programs of,
        165–166
JOBS. See Job Opportunities and Basic
    Skills training program
Jobs Plus, employment rates and, 158,
    160n2
JTPA. See Job Training Partnership Act

Kentucky, UI claimants and WPRS in,
    169
Kerner Commission, inner-city riots and,
    23
Kingsborough Community College, New
    York, Opening Doors project at,
    95t
Kotlowitz, Alex, conference participant,
    40

Labor market intermediaries, 27, 33,
    156–157
Labor market reentry programs
    formerly incarcerated persons and, 3,
        4, 6, 27, 29–31, 158, 159
    welfare reform and, 12, 17
Labor markets, 61n6
    lack of attachment to, 153–156
    policies to improve participation in,
        156–159, 171–172
    residential mobility and, 127, 137–
        138, 142–143

supply disincentives and, 66–67, 156,
    158
LaLonde, Robert J., conference
    participant, 40
Lazear, Edward, conference participant,
    19, 40
Legal Action Center, New York, 160n5
Lifelong Learning Accounts, support for,
    121
Lifetime Learning Tax Credit (LLTC),
    114
LLTC. See Lifetime Learning Tax Credit
Loan programs, education and, 114
Long, Bridget Terry, conference
    participant, 40
Lorain County Community College,
    Ohio, Opening Doors project
    at, 94–96, 95t, 98t–99t, 102t–103t,
    104n1
Los Angeles, California, Watts riots in,
    23
Louisiana, 116
    community college projects in, 95t,
        98t–99t, 102t–103t, 104–105n2
Louisiana Technical College–West
    Jefferson, Opening Doors project
    at, 95t, 96–101, 102t–103t, 104–
    105n2
Low-income assistance, 3–6, 14, 16–19,
    35–36, 65
    effects on children, 17–18
    residential mobility as, 127–149
    See also Financial aid
Low-wage occupations, 12, 56t, 58, 59t
Low-wage workers, 41n4
    earnings improvements for, 160nn2–3
    education and, 89–92, 101, 104, 110,
        115
    material circumstances of, 4, 5, 14–
        15, 79, 82–83, 84f, 109
    opportunities for, 7, 12–14, 21
    policies affecting, 3–6, 15
Low wages
    consequences of, 7–8, 12, 15, 138
    trends in, 4, 5, 13f, 51–52, 52f, 53f

Maine, Parents as Scholars program in, 93
Managerial occupations, 56*t*, 59*t*, 62*n*10
Manpower Demonstration Research Corporation. *See* MDRC
Manpower Development and Training Act (MDTA), 26, 165–166
Manual occupations, characteristics of, 56*t*, 59*t*
Manufacturing sector, 154, 155
Maryland, court decision in, 149
Massachusetts, TANF-eligible students in, 93
Mazumder, Bhashkar, conference participant, 39
McCone Commission, inner-city riots and, 23
McMillen, Daniel, conference participant, 39
MDRC (Manpower Demonstration Research Corporation), 194*n*6
    Opening Doors demonstration, 21, 93–104, 104–105*nn*1–3
    Welfare-to-Work income supplements, 17–18
MDTA. *See* Manpower Development and Training Act
Median income measurements, 82–83, 83*f*
Meléndez, Edwin, conference participant, 33–34, 40
Mental health, residential mobility and, 140, 145
Meyer, Bruce D., conference participant, 40
MFIP. *See* Minnesota Family Investment Program
Michigan, improved productivity in, 160*n*2
Microneighborhoods, residential mobility placement and, 133*t*, 134–135, 146
Milwaukee, Wisconsin, New Hope program in, 18–19
Minimum wage, 159, 170

Minnesota Family Investment Program (MFIP), 18
Minnesota programs, 18, 76*n*3, 116
Minorities, 8, 91–92, 137
    employer discrimination and, 154, 156
    See also Black workers; Hispanic workers; Nonwhite workers
Minority Female Single Parent Demonstration program, effectiveness of, 91–92
Missouri, earnings impact of JTPA in, 167
Mobility issues. *See* Economic mobility; Residential mobility programs
Moving to Opportunity for Fair Housing (MTO) program, Chicago, 23–24
    design, 131–136, 133*t*
    policy implications of, 147–149
    social influences on clients, 133*t*, 136–140, 146
    study conclusion, 145–146
MTO. *See* Moving to Opportunity for Fair Housing

National Advisory Commission on Civil Disorders, unemployment role in, 23
National Evaluation of Welfare-to-Work Strategies (NEWWS), 17–18, 90–91, 157, 160*n*1
National JTPA Study (NJS), JTPA evaluation known as, 166, 173
Natural resources occupations, characteristics of, 56*t*, 59*t*
NCLB. *See* No Child Left Behind Act of 2001
Negative income tax (NIT), EITC and, 66–67, 76*n*5
Neighborhoods, 25, 33, 158
    in Chicago, 9, 132–136, 133*t*, 140
    low-income, 28, 140
    poverty in, 80, 129, 130, 160*n*4
    safety in, 42–43*n*14, 128, 140, 145, 168
    schools in, 127, 137, 141–142
New Hope program, 18–19, 158

New Visions program, 91, 93
New York, 93, 95*t*, 160*n*5
  Harlem Children's Zone in, 27, 158
NEWWS. *See* National Evaluation of
  Welfare-to-Work Strategies
NIT. *See* Negative income tax (NIT)
NJS. *See* National JTPA Study (NJS)
No Child Left Behind Act of 2001
  (NCLB), 19
Noncustodial fathers, 156, 158, 159
Nonfarm employment, service sector in,
  61*n*8
Nonprofit community organizations, 26
  as labor market intermediaries, 27, 157
Nontraditional students, 109–123
  defined, 111–112
  employer investment in, 117–118
  federal aid programs for, 114–116,
    121–122
  financial aid for, 21–22, 110, 112–
    123, 122*n*2
  need analysis for, 112–114, 118–119
  older workers as, 21–22, 109–111
  state aid programs for, 116–117
Nonwhite workers, 56*t*, 59*t*, 194*n*10
  See also Black workers; Hispanic
    workers

OBRA90. *See* Omnibus Reconciliation
  Act of 1990
OBRA93. *See* Omnibus Reconciliation
  Act of 1993
Occupations, 154
  census IPUMS data on, 56*t*, 61*nn*7–8
  education levels and, 55, 56*t*
  employment growth rates in, 58–60,
    59*t*
  trends in, 4, 5, 55–60, 57*f*
Ohio, 116
  community college with employment
    services in, 94–96, 95*t*, 98*t*–99*t*,
    102*t*–103*t*, 104*n*1
OJT. *See* On-the-job training
Older workers
  financial aid for education of, 110,
    111–120, 122*n*2

as nontraditional students, 21–22,
  109–111
support systems for, 120–122, 122*n*3
Omnibus Reconciliation Act of 1990
  (OBRA90), 16, 68, 69*f*
Omnibus Reconciliation Act of 1993
  (OBRA93), 16, 68, 69*f*
On-the-job training (OJT), 6, 28, 171
  combating spatial mismatch with,
    42*n*14
  employers receive subsidies for,
    169–170
  evaluation of, 29, 91
  federal programs with, 26, 166
One-Stop Career Centers, 121
Opening Doors demonstration, MDRC,
  21, 93–104, 104–105*nn*1–3
Oregon, 116, 157, 160*n*1
Outsourcing, 35, 61*n*6
  displaced worker assistance due to,
    21, 26–27, 42*n*12
Owens Community College, Ohio,
  Opening Doors project at, 94–96,
    95*t*, 98*t*–99*t*, 102*t*–103*t*, 104*n*1

Palms-Barber, Brenda, conference
  participant, 40, 41*n*3
Panel Study of Income Dynamics
  (PSID), income volatility and, 80
Parent Loans for Undergraduate Students
  (PLUS), 115
Parents
  single, and effective programs, 91–92
  state aid to, for education, 93, 117
  subsidies in compensation patterns of,
    42*n*14, 120, 121–122
  See also Noncustodial fathers; Single
    mothers with children
Parents as Scholars program, 93
Pell Grants, 19, 20
  advancement of working poor and,
    157, 159
  college retention and, 104–105*n*3,
    119–120
  eligibility for, 113, 114–115

Pennsylvania, workforce development in, 33

Perkins Loan Program, 115

Personal Responsibility and Work Opportunity Reconciliation Act of 1996 (PRWORA), 16, 66

Philanthropy, 209n1

Plant closings, displaced workers and, 42n12

PLUS. *See* Parent Loans for Undergraduate Students

Portland, Oregon, NEWWS and, 157, 160n1

Poverty, 14, 80
educational aid and, wages, 113, 114, 117, 122n2
low-wage workers and, 41n4, 89–90
measurements, 82–83, 84f
neighborhoods with, 8–9, 23, 80, 130, 140, 160n4
NIT to reduce, 66–67
trends in work and, 11–15, 11f, 13f

Princeton University. Center for Economic Policy Studies, working papers from, 42n11

Production occupations, characteristics of, 56t, 59t

Productivity, 154, 160n2

Professional occupations, 56t, 59t, 62n10

Project Upward Bound, 19

PRWORA. *See* Personal Responsibility and Work Opportunity Reconciliation Act of 1996

PSID. *See* Panel Study of Income Dynamics

Public transit, 25
limitations of, 22, 23, 138

Racial differences. *See specific cohorts, e.g.,* Black men; White men

Racial integration/segregation, 23, 43n14, 131, 155

Residential mobility programs, 149n2
effectiveness of, 4, 23–24
Gautreaux compared to MTO, 130–146

policy implications of, 147–149
individual outcomes of, 141–145
social mechanisms of, 24–26, 127–140

Richburg-Hayes, Lashawn, conference participant, 40

Riverside Community College, California, New Visions program at, 91, 93, 160n3

Rosenbaum, James E., conference participant, 39

San Jose, California, CET cost effectiveness in, 157, 160n1

Scholarships, 94–97, 95t, 100, 101, 104

School integration, combating spatial mismatch with, 43n14, 144–145

School quality, 155
residential mobility and, 127, 129, 136–137, 141–142

Second chance programs, 28, 158, 159

Sentencing Project, Washington, D.C., 160n5

Serious and Violent Offender Reentry Initiative (SVORI), 30, 188–189, 193

Service occupations, 127
calculation discrepancies and data sets on, 61–62n9
low education and, 58, 60, 61n8
low-wage workers in, 12, 17, 56t, 57–58, 59t

Service sector *vs.* service occupations, 61n8

Single women with children, 149n2
as AFDC/TANF recipients, 16, 65, 66, 76n4
annual income percentiles of, 85, 86t
education and, 91–92, 93, 104, 120
EITC and, 4, 5, 16–17, 65–76, 69ff, 160n2
employment rates and, 65–66, 66, 71–75, 72f, 73ff, 153
welfare reform and, 4, 5, 16–17, 65–68

SIPP. *See* Survey of Income and Program Participation
Snyderman, Robin, conference participant, 25–26, 39, 43*n*15
Social interaction, residential mobility and, 127–128, 138–140, 144–145, 148–149
Social Security Act of 1935, 16, 66, 166–167
Song, Unmi, conference participant, 40
Spatial mismatch, 42*n*13, 80
   housing allowance programs and, 3, 5, 23–26, 36–37
   mobility strategies to combat, 42–43*n*14, 127, 129, 137–138
Spriggs, William, conference participant, 41
Stafford loan program, 114
Straits, Robert, conference participant, 40, 41*n*3
Student services
   counseling, 94–96, 95*t*, 148
   employment, 94–96, 95*t*, 98*t*–99*t*, 102*t*–103*t*, 104*n*1
Suburban areas
   job growth in, *vs.* worker residences (*see* Spatial mismatch)
   racial mix of, and resident choices, 130, 144, 146
   zoning regulations in, 24, 25
Suburban compared to urban residents, 130
   educational outcome differences between, 141–142
   employment characteristics, 142–143
   strategies to combat mismatches of, 22–26, 36–37, 43*n*14, 127
Sullivan, Daniel, conference participant, 40
Survey of Income and Program Participation (SIPP), income volatility and, 80
SVORI. *See* Serious and Violent Offender Reentry Initiative
Sykes, Donald, conference participant, 40, 41*n*3

TANF. *See* Temporary Assistance for Needy Families
Tax credits, 26, 114–115
   See also Earned Income Tax Credit (EITC)
Tax Reform Act of 1986 (TRA86), 16, 68, 69*f*
Tech Prep model, positive impact of, 160*n*4
Technician occupations, characteristics of, 56*t*, 59*t*
Technological changes, wage inequality and, 20, 42*nn*9–10
Temporary Assistance for Needy Families (TANF)
   caseloads, 66, 67*f*
   costs of, *vs.* EITC, 65, 68, 70*f*
   eligibility for, and college training, 22, 35, 93, 116–117, 121
   PRWORA and, 16, 66, 138, 143
Temporary help sector, 17
Testa, William, conference participant, 39
Texas, earnings subsidies in, 160*n*3
Thompson decision, Baltimore, 149
Title III, Workforce Investment Act (WIA), displaced workers and, 42*n*12
Title IV, Pell Grants and, 114
Toussaint-Comeau, Maude, conference participant, 39
TRA86. *See* Tax Reform Act of 1986 (TRA86)
Trade adjustment assistance, 42*n*12, 174
Trade unions, 41–42*n*9, 101, 160*n*6
Transportation restructure
   combating spatial mismatch with, 22–23, 42*n*14
   commuters with private cars in, 24–25
   need for, 154–155, 156
   See also Public transit
Transportation sector, wages and skills for, 154
Tyler, John H., conference participant, 40

UI. *See* Unemployment insurance (UI)
Unemployment, 23 116
Unemployment insurance (UI), 42*n*12,
173, 194*n*5
    claimants of, and WPRS, 28–29,
    168–169
U.S. Dept. of Health and Human
Services, 188
U.S. Dept. of Housing and Urban
Development (HUD), 43*n*14, 188
U.S. Dept. of Justice, 188
U.S. Dept. of Labor (USDOL), 62*n*9, 188
    program evaluation by, 28, 159, 166–
    167
U.S. General Accounting Office
(USGAO), 33, 166–167
U.S. law and legislation, 16, 19, 160*n*6
    workforce development, 26, 159
U.S. Secretary of Education, commission
appointed by, 121
U.S. Senate, commission appointed by,
82
Urban areas, 22, 23, 130

Violent behaviors, 23
    debilitating effects from, 42–43*n*14,
    128, 140, 145
    rehabilitation of, 30, 188–189, 193
Vocational education, 35, 117, 156
    effects of, *vs.* work experience, 190–
    191
    federal programs with, 28, 166
    prison-based programs for, 180–181,
    182

Wages, 160*n*6, 170
    causes of inequality in, 20, 41–42*n*9,
    52–53, 89–90, 154–156
    college differential on, 62*n*11, 91, 110
    higher minimum, with caveat, 159,
    170
    trends in inequality of, 12, 13*f,* 51–52,
    52*f,* 53*f,* 79–80
    See also Minimum wage
Washington, D.C., civil rights review in,
160*n*5

Washington (state), 116, 117
W.E. Upjohn Institute, conference
sponsorship by, 3–6, 39–40
Welfare reform
    effectiveness of, 15, 143
    EITC and, 66–68, 70*f,* 74–75
    employment training programs and, 3,
    90–91, 110
    impact of work incentives on, 17–19
    income assistance policy and, 16–17
    labor market entry at, 12, 17, 138,
    153
    single women with children and, 4, 5,
    16–17, 65–68
Welfare-to-Work programs
    education first *vs.* job search first as,
    90–91
    evaluation of, 157, 160*n*1, 174
    income supplements in, 17–18
West Virginia, tuition program in, 116
White men
    earnings of, *vs.* nonwhite, 194*n*10,
    194–195*n*11
    incarcerated, as school dropouts, 180,
    194*n*2
WIA. *See* Workforce Investment Act
Williams, Alicia, conference participant,
40
Wisconsin
    New Hope program in, 18–19
    state EITC supplement to federal
    program, 76*n*3
Work-Based Learning Tuition Assistance
Program, 117
Work experience *vs.* classroom training,
190–191
Work-study programs, 116–117
Worker Profiling and Reemployment
Services (WPRS), 6, 28–29, 168–
169
Workforce development initiatives
    access to education, 92–93, 116–117
    best practices for, 3–6
    impacts of, 165–174
    policy and evaluation of, 26–31,
    33–34, 37–38

Workforce development initiatives, *cont.*
    See also Employment training
        programs
Workforce Investment Act (WIA), 6,
        26–27, 43n16, 159
    evaluation of, 28, 116, 167
    services provided by, 42n12, 121,
        165–166
    training ties to, 22, 35
Working poor, 154
    education and, 89–92, 101, 104, 110
    EITC eligibility and, 67–68
    employment and advancement of, 6,
        27, 92, 153–159
    policies for success of, 83–84, 156–
        159
    trends in, 11–15, 11f, 13f, 109
    See also Low-wage workers
WPRS. *See* Worker Profiling and
        Reemployment Services

Youth, 9, 155, 166
    employment and advancement of, 6,
        27–28, 158, 159, 166
    Job Corps for disadvantaged, 6, 28,
        167–168
Youth Opportunity Program, 28, 158,
        160n4
Youth Service program, 28, 158, 160n4
YouthBuild program, 28, 158

About the Institute

The W.E. Upjohn Institute for Employment Research is a nonprofit research organization devoted to finding and promoting solutions to employment-related problems at the national, state, and local levels. It is an activity of the W.E. Upjohn Unemployment Trustee Corporation, which was established in 1932 to administer a fund set aside by Dr. W.E. Upjohn, founder of The Upjohn Company, to seek ways to counteract the loss of employment income during economic downturns.

The Institute is funded largely by income from the W.E. Upjohn Unemployment Trust, supplemented by outside grants, contracts, and sales of publications. Activities of the Institute comprise the following elements: 1) a research program conducted by a resident staff of professional social scientists; 2) a competitive grant program, which expands and complements the internal research program by providing financial support to researchers outside the Institute; 3) a publications program, which provides the major vehicle for disseminating the research of staff and grantees, as well as other selected works in the field; and 4) an Employment Management Services division, which manages most of the publicly funded employment and training programs in the local area.

The broad objectives of the Institute's research, grant, and publication programs are to 1) promote scholarship and experimentation on issues of public and private employment and unemployment policy, and 2) make knowledge and scholarship relevant and useful to policymakers in their pursuit of solutions to employment and unemployment problems.

Current areas of concentration for these programs include causes, consequences, and measures to alleviate unemployment; social insurance and income maintenance programs; compensation; workforce quality; work arrangements; family labor issues; labor-management relations; and regional economic development and local labor markets.